CLARENDON ARISTOTLE SERIES

General Editors
J. L. ACKRILL AND LINDSAY JUDSON

Also published in this series

Categories and *De Interpretatione*
J. L. ACKRILL

De Anima Books II and III
D. W. HAMLYN
New impression with supplementary material by Christopher Shields

De Generatione et Corruptione
C. J. F. WILLIAMS

De Partibus Animalium I and *De Generatione Animalium* I
D. M. BALME
New impression with supplementary material by Allan Gotthelf

Eudemian Ethics Books I, II, and VIII
MICHAEL WOODS
Second edition

Metaphysics Books Γ, Δ, and E
CHRISTOPHER KIRWAN
Second edition

Metaphysics Books M and N
JULIA ANNAS

Metaphysics Books Z and H
DAVID BOSTOCK

Physics Books I and II
WILLIAM CHARLTON
New impression with supplementary material

Physics Books III and IV
EDWARD HUSSEY
New impression with supplementary material

Politics Books III and IV
RICHARD ROBINSON
New impression with supplementary material by David Keyt

Posterior Analytics
JONATHAN BARNES
Second edition

Other volumes are in preparation

ARISTOTLE
Politics

BOOKS I AND II

Translated
with a Commentary
by

TREVOR J. SAUNDERS

CLARENDON PRESS • OXFORD
1995

Oxford University Press, Walton Street, Oxford OX2 6DP

Oxford New York
Athens Auckland Bangkok Bombay
Calcutta Cape Town Dar es Salaam Delhi
Florence Hong Kong Istanbul Karachi
Kuala Lumpur Madras Madrid Melbourne
Mexico City Nairobi Paris Singapore
Taipei Tokyo Toronto
and associated companies in
Berlin Ibadan

Oxford is a trade mark of Oxford University Press

Published in the United States
by Oxford University Press Inc., New York

British Library Cataloguing in Publication Data
Data available

Library of Congress Cataloging in Publication Data
Aristotle.
[Politics. Book 1–2. English]
Politics. Books I and II/Aristotle; translated with a
commentary by Trevor J. Saunders.
— (Clarendon Aristotle series)
Includes bibliographical references and index.
1. Political science—Early works to 1800. I. Saunders, Trevor
J., 1934– . II. Title. III. Series.
JC71.A41S3 1995 320′.01′1—dc20 95–9279

ISBN 0-19-824892-X
ISBN 0-19-824894-6 (Pbk)

Typeset by Best-set Typesetter Ltd., Hong Kong
Printed in Great Britain
on acid-free paper by
Bookcraft (Bath) Ltd
Midsomer Norton, Avon

To
Clare and Angela

ACKNOWLEDGEMENTS

Most of the work on this book was done during the academic year 1992–3, when the generosity of two major benefactors enabled me to take research leave. The Leverhulme Trust appointed me to a Research Fellowship for that year, and the Research Committee of the University of Newcastle upon Tyne made a further grant towards costs. It is an agreeable duty to express my gratitude to these bodies, without whom the book would still be in gestation. In addition, during the Hilary term of 1993 I benefited greatly from a Visiting Fellowship at Brasenose College, Oxford, and enjoyed splendid hospitality both there and at St Benet's Hall; and the following term I derived much pleasure and profit from a Summer Visitorship at the Institute for Advanced Study, Princeton. To these institutions also my warmest thanks are due.

I am delighted to offer my cordial gratitude to the many scholars who have read and criticized parts of the translation and/or other material: Dr P. A. Cartledge, Dr R. Crisp, Dr S. J. Hodkinson, Dr L. Judson (Joint General Editor), Professor J. F. Lazenby, Dr R. Mayhew, Dr S. Meikle, Professor C. Natali, Dr R. G. Osborne, Professor C. J. Rowe, and Mr C. C. W. Taylor. It is a particular pleasure to acknowledge the help of the Joint General Editor of this series, Professor J. L. Ackrill, who in addition to endless patience and constant encouragement provided invaluable comments on my drafts.

I am also grateful to Penguin Books Ltd for permission to adapt my version of books I and II of the *Politics* in: *Aristotle, The Politics*, translated by T. A. Sinclair, revised and re-presented by Trevor J. Saunders (Penguin Classics, Harmondsworth 1981, copyright © Trevor J. Saunders).

October 1994   T. J. S.

CONTENTS

INTRODUCTION   xi

REFERENCES AND ABBREVIATIONS   xiv

TRANSLATION
  Book I   1
  Book II   22

COMMENTARY
  Book I   55
  Book II   104

APPENDIX: THE ALLEGED OLIGARCHIC
BIAS IN PLATO'S *LAWS*   171

LIST OF DEPARTURES FROM THE OXFORD
CLASSICAL TEXT   173

BIBLIOGRAPHY   175

SELECTIVE GLOSSARIES   182
  English–Greek   182
  Greek–English   186

SELECTIVE INDEX   191

GUIDE TO TRANSLATION AND COMMENTARY

(Page numbers of the translation are given in square brackets)

Book I
    i Varieties of Rule in State and Household [1] 55
   ii Origin, Growth, and Purpose of the State [2] 59
  iii Preliminary Analysis of the Household [4] 71
   iv The Slave as the Tool of his Master [5] 73
    v Natural Patterns of Rule as a Justification of
       Slavery [6] 75
   vi The Controversy about the Justification of
       Slavery [7] 79
  vii The Skill Needed to Rule Slaves [9] 82
 viii Household Management and Natural
       Acquisition [10] 83
   ix Origin, Development, and Varieties of Exchange [12] 87
    x Household Management in Relation to
       Acquisition, Trade, and Money-Lending [15] 94
   xi Modes of Acquisition, including Monopoly:
       Analysis and Assessment [16] 95
  xii Rule in the Household: Husbands and Fathers [18] 96
 xiii The Moral Virtues of Members of the Household [18] 97

Book II
    i Programme: Ideal States, Real and Proposed;
       the Limits of Sharing [22] 104
   ii Criticism of Social and Political 'Oneness' in
       Plato's *Republic* [22] 106
  iii Language and Psychology of Possession in a
       System of 'Oneness' [24] 110
   iv Drawbacks of Community of Wives and Children
       in Plato's *Republic* [25] 113
    v Drawbacks of Community of Property in Plato's
       Republic; the Constitution [27] 116
   vi Criticism of Plato's Second-Best 'Ideal' State in
       the *Laws* [31] 126
  vii The Constitution of Phaleas: The Problems of
       Egalitarianism [34] 135
 viii The Constitution of Hippodamus: Problems of
       Property, Law, and Innovation [37] 140

CONTENTS

ix Criticism of the Constitution and Social System
   of Sparta   [41] 149
 x Criticism of the Constitution and Social System
   of Crete   [46] 158
xi Criticism of the Constitution and Social System
   of Carthage   [48] 161
xii Defence of the Constitution of Solon; Significant
   Measures of Certain Other Lawgivers   [51] 166

INTRODUCTION

A

If volumes in this series had subtitles, a good one for this volume would be *Aristotle and his Rivals*. In book I he develops the central idea of his political theory: natural teleology. In rich and vivid detail, he applies it in four connected areas: the historical growth of the state from primitive beginnings, slavery, economics, and the household. It is in this book that we find his defence of natural slavery, and of the subordinate status of women. Then in book II he launches a vigorous and penetrating polemic against four theoretical 'utopias' (Plato's *Republic* and *Laws*, Phaleas' state, Hippodamus' state), and against three actual states which enjoyed a high reputation for good government (Sparta, Crete, Carthage). All, he claims, fail; for the central ideas on which they are based are fundamentally mistaken.

So much is easy to recount; and it makes the two books look tightly connected. In fact, their historical and philosophical relationships are not certain. The *Politics* as a whole is studded with references from one part to another ('as been said in . . .', 'as we shall enquire later', *vel sim.*); but between books I and II the silence is total, apart from a few (possibly non-authentic) transitional words at the end of I. In particular, it is remarkable that in his many and various arguments against his rivals in the second book Aristotle very rarely appeals to nature; and even when he does, it is far from clear that he has book I in mind.

An obvious recourse is to suppose that II was written earlier than I, and that it was never revised in the light of I's existence. We need not believe that II was *composed* first in the course of Aristotle's work on the *Politics* as a whole, merely that it was composed to *stand* first; and if that is so, it would fit (1) Aristotle's well-known practice of starting a work with a survey of his predecessors' opinions, (2) his stated intention, in the 'bridging' passage between the *Nicomachean Ethics* and the *Politics* (*EN* 1181^{b}12–23), 'to review first whether anything of merit has been said on particular questions by our predecessors'. This passage contains what seems intended as a rough and rapid overview of the *Politics* as we have it; but among other omissions it says nothing of the themes of I. This permits the twin conjectures (1) that I was written quite late in Aristotle's work on politics (though not last, as III 1278^{b}17–19 refers explicitly to I 1253^{a}1), and became the new first book, (2) that the brief transitional passage at its end indicates merely that he placed next the already written II, preferring that order to II then I.

However, irrespective of its location, it is perhaps not difficult to divine what led Aristotle to write I. If his political work was to consist of more than a series of pragmatic assertions locked in inconclusive conflict with the pragmatic assertions of others, it needed to be placed on some impregnable foundation. This, in his view, was the natural needs, natural activities, and natural fulfilment of the animal man. In effect he extended natural teleology from biology to social and political life (on the problems inherent in this manœuvre, see esp. introduction to I ii). Hence there is no reason to suppose that the pragmatic author of book II is not on nodding terms with the philosopher who wrote book I. On the contrary: if we wish to find some sort of 'ultimate' justification for the practical judgements of II, it is to the theory of I that we must turn (see e.g. the comments on $1269^b12-1270^b6$).[1]

B

The extreme range and variety of the subject-matter of the two books pose a severe problem for the commentator. Aristotle discusses, often in allusive detail, constitutional, social, and legal theory and practice; economics; military policy; slavery; psychology, education, and ethics; historical and comparative anthropology; and even (briefly) religion, logic, and sex. Historical elucidation of these topics could easily have filled this entire volume; yet Aristotle's political theory is so thoroughly saturated with the opinions and institutions of his day and their historical origins that they cannot be omitted entirely. So my policy has been this: in order to conserve space in which to elucidate and discuss what seem to me the central issues, I have confined myself to rather compendious and even dogmatic statements of the historical facts, even though in view of the state of our evidence they are often in dispute. I have also been fairly summary with certain substantive issues which seemed not crucial to the concerns of these two books. But compendiousness brings the obligation to give the reader a

[1] Readers new to the *Politics* ought however to be aware that the above account cuts a broad swath, and that the problems concerning the dating, composition, and structure of the work as a whole are decidedly complex: see Rowe (1977), Keyt and Miller (1991) 3–6, Schütrumpf i. 129–34, ii. 95–108, esp. 108. Both books are probably datable to Aristotle's residence in Athens, 335–323, as head of his Lyceum.

chance to go further if he wishes. Hence the generous supply of references, not only to the *Politics* and other texts of Aristotle (he is often his own best commentator), but also to other ancient authors (notably Plato) and to modern literature (often articles, and specific pages of books, selected for the sharpness of their focus on particular passages and problems).

C

The translation is a fairly extensive revision of my own 1981 revision of T. A. Sinclair's version of 1962 (both in the Penguin Classics series). I have sought exact conformity with the Greek, but have occasionally been forced into minor compromises of a kind familar to anyone who has wrestled with the problems of translating; difficulties that appreciably affect translation and interpretation are dealt with in the commentary. The text used is Ross's Oxford Classical Text of 1957; my few departures from it are listed at the end of the volume.

As in the Penguin, I have attempted to maintain a high degree of consistency in the rendering of key terms; total consistency, however, is impossible (see Glossaries). My choice of 'equivalents' for certain technical words for which no exact equivalent exists in English is generally conservative. Some will frown at this, and one can indeed argue; but whatever one prints, the reader is still in need of exegesis. The traditional renderings seem to me have merits in their own right; at the very least, they have the advantage of familiarity.

D

Brief Guide to Reading. For readers new to Aristotle, the best introduction to his thought is Ackrill (1981); the best introduction to the *Politics* is Mulgan (1987). The essays collected in Patzig (1990) and Keyt and Miller (1991) are excellently stimulating. For reading beyond book II, Robinson's volume in this series on III and IV (1962, rev. edn., 1995, by D. Keyt) is essential; two other volumes, on V–VI and VII–VIII, are in preparation. Though Newman remains useful, the standard commentary is now Schütrumpf (1991–), a most learned work to which I owe much.

REFERENCES AND ABBREVIATIONS

1. The standard mode of reference to the text of Aristotle is by page, column, and line (e.g. 1256ª34) in the edition of Immanuel Bekker (Berlin, 1831). The pages containing the *Politics* run from 1252 to 1342; references from 1252ª1 to 1260ᵇ24 are to book I, those from 1260ᵇ27 to 1274ᵇ28 are to book II. The Bekker lineation is given in the translation for each paragraph at its start, and at 5-line intervals in the margin. However, between any two such consecutive marginal numbers there may for obvious reasons be more or fewer than 5 lines of printed translation. The awkwardness when one looks up references is unavoidable but slight.

2. The numbering of the paragraphs of the translation and of the matching sections of the commentary is intended to provide a means of rapid referring *within* individual chapters, notably in surveys of their structure and argument. The system is not used in references from one chapter to another.

3. Apart from that, and general references to books and chapters (e.g. II iii), all references to the text of the *Politics* are given in the form of plain Bekker numbers, bare of author and title. References to the text of other works of Aristotle are given in Bekker form, bare of author, and with the following abbreviations of titles:

AP	*Constitution of the Athenians* (*Athènaiōn Politeia*).
Anim.	*On the Soul* (*De Anima*)
Cael.	*On the Heavens* (*De Caelo*)
EE	*Eudemian Ethics* (*Ethica Eudemia*)
EN	*Nicomachean Ethics* (*Ethica Nicomachea*)
GA	*On the Generation of Animals* (*De Generatione Animalium*)
GC	*On Generation and Corruption* (*De Generatione et Corruptione*)
HA	*History of Animals* (*Historia Animalium*)
MA	*On the Movement of Animals* (*De Motu Animalium*)
Met.	*Metaphysics* (*Metaphysica*)
[MM]	*Great Ethics* (*Magna Moralia*)
[Oec.]	*Matters of Household-Management* (*Oeconomica*)
PA	*On the Parts of Animals* (*De Partibus Animalium*)
Phys.	*Physics* (*Physica*)

Poet.	*On the Art of Poetry* (*De Arte Poetica*)
Soph. Ref.	*Sophistical Refutations* (*Sophistici Elenchi*)

4. References to Plato are often given bare of author, with the following abbreviations:

Crit.	*Critias*
Gorg.	*Gorgias*
Ph.	*Phaedo*
Pol.	*Politicus* (*Statesman*)
Prot.	*Protagoras*
Rep.	*Republic*
Tim.	*Timaeus*

5. References to other authors employ the following abbreviations:

Aes.	Aeschylus
	PV (*Prometheus Bound*)
Aesch.	Aeschines
Eur.	Euripides
	Bac. (*Bacchants*)
	IA (*Iphigenia in Aulis*)
Dem.	Demosthenes
Diod. Sic.	Diodorus Siculus
D.L.	Diogenes Laertius
Her.	Herodotus
Hes.	Hesiod
	WD (*Works and Days*)
Hipp.	Hippocrates
	AWP (*On Airs, Waters, Places*)
Hom.	Homer
	Il. (*Iliad*)
	Od. (*Odyssey*)
Isoc.	Isocrates
Paus.	Pausanias
Plut.	Plutarch
	Lyc. (*Life of Lycurgus*)
	Fort. Alex. (*On the Fortune or Virtue of Alexander the Great*)
Thuc.	Thucydides
Xen.	Xenophon
	Cyr. (*Education of Cyrus*)
	Hell. (*History of Greece*)
	Mem. (*Memoirs of Socrates*)
	Oec. (*Household-Manager*)
[Xen.]	*AP* (*Constitution of the Athenians*)

Square brackets indicate doubtful authenticity. For the character and status of the *AP* attributed to Aristotle, see Rhodes (1981) 58–63.

6. DK   Diels, H. and Kranz, D. (1951–2), *Die Fragmente der Vorsokratiker* (6th edn., 3 vols., Berlin).

TRANSLATION

I i

VARIETIES OF RULE IN STATE AND HOUSEHOLD

1 (1252ᵃ1–7) We observe that every state is a certain sort of association, and that every association is formed for some good purpose; for in all their actions all men aim at what they think good. Clearly, then, while all associations aim at some good, the association which is the most sovereign of all and embraces all the others ᵃ5 aims highest, i.e. at the most sovereign of all goods. This is the association called the state, the association which takes the form of a state.

2 (1252ᵃ7–16) Now those who suppose that the roles of a statesman, of a king, of a household-manager, and of a master of slaves are the same, put the matter badly; for they think that each of these differs in point of large or small numbers, but not in kind: ᵃ10 that if, for example, a man rules few people, he is a slave-master, if several, a household-manager, and if still more, he has the role of a king or statesman—on the assumption that there is no difference between a large household and a small state. And as for the roles of a statesman and a king, they reckon that when a man is in personal control he has the role of a king, whereas when he takes his turn at ruling and at being ruled according to the principles of that sort of ᵃ15 knowledge, he is a statesman. But these assertions are false.

3 (1252ᵃ17–23) The point will be clear if we examine the matter according to the mode of inquiry that has guided us. For in other fields we have to analyse a composite into its irreducible elements, the smallest parts of the whole. So let us in the same ᵃ20 way examine the component parts of the state also, and we shall see better both how these too differ from each other and whether we can acquire some skilled understanding of each of the roles mentioned.

I ii

ORIGIN, GROWTH, AND PURPOSE OF THE STATE

1 (1252ᵃ24–34) Now in this as in other fields we shall get the best
ᵃ25 view of things if we look at their natural growth from their beginnings. First, those which are incapable of existing without each
other must unite as a pair. For example, (a) male and female, for
breeding (and this not from choice; rather, as in the other animals
too and in plants, the urge to leave behind another such as one is
ᵃ30 oneself is natural); (b) that which naturally rules and that which is
ruled, for preservation. For that which can use its intellect to look
ahead is by nature ruler and by nature master, while that which has
the bodily strength to labour is ruled, and is by nature a slave.
Hence master and slave benefit from the same thing.

2 (1252ᵃ34–ᵇ9) So it is by nature that a distinction has been
ᵇ1 made between female and slave. For nature produces nothing
skimpily (like the Delphic knife that smiths make), but one thing
for one purpose; for every tool will be made best if it subserves not
many tasks but one. Non-Greeks, however, assign to female and
ᵇ5 slave the same status. This is because they do not have that which
naturally rules: their association comes to be that of a male slave
and a female slave. Hence, as the poets say, 'It is proper that
Greeks should rule non-Greeks', on the assumption that non-
Greek and slave are by nature identical.

3 (1252ᵇ9–15) Thus it was from these two associations that a
ᵇ10 household first arose, and Hesiod was right in his poetry when he
said, 'first of all a house and a wife and an ox to draw the plough.'
(The ox is the poor man's slave.) So the association formed according to nature for the satisfaction of the purposes of every day is a
household, the members of which Charondas calls 'bread-fellows',
and Epimenides the Cretan 'stable-companions'.

ᵇ15 **4 (1252ᵇ15–27)** The first association, from several households,
for the satisfaction of other than daily purposes, is a village. The
village seems to be by nature in the highest degree, as a colony of
a household—children and grandchildren, whom some people call
'homogalactic'. This is why states were at first ruled by kings (as are
ᵇ20 the nations to this day): they were formed from persons who were
under kingly rule. For every household is under the kingly rule of
its most senior member; so too the colonies, because of the kinship.
This is what is mentioned in Homer: 'Each one lays down the law
to children and wives.' For they were scattered; and that is how
they dwelt in ancient times. For this reason the gods too are said by

everyone to be governed by a king—namely because men them- ᵇ25
selves were originally ruled by kings and some are so still. Men
model the gods' forms on themselves, and similarly their way of life
too.

5 (1252ᵇ27–1253ᵃ1) The complete association, from several
villages, is the state, which at once reaches the limit of total self-
sufficiency, so to say. Whereas it comes into existence for the sake
of life, it exists for the sake of the good life. Therefore every state ᵇ30
exists by nature, since the first associations did too. For this association is their end, and nature is an end; for whatever each thing is in
character when its coming into existence has been completed, that
is what we call the nature of each thing—of a man, for instance, or
a horse or a house. Moreover the aim, i.e. the end, is best; and self-
sufficiency is both end and best.

6 (1253ᵃ1–7) These considerations make it clear, then, that the **1253**
state is one of those things which exist by nature, and that man is by
nature an animal fit for a state. Anyone who by his nature and not
by ill-luck has no state is either a wretch or superhuman; he is also
like the man condemned by Homer as having 'no brotherhood, no ᵃ5
law, no hearth'; for he is at once such by nature and keen to go to
war, being isolated like a piece in a game of *pettoi*.

7 (1253ᵃ7–18) The reason why man is an animal fit for a state
to a fuller extent than any bee or any herding animal is obvious.
Nature, as we say, does nothing pointlessly, and man alone among
the animals possesses speech. Now the voice is an indication of ᵃ10
pleasure and pain, which is why it is possessed by the other animals
also; for their nature does extend this far, to having the sensations
of pleasure and pain, and to indicating them to each other. Speech,
on the other hand, serves to make clear what is beneficial and what
is harmful, and so also what is just and what is unjust. For by ᵃ15
contrast with the other animals man has this peculiarity: he alone
has sense of good and evil, just and unjust, etc. An association in
these matters makes a household and a state.

8 (1253ᵃ18–29) Furthermore, the state is by nature a thing
prior to the household and to each of us individually. For the whole ᵃ20
must be prior to the part. If the body is put to death as a whole,
there will no longer be hand or foot except in name, as one might
speak of a 'hand' made of stone. The killed hand will be like that;
for everything is defined by its capacity and function. So when they
are no longer in that condition, we must not say they are the same
things, but that they have the same names. It is clear then that the
state is both natural and prior to the individual. For if an individual ᵃ25
is not self-sufficient after separation, he will stand in the same
relationship to the whole as the parts in the other cases do.

3

Whoever is incapable of associating, or has no need to because of self-sufficiency, is no part of a state; so he is either a beast or a god.

9 (1253ᵃ29–39) Thus although the impulse towards this kind of
ᵃ30 association exists by nature in all men, the first person to have set one up is responsible for very great benefits. For as man is the best of all animals when he has reached his full development, so he is worst of all when divorced from law and justice. Injustice armed is at its harshest; man is born with weapons to support practical
ᵃ35 wisdom and virtue, which are all too easy to use for the opposite purposes. Hence without virtue he is the most savage, the most unrighteous, and the worst in respect of sex and food. The virtue of justice is a characteristic of a state; for justice is the arrangement of the association that takes the form of a state, and the virtue of justice is a judgement about what is just.

I iii

PRELIMINARY ANALYSIS OF THE HOUSEHOLD

ᵇ1 **1 (1253ᵇ1–11)** Now that it is clear from what parts the state is composed, it is essential to speak of household-management first; for every state consists of households. The parts of household-management match the parts that go to make up the household in its turn; and a complete household is made up of slaves and free men. But we have first to investigate each thing in terms of its
ᵇ5 smallest elements, and the first and smallest parts of a household are: master and slave, husband and wife, father and children. So we should have to examine what each one of these three is, and what sort of thing it ought to be. They are: the skill 'of a master', 'marital' skill (there is no term for the union of man and woman), and thirdly
ᵇ10 'procreative' skill (this too has not been given a name peculiar to itself).

2 (1253ᵇ11–14) These three skills which we have mentioned should stand; but there is a certain part which some people regard *as* household-management, others as its most extensive part; and our task is to consider its position. I refer to what is called 'the skill of acquiring goods'.

3 (1253ᵇ14–23) First let us discuss master and slave, in order to
ᵇ15 see both the position regarding essential needs, and whether we can find a better means of understanding them than the assumptions usually made. For some people suppose that mastership is a certain kind of knowledge, and that household-management,

mastership, a statesman's knowledge, and a king's are the same, as
we said at the beginning. Others think that it is contrary to nature ᵇ20
to be a master, because the fact that one man is a slave and another
free is by convention, whereas in nature they do not differ at all,
which is why it is not just either; for it is the result of force.

I iv

THE SLAVE AS THE TOOL OF HIS MASTER

1 (1253ᵇ23–1254ª1) Now property is part of the household, and
the art of acquiring property is part of household-management; for
both life itself and the good life are impossible without the essentials. Hence just as in the special skills the proper tools will have to ᵇ25
be available if the task is to be performed, so too a person concerned with household-management must have his. Of tools, some
are animate, some inanimate; for instance, for a ship's captain the
rudder is an inanimate tool, the look-out an animate one; as far as
the skills are concerned, an assistant is in the category of tools. So ᵇ30
a possession also is a tool for purposes of living, and property is an
assemblage of tools; a slave is a sort of living possession, and every
assistant is like a superior tool among tools. (For if each tool could
perform its own task either at our bidding or anticipating it, and
if—as they say of the statues made by Daedalus or the tripods of ᵇ35
Hephaestus, of which the poet says, 'self-moved they enter the
assembly of the gods'—shuttles shuttled to and fro of their own
accord, and pluckers played lyres, then master-craftsmen would
have no need of assistants nor masters any need of slaves.)
2 (1254ª1–8) Tools in ordinary parlance are productive tools, 1254
whereas a possession is meant for action. For from a shuttle there
comes something other than its use, from a bed or a garment the
use alone. Moreover, since production and action differ in kind, ª5
and both require tools, the difference between their tools also must
be the same. Now life is action, not production: therefore the slave
too is an assistant in the class of things that promote action.
3 (1254ª8–17) A possession is spoken of in the same way as a
part; for a part is not only part of another but belongs to another
wholly; and so too similarly does a possession. Accordingly, ª10
whereas the master is only master of his slave, but does not belong
to him, the slave is not only the slave of his master, but belongs to
him wholly. These considerations make clear what the nature and
capacity of the slave are: anyone who, though human, belongs by

ᵃ15 nature not to himself but to another is by nature a slave; and a human being belongs to another if, in spite of being human, he is a possession; and a possession is a tool for action and has a separate existence.

I v

NATURAL PATTERNS OF RULE AS A JUSTIFICATION OF SLAVERY

1 (1254ᵃ17–28) But whether there is anyone like that by nature, or not, and whether it is better and just for anyone to be a slave, or not (all slavery being on the contrary opposed to nature)—these
ᵃ20 points must be considered next. Neither theoretical examination nor learning from what occurs presents any difficulty. For ruling and being ruled come not only under essentials but also under benefits; and some things are differentiated right from birth, some to rule, some to be ruled. There are many species of ruler and ruled,
ᵃ25 and the rule is always better when the ruled are better, for instance better over a man than over an animal; for that which is produced by the better is a better piece of work; and where one element rules and another is ruled, they have a certain work.

2 (1254ᵃ28–ᵇ2) For wherever there is a combination of elements, continuous or discontinuous, and something in common
ᵃ30 results, in all cases the ruler and the ruled appear; and living creatures acquire this feature from nature as a whole. (Some rule exists also in things that do not share in life, for instance over a musical mode; but an investigation of these topics would perhaps take us somewhat far afield.) First, the living creature consists of soul and
ᵃ35 body; and of these the former is ruler by nature, the latter ruled. Now we ought rather to contemplate the natural in things whose condition is according to nature, not in corrupted ones. We must therefore consider the person too who is in the best condition, both of soul and of body, one in whom this is conspicuous—because the poor and unnatural condition of wretched persons, or of those in a
ᵇ1 wretched state, will often give the impression that the body is ruling over the soul.

3 (1254ᵇ2–16) However that may be, it is, as I say, within a living creature that we first find it possible to see both the rule of a master and that of a statesman. For the rule of soul over body is a
ᵇ5 master's rule, while the rule of mind over appetition is a statesman's or a king's. In these cases it is clear that it is both natural and beneficial for the body to be ruled by the soul, and for the emo-

6

tional part to be ruled by the mind, the part which possesses reason.
The reverse, or parity, would be damaging to everything. And
again, as regards man and the other animals, in the same way: for ᵇ10
tame animals are by nature better than wild, and it is better for all
of them to be ruled by men, because it secures their safety. Again,
the relationship of male to female is that the one is by nature
superior, the other inferior, and the one is ruler, the other ruled.
And this must hold good of all mankind.   ᵇ15

4 (1254ᵇ16–26)   Therefore those persons who exhibit the same
wide difference as there is between soul and body or between man
and beast (people whose function is to use their bodies, and this is
the best forthcoming from them, are in this condition)—these persons are natural slaves, for whom it is better to be subject to this
rule, given that it was also for the cases already cited. For he who ᵇ20
can belong to another (and that is why he does belong to another),
and he who participates in reason so far as to apprehend it but not
so far as to possess it (for the other animals obey not reason but
feelings), is a slave by nature. The use made of them differs little;
for from both—slaves and tame animals—comes bodily help in the ᵇ25
supply of essentials.

5 (1254ᵇ27–34)   It is, then, nature's purpose to make the bodies
too of freemen and of slaves different, the latter strong enough to
be used for essentials, the former erect and useless for that kind of
work, but fit for the life of a citizen (this too acquires a differentia- ᵇ30
tion, between the needs of war and those of peace). But the opposite also often occurs: some people have the body of a free man,
others the soul.

6 (1254ᵇ34–1255ᵃ3)   This much is clear: if they were to become,
in body alone, as splendid as representations of the gods, then all ᵇ35
would agree that those who fell short would deserve to be their
slaves. And if this is true of the body, it is far more just to make a
decisive distinction in respect of the soul; but it is not equally easy
to see the beauty of the soul as it is to see that of the body. It is clear **1255**
then that there are some people, of whom some are by nature free,
others slaves, for whom the state of slavery is both beneficial and
just.

I vi

THE CONTROVERSY ABOUT THE JUSTIFICATION OF SLAVERY

1 (1255ᵃ3–12)   But it is not hard to see that those who make the
opposing claims are also right in a way. We say 'state of slavery',

ᵃ5 and 'slave', with a double meaning; for by law too a person is a
slave, and in a state of slavery. The law is a kind of agreement, by
which people say that things conquered in war belong to the conquerors. Against the justice of this many of those versed in law
bring a charge analogous to that of 'illegality' brought against an
orator, on the ground that it is dreadful if what has been over-
ᵃ10 powered is going to be the slave of and ruled by someone who is
able to use force and has superior power. Some take this view,
others the other; and both views are held even among the learned.

2 (1255ᵃ12–21) The reason for this difference of opinion, and
for the overlap in the arguments, lies in this, that in a way virtue,
when it acquires resources, is best able actually to use force; and
ᵃ15 that which conquers always excels in *some* good. It seems therefore
that force is not without virtue, and that the dispute is only about
what is just. Consequently some think that 'just' is a nonsense,
others that justice is precisely this, the rule of the stronger—
although when these arguments are disentangled, the other argu-
ᵃ20 ments contain neither strength nor anything to persuade us that the
superior in virtue ought not to rule and be master.

3 (1255ᵃ21–1255ᵇ4) Some cleave exclusively (as they suppose)
to a kind of justice (for law is a kind of justice), and claim that
enslavement in war is just; but they simultaneously deny it, since it
ᵃ25 is possible for wars to be started unjustly, and in no way could one
call someone a slave who does not deserve to be a slave; otherwise,
it will turn out that those considered to be of the noblest birth are
slaves and descendants of slaves, should any of them be captured
and sold. For this reason they are not prepared to describe them,
but only non-Greeks, as slaves. And yet when they say that, they
ᵃ30 are seeking precisely the slave by nature, which was our starting
point; for one has to say that some people are slaves everywhere,
others nowhere. This applies in the same way to noble birth: nobles
regard themselves as of noble birth not only among their own
people but everywhere, but non-Greeks as noble only in their
ᵃ35 homelands. They imply that freedom and noble birth have two
senses, one absolute, the other not. (As the Helen of Theodectes
says, 'Who would think it proper to call me a servant, who am
sprung of divine roots on both sides?') But when they say that, they
ᵃ40 are distinguishing freedom and slavery, nobly born and base born,
ᵇ1 by nothing but virtue and vice. For they claim that as man is born
of man, and beast of beast, so good is born of good. But frequently,
though it may be nature's intention to do this, she is nevertheless
incapable of it.

4 (1255ᵇ4–15) It is clear then that there is justification for the
ᵇ5 difference of opinion, and that it is not always true that some are

slaves by nature and others free; it is clear also that such a distinction does in some cases exist—cases where it is expedient and just for the one to be master, the other to be slave, and where the one ought to be ruled, and the other ought to exercise the rule he is fitted to exercise by nature—so as to be, in fact, a master. If it is exercised badly, that is contrary to the interest of both; for the same thing benefits the part and the whole, the soul and the body; and ᵇ10 the slave is a sort of part of his master like a sort of living but detached part of his body. For this reason there is actually a certain advantage for master and slave, and mutual friendship, for those of them deemed to deserve their condition by nature; but when the position is not like that but rests on law, and they have been subjected to force, the opposite occurs. ᵇ15

I vii

THE SKILL NEEDED TO RULE SLAVES

1 (1255ᵇ16–20)   From this too it is clear that the rule of a master and the rule of a statesman are not the same thing, and that the forms of rule are not all the same as one another, though some say that they are. The one is rule over naturally free men, the other over slaves; rule by a household-manager is a monarchy, since every household has one ruler; the rule of a statesman is rule over free and equal persons. ᵇ20

2 (1255ᵇ20–30)   A master is not so styled in virtue of knowledge, but in virtue of being that kind of person; and a similar point applies both to slave and to free. Still, there *could* be such a thing as a master's knowledge, and a slave's knowledge, such as was taught by the man in Syracuse, who, for a fee, trained the slaves in their routine services; and the learning of such things as these could ᵇ25 be extended even further, for instance to cookery and the other services of that kind. For different personnel have different tasks, some of which are more prestigious, others more in the way of essential chores (as the proverb has it, slave before slave, master before master).

3 (1255ᵇ30–40)   All such fields of knowledge are the business of ᵇ30 slaves, whereas a master's knowledge is of how to put slaves to use; for it is not in his acquiring of his slaves but in his use of slaves that he is master. But this form of knowledge has no great importance or dignity, since he has to know how to direct slaves to do the things which they have to know how to do. Hence for those in a position ᵇ35 to avoid bothering personally an overseer takes on this office, while they themselves engage in statesmanship or philosophy. The knowledge of how to *acquire* slaves is different from both these—that is, knowing how to acquire them justly is a kind of military or hunting knowledge. As for master and slave, then, these are the b40 distinctions that should stand.

I viii

HOUSEHOLD-MANAGEMENT AND NATURAL ACQUISITION

1256 **1 (1256ᵃ1–10)** Let us then, since the slave too has proved to be part of property, go on to consider property and the art of acquiring goods in general, in accordance with our guiding method. The first question one might ask is this: Is the art of acquiring goods the same as that of household-management, or a part of it, or subsidi-ᵃ5 ary to it? And if it is subsidiary, is it so in the same way as the art of shuttle-making is subsidiary to that of weaving, or as that of bronze-founding is to the making of statues? For they are not subsidiary in the same way: the one provides tools, the other the material—I mean by 'material' the underlying stuff out of which a product is made, for example wool for the weaver, bronze for the sculptor.

ᵃ10   **2 (1256ᵃ10–19)** Now it is obvious that the art of household-management is not the *same* as that of acquiring goods, because it is the role of one to provide, the other to use; for what skill will there be which will make use of what is in the house, except that of household-management? But whether the skill of acquisition is some *part* of it, or a different kind of thing, is a question for debate. ᵃ15 For if it is the task of a person concerned with acquiring goods to consider from what sources goods and property will come, and property and riches embrace many parts, the first question will be whether the skill of farming is some part of the skill of household-management or some different type of thing—and the same considerations apply generally to the superintendence and provision of food.

   3 (1256ᵃ19–29) But again, there are many different types of ᵃ20 food, which is why there are also many different ways of life, both of animals and of humans; for no life is possible without food, so that differences of food have produced among animals different ways of life. Some animals live in herds and others scattered about, whichever helps them to find their food, because some of them are

10

carnivorous, some frugivorous and others omnivorous. So, to serve ᵃ25
their convenience and help them get hold of these foods, nature has
made their ways of life different; and since by nature the same thing
is not found tasty by each, but some things by some and some by
others, among the carnivorous and frugivorous animals themselves
the ways of life are different.

4 (1256ᵃ29–40)   Similarly among human beings too: for their
ways of life differ widely. The most idle are the nomads, for food ᵃ30
from tame animals comes to them without toil as they take their
leisure; but when it is necessary for the flocks to change location
because of the pastures, the human beings themselves have to go
along with them, farming as it were a living farm. Others live from
hunting, and different kinds from different kinds of it: some from ᵃ35
raiding, others—people who live near lakes, marshes, rivers, or a
fish-bearing area of the sea—from fishing; others live off birds and
wild beasts. But the most numerous type lives off the earth and its
cultivated crops.

5 (1256ᵃ40–ᵇ7)   The ways of life are then roughly of that ᵃ40
number, at any rate those that have their work self-engendered,
and do not procure their food through exchange or trade. They are ᵇ1
the nomadic, the agricultural, and those of raiding, fishing, and
hunting. Some men live agreeably by some combination of them,
making up for the inadequacies of their way of life where it falls
short in regard to self-sufficiency; for instance, some simultaneously pursue the nomadic and the raiding life, others the farming ᵇ5
and the hunting life; and similarly in the case of the others also.
They live in whatever way need joins in compelling them.

6 (1256ᵇ7–20)   Such acquisition is clearly given by nature her-
self to all, both straight away at the first moment of birth, and so too
when they are fully grown. For some animals produce at the start, ᵇ10
to accompany the birth, sufficient food to last until such time as the
offspring is able to get it for itself, for example those which produce
grubs or eggs. The viviparous carry for some time within themselves food for the offspring being born—the natural substance we
call milk. So similarly it is clear we have to suppose that, for ᵇ15
developed things also, plants exist for the sake of animals, and that
the other animals exist for the sake of man, tame ones both for use
and for food, and most but not all wild animals for food and other
support—in order that we may obtain clothing and other instru-
ments from them. ᵇ20

7 (1256ᵇ20–6)   If then nature makes nothing either incomplete
or to no purpose, it must be that nature has made all of them for the
sake of man. That is why even the art of war, since hunting is a part
of it, will in a sense be by nature an art of acquiring property, which

ᵇ25 must be used both against wild animals and against such men as are by nature intended to be ruled over but refuse, on the ground that this kind of warfare is just by nature.

8 (1256ᵇ26–39) So one type of the art of acquiring property is by nature a part of the art of household-management, in that either there must be available, or it must itself contrive that there is available, a supply of those things which go to make up a store of goods that are essential for life and useful for the association of ᵇ30 state or household. And it looks as if true wealth consists of these things. For self-sufficiency in this kind of property, for purposes of a good life, is not limitless. Solon in his poetry says it is: 'No end to riches lies stated for men.' But one does lie, as in the other skills ᵇ35 too; for none has any tool which is unlimited in size or number, and wealth is a collection of tools of statesmen and of persons concerned with household-management. So then, that there is by nature a certain kind of skill in property-acquisition for household-managers and statesmen, and the reason why, is clear.

I ix

ORIGIN, GROWTH, AND VARIETIES OF EXCHANGE

ᵇ40 **1 (1256ᵇ40–1257ᵃ5)** But there is another type of skill in acquisition, which people call 'skill in acquiring goods' *par excellence*; and it is just to call it that. Because of it, there is thought to be no **1257** limit to wealth or property: many people suppose that it is one and the same as the kind we spoke of, because of their closeness. But it is neither the same as the one we mentioned, nor far from it: one of them is natural, the other is not, but comes more from a certain kind of experience and skill.

ᵃ5 **2 (1257ᵃ5–19)** Let us begin our discussion of it thus: Every possession has a double use; both are uses of it in itself, but they are not similar uses of it in itself; for one is proper to the thing, the other is not; for example, the wearing of a sandal, and its use in ᵃ10 changing-round. Both are uses of the shoe; for he that exchanges a shoe, for coins or food, with someone who needs a shoe, makes use of the shoe as a shoe, but not the use proper to it; for it does not come to exist for the purpose of exchange. The same is the case with other possessions: the technique of changing-round embraces ᵃ15 them all, and had its first origin in natural conditions, from men having less than sufficient of this and more than sufficient of that. In the light of this, it is clear also that that branch of the skill of

acquiring goods which is skill in trade does not exist by nature; for
it was up to the point where they had *enough* that they were forced
to engage in exchange.

3 (1257ᵃ19–28)   So then, exchange obviously has no function in
the first association, i.e. the household, but only when the associa- ᵃ20
tion has now come to consist of larger numbers. In the former case
people used to share all the same things, whereas those who were
separated shared next many other things too, of which they were
forced to make exchanges in accordance with their needs—as many
of the non-Greek nations too still proceed, by exchange. For they ᵃ25
exchange real things of use for real things of use, but no more than
that—for example they take and give wine for corn, and everything
else of this kind.

4 (1257ᵃ28–41)   So then, such a technique of changing-round is
neither contrary to nature nor is it any type of skill in acquiring
goods; for it served to make up for gaps in natural self-sufficiency. ᵃ30
All the same, it was out of it that that skill arose, and intelligibly
so—for when supplies came increasingly from foreign sources, because of the import of needs and export of surplus goods, then the
use of coinage was contrived under pressure of necessity. For not
every natural necessity is easily carried; and that is why for pur- ᵃ35
poses of exchange they entered into an agreement to give each
other and accept from each other something which was included in
its own right among useful objects and offered easy handling in use
for the purposes of life—iron, silver, and anything else like that. It
was at first determined simply by size and weight; but finally they
also put a stamp on it, by which to free themselves from measuring, ᵃ40
since the stamp was put on as an indication of the amount.

5 (1257ᵃ41–ᵇ10)   Once a currency had been provided, out of
necessary exchange the other type of skill in acquiring goods arose: ᵇ1
trade. At first it was probably quite a simple affair, but then it
became more skilled, through experience of the sources and methods from which the greatest profit would be made out of the changing-round. That is why the technique of acquiring goods is held to ᵇ5
be concerned primarily with coinage, and its function to be the
ability to look out for sources from which a lot of money will come;
for it is productive of wealth and money. And people often regard
wealth as a large quantity of coin, because coin is what the tech-
niques of acquiring goods and of trading are concerned with.

6 (1257ᵇ10–17)   But sometimes coinage is on the contrary re- ᵇ10
garded as trumpery and as entirely a convention, not natural at all,
since, if those who employ coinage alter it, it has no value and
cannot be used to obtain any necessity; and often a man with
wealth in coin will not have the necessities in food. Yet it *is* ridicu-

lous that there should be wealth such that someone who is rolling
ᵇ15 in it will die of hunger. It is like the story they tell of that fellow
Midas' death: because of the insatiable greed of his prayer everything that was set before him turned to gold.

7 (1257ᵇ17–23) Hence men seek some different sense of
wealth and of skill in the acquisition of goods, and are right to do
so. For natural wealth, and skill in the acquisition of goods, are a
ᵇ20 distinct thing, and this skill belongs to household-management; but
skill in trading is to do with the production of goods, not in the full
sense, but through their changing-round. And it is thought to be
concerned with coinage because coinage is both the unit of exchange and its limit.

8 (1257ᵇ23–31) And to the wealth that comes from this mode
ᵇ25 of acquiring goods there is in fact no limit. For the art of medicine
aims at unlimited health, and every other skill aims at its own end
without limit; for they wish to achieve that to the maximum extent.
But none of their means towards the end are unlimited, since the
end is the limit for all skills. Similarly, there is no limit to the end of
this skill in acquiring goods, because the end is wealth in that
ᵇ30 form, i.e. the possession of goods. The skill of acquiring goods that
is involved in household-management, on the other hand, does
have a limit, since this is not the function of skill in household-
management.

9 (1257ᵇ32–40) So while in one way it seems there is necessarily a limit to wealth, in the event we observe that the opposite
occurs: all those engaged in acquiring goods go on increasing their
ᵇ35 coin without limit. The cause is the closeness of the two things.
Each of the two skills in acquiring goods makes use of the same
thing, so their uses overlap, since they are uses of the same property, but not on the same principle. In one case increase, in the
other something different, is the end. So some people imagine that
this is the job of household-management, and go on thinking that
they ought either to maintain their resources in coin or to increase
ᵇ40 them without limit.

10 (1257ᵇ40–1258ᵃ14) The cause of this disposition is pre-
1258 occupation with life but not with the good life; so, desire for the
former being unlimited, they also desire productive things without
limit. Those who do actually aim at the good life seek what brings
the pleasures of the body; so, as this too appears to lie in property,
ᵃ5 their whole activity centres on getting goods; and the second type
of skill in acquiring goods has come about because of this. For since
their pleasure is in excess, men look for the art which produces the
excess that brings the pleasure. And if they cannot procure it by
means of the skill of acquiring goods, they attempt to do so by

means of something else that causes it, using each of their faculties
in a manner contrary to nature. For it is not the job of courage to   ᵃ10
produce goods, but boldness; nor is it the job of a general's skill or
a doctor's, but victory and health respectively. But these people
make all skills into skills of acquiring goods, in the belief that this is
the end, and everything has to be directed towards the end.

11 (1258ᵃ14–18)   We have now discussed both the non-necessary acquisition of goods, what it is and what the reason is why we   ᵃ15
employ it, and the necessary, stating both that it differs from the
other and that it is by nature that skill in household-management
which has to do with food, being not unlimited like this one, but
with a limit.

I x

HOUSEHOLD-MANAGEMENT IN RELATION TO ACQUISITION,
TRADE, AND MONEY-LENDING

1 (1258ᵃ19–27)   The answer is clear also to the problem posed at
the start, namely whether the skill of acquiring goods is the business of the statesman, and of the household-manager's role, or   ᵃ20
not—this having rather to be on hand. For just as the skill of the
statesman does not make men, but takes them from nature and
uses them, so too nature has to provide land or sea or something
else to yield food, and from these the household-manager should
draw these supplies and administer them in the manner required.   ᵃ25
For the job of weaving is not to make wool but to use it, and
to know what sort is usable and suitable, or substandard and
unsuitable.

2 (1258ᵃ27–38)   For one might raise the problem of why the
skill of acquiring goods is part of household-management, whereas
the art of medicine is not a part, even though the members of a
household have to be healthy, just as they have to live or meet some   ᵃ30
other essential need. In one sense it *is* the business of household-
manager or ruler to see to health also, but in another it is not their
business, but the doctor's. So too in the matter of goods: in one
sense they *are* the concern of the manager, but in another sense not
his concern, but that of the subsidiary skill. But above all, as has
been said earlier, this should be on hand by nature. For it is a   ᵃ35
function of nature to provide food for what is born, since the
residue of that from which it is born is food for every one of them.
That is why the skill of acquiring goods from crops and animals is
in accordance with nature for all men.

3 (1258ᵃ38–ᵇ8) The skill of acquiring goods is, then, as we have said, of two kinds. One is to do with trade, the other with house-
ᵃ40 hold-management. The latter is necessary and commended, but the
ᵇ1 kind to do with changing-round is justly censured, since it is not in accordance with nature, but is from each other. Hence the technique of charging petty interest is very reasonably hated, for the acquisition comes from the coinage itself, not from the purpose for which coinage was provided. For coinage came into being for the sake of changing-round, whereas interest increases the amount of
ᵇ5 the thing itself. That is where it got its name from: for what resembles a parent is precisely the offspring, and interest is born as coinage from coinage. And so, of all ways of acquiring goods, this one is actually the most contrary to nature.

I xi

MODES OF ACQUISITION, INCLUDING MONOPOLY: ANALYSIS AND ASSESSMENT

1 (1258ᵇ9–21) Now that we have adequately discussed what bears on knowledge, we ought to go through what bears on prac-
ᵇ10 tice. In all subjects of this kind speculation befits a free man, whereas experience meets essential needs. Useful parts of the skill of acquiring wealth are experience of: (1) *stock-rearing*, of what kinds are most profitable and where and how, e.g. what sort of property in the form of horses, cattle, sheep, and of other animals
ᵇ15 similarly; for one has to have experience of which of these are most profitable, when compared with each other, and what kinds in what kinds of location, since some flourish in some districts, others in others. (2) *Tillage* of land, which immediately divides into land planted for grain and land planted for fruit. (3) *Bee-keeping*, and the rearing of other animals—birds or fishes—from which one can
ᵇ20 derive advantage. These, then, are the parts of the primary and most authentic kind of acquisition of goods.

 2 (1258ᵇ21–33) Of the technique of changing-round, the main branch is (1) *commerce*, subdivided into (*a*) shipping, (*b*) carrying goods, (*c*) offering them for sale. These differ one from another in that some are more secure, others offer a greater return. Then (2)
ᵇ25 *money-lending*, and (3) *working for pay*, whether (*a*) as a skilled mechanic, or (*b*) as an unskilled worker useful in body only. Between this form and the primary type of skill in the acquisition of goods there comes a third, in that it partakes to some extent both of

the natural form and of the form based on changing-round; it has to
do with such things as are from the earth and from barren but
useful things which come from the earth: timber-working, for ex- ᵇ30
ample, and mining of every description. This latter immediately
embraces many categories, for the substances mined from the earth
are of many types.

3 (**1258ᵇ33–1259ᵃ6**)　About each of these I have still spoken
only in a general way; a detailed account of them would be useful
for performing the operations, but it would be a low thing to linger ᵇ35
over them. The operations which are most skilled are those in
which there is the smallest element of chance; the most mechanical
are those which most harm the body; the most slavish are those in
which the body is used most often; and the most ignoble are those
in which there is least need of virtue too. Since some people have
written on these topics, for instance Charetides of Paros and ᵇ40
Apollodorus of Lemnos on tillage of land for grain and land **1259**
planted for fruit, and others too on other subjects similarly, anyone
who is interested may study them in their works. A collection ought
to be made of the scattered reports of methods by which some
people have succeeded in acquiring wealth; for those who value ᵃ5
that skill can make use of them all.

4 (**1259ᵃ6–23**)　Take for instance that of Thales of Miletus. This
is a device for getting wealth which, though ascribed to him because
of his wisdom, is in fact applicable generally. People were re-
proaching him for his poverty, claiming that philosophy was useless; and the story is that when he realized from his astronomy that ᵃ10
there would be a harvest of olives, then while it was still winter and
he had a little money to spare, he handed round deposits on all the
oil-presses in Miletus and Chios, hiring them for a small sum, as no
one was outbidding him. When the time came, and many people
suddenly and simultaneously sought them, he hired them out on ᵃ15
what terms he wished. He raked in a lot of money, and so demonstrated that it is easy for philosophers to become rich, if they want
to, but that this is not their concern. This is the manner in which
Thales is said to have given proof of his wisdom; but, as we have
said, such a device for getting wealth—seeing if one can contrive a ᵃ20
monopoly for oneself—applies generally. Hence some states too
raise revenue thus when they are short of money: they secure
themselves a monopoly of things for sale.

5 (**1259ᵃ23–36**)　There was a man in Sicily who, when a sum of
money had been deposited with him, bought up all the iron from
the foundries, and later, when the merchants arrived from their ᵃ25
warehouses, he used to be the only seller, though without raising
the price by much; nevertheless, he took a hundred talents to add to

his fifty. When Dionysius heard of this he told the man to take his
ᵃ30 money out, but to remain in Syracuse no longer, as he was finding
ways of raising revenue that were prejudicial to his own affairs. Yet
Thales and this man had their eyes on the same thing: for they both
contrived to create a monopoly for themselves. It is useful for
statesmen too to know these things; for many states are in need of
business and the associated revenues, just as a household is, indeed
ᵃ35 more so. That is precisely why some of those involved in affairs of
state actually involve themselves in these affairs of state alone.

I xii

RULE IN THE HOUSEHOLD: HUSBANDS AND FATHERS

1 (1259ᵃ37–ᵇ10)   The skill of household-management proved to
have three parts, one being the skill of a master, which has already
been dealt with, next that of a father, and a third marital. For he
rules over wife and children, over both as free persons, but not with
ᵃ40 the same style of rule: over a wife he rules in the manner of a
ᵇ1 statesman, over children in that of a king; for by nature the male is
more fitted to be in command than the female, unless conditions in
some respect contravene nature; and the elder and fully grown is
more fitted than the younger and underdeveloped. Now in most
cases of rule by statesmen there is an interchange of the role of
ᵇ5 ruler and ruled, since they tend to be equal by nature and not to
differ at all. (Nevertheless, while one is ruling and the other is being
ruled, the former seeks to have a distinction made in outward
dignity, in style of address, and in honours, as for example in what
Amasis said about his foot-basin.) But that is the permanent relationship of male to female.
ᵇ10   **2 (1259ᵇ10–17)**   Rule over children is royal, for the begetter is
ruler by virtue both of affection and of seniority, and this is a
species of royal rule. Homer's term for Zeus was therefore right
when he called the king of them all, 'father of gods and men'. For
ᵇ15 a king ought to have a natural superiority, but to be the same in
stock; and this is just the condition of elder in relation to younger
and of the begetter to the child.

I xiii

THE MORAL VIRTUES OF THE MEMBERS OF THE HOUSEHOLD

1 (1259ᵇ18–32)   It is clear then that household-management is
more seriously concerned with the human beings than with the

inanimate property, and with their virtue than with the virtue, which we call wealth, of acquisition, and with the virtue of the free ᵇ20 than with that of slaves. Now the first question one could ask about slaves is whether, in addition to his virtues as tool and his virtues as servant, a slave has some other virtue, more valuable than these, such as restraint, courage, justice, and every other condition of that kind. Or has he none but his bodily services? Either answer ᵇ25 presents a problem. For if they do have such a virtue, in what respect will they differ from free men? If they have not, that is curious, since they are human beings and share in reason. The question that is put concerning both woman and child is broadly the same. Have these also virtues, and ought a woman to be tem- ᵇ30 perate, brave, and just, and is a child both intemperate and temperate? Or not?

2 (1259ᵇ32–1260ᵃ2) This question about the natural subject and ruler, whether their virtue is the same or different, needs to be examined in general terms. For if both have to partake of a high moral character, why should one have to rule unqualifiedly, and the ᵇ35 other unqualifiedly obey? (A distinction of more or less is not possible: the difference between ruling and obeying is one of type, and the more and the less do not differ like that at all.) But if the one is to have virtues, and the other not, that is surprising. For if the ruler is not going to be moderate and just, how shall he rule well? And if the ruled is not going to be, how shall he *be* ruled well? For ᵇ40 if he is intemperate and corrupt, he will perform none of his duties. **1260**

3 (1260ᵃ2–14) Thus it becomes clear that both must have a share in virtue, but that there are differences in it, just as there are among those who are by nature ruled. We have an immediate guide in the position in the case of the soul, where we find natural ruler ᵃ5 and natural subject, whose virtues we say are different—that is, one belongs to the rational element, the other to the non-rational. Well then, it is clear that the same applies in the other cases too, so that most instances of ruling and being ruled are natural. For rule of free over slave, male over female, man over child, is exercised in ᵃ10 different ways, because, while the parts of the soul are present in all of them, they are present in them in different ways. The slave is completely without the deliberative element; the female has it, but it has no authority; the child has it, but undeveloped.

4 (1260ᵃ14–24) Well then, we should take it that a similar situation inevitably prevails in regard to the moral virtues also, namely ᵃ15 that all must participate in them, but not in the same fashion, but only so far as suffices for each for his own function. That is why the ruler must have moral virtue complete; for his function is without qualification that of a master-craftsman, and reason is a master-

craftsman; and each of the others ought to have as much as pertains
to them. So it is evident that all those mentioned have moral virtue,
and that the same moderation does not belong to a man and to a
woman, nor justice and courage, as Socrates used to think; the one
courage is that of a ruler, the other that of a servant, and likewise
with the other virtues too.

5 (1260ª24–36) If we look at this matter in detail it will become
clear. For those who talk in generalities and say that virtue is 'a
good condition of the soul', or that it is 'right conduct', or the like,
delude themselves. Those who, like Gorgias, *enumerate* the virtues,
give a better account than those who frame definitions in this
manner. That is why in all cases one ought to think like the poet
who said of a woman, 'to a woman silence brings refinement'—
whereas this does not apply to a man. Since the child is not fully
developed, it is clear that his virtue too is not his in relation to
himself, but in relation to his end and his guide. So too is that of a
slave in relation to his master: we laid it down that a slave is useful
in relation to necessities, so obviously of virtue too he needs but
little—enough to ensure that he does not neglect his work through
intemperance or corruption.

6 (1260ª36–ᵇ7) If what has now been said is true, one would
naturally ask whether skilled workers too will have to possess
virtue; for they often skimp their work through intemperance. Or is
this a very different thing? For the slave shares his master's life,
whereas the workman is further off, and virtue pertains to him to
the precise extent that slavery does; for the skilled mechanic has a
kind of delimited slavery, and the slave is one of those things that
exist by nature, whereas no shoemaker is, nor any other skilled
worker. So then, it is clear that it is the master who ought to be the
cause of such virtue in his slave, not the man who has the skill of
instructing him in his tasks. That is why those who deny reason to
slaves, and bid one use orders only, are wrong in what they say; for
slaves ought to be admonished more than children.

7 (1260ᵇ8–20) But let us take these matters as settled in this
way. As for man and woman, children and father, the virtue relevant to each, and what is admirable in their intercourse among
themselves and what is not, and the way they ought to aim at good
practice and avoid the bad—it will be necessary to go through these
topics in connection with the constitutions. For every household is
part of a state, and these persons are part of the household; and the
virtue of the part ought to be examined in relation to that of the
whole. So both children and women must be educated with an eye
to the constitution, since it does indeed make a difference to the
soundness of a state that its children should be sound, and its

women too. The difference made is inevitable: women are half the free persons, and from children come those who participate in the constitution.

8 (1260ᵇ20–4) So now that we have settled these matters, and ᵇ20 have to discuss the rest in another place, we will dismiss the present subjects as concluded, and make another beginning to our discussion. And let us first review those who have pronounced an opinion on the best constitution.

PROGRAMME: 'IDEAL' STATES, REAL AND PROPOSED:
THE LIMITS OF SHARING

1 (1260ᵇ27–36) We propose to consider which form of association that is the state is best of all for persons able to live a life as
close as possible to the ideal. So we must look at the other consti-
ᵇ30 tutions too, both those in use in certain of the states that are
reputed to be governed by good laws, and any others which we find
set forth by any one and are thought to be of good quality. Our
purpose is to see what is right and useful in them—but also to avoid
giving the impression that a search for something different from
them is the result of a desire to be clever at all costs; let it be
thought, rather, that we have embarked on this mode of inquiry
ᵇ35 precisely because these constitutions currently existing are *not* of
good quality.
 2 (1260ᵇ36–1261ᵃ9) We must begin at the natural starting-
point of this inquiry. All the citizens must either share all things, or
none, or some but not others. It is clearly impossible that they
ᵇ40 should share nothing: a constitution being a form of association,
they must share the territory, the single territory of a single state, of
1261 which single state the citizens are sharers. But is it better that a
state which is to be run well should share all things capable of being
shared, or is it better for it to share some things but not others? It
is possible for citizens to go shares with each other in children, in
ᵃ5 wives, and in possessions, as in the *Republic* of Plato. For in that
work Socrates says that children, wives, and property ought to be
held in common. So is present practice better, or observance of the
law proposed in the *Republic*?

II ii

CRITICISM OF SOCIAL AND POLITICAL 'ONENESS' IN
PLATO'S *REPUBLIC*

ᵃ10 **1 (1261ᵃ10–22)** That wives should belong in common to all has
many other disadvantages, on top of these: (*a*) his reason for claiming the necessity for legislation laid down in these terms obviously
does not emerge from his arguments; (*b*) further, the end which he
says the state should have is, as it is there described, impossible; yet

(*c*) nothing has been settled about how one ought to define it. I'm
speaking of the greatest possible oneness of the entire state, as ᵃ15
allegedly best; for this is the assumption Socrates adopts. But obviously a state which becomes progressively more and more one will
not be a state at all. For a state is by nature a plurality of some sort,
and the more it becomes one, it will turn from a state into a
household, and from a household into an individual person. For we
would say that the household is more one than the state, and the ᵃ20
single individual than the household. So, even if someone proved
able to achieve this, it ought not to be done; for it will destroy the
state.

   2 (1261ᵃ22–37)   The state consists not merely of a plurality of
persons, but of persons who differ in type; for a state does not come
from people who are alike. A state and an alliance are different:
the latter is useful in point of quantity, even if it is the same in type ᵃ25
(the natural purpose of an alliance to military assistance)—like the
effect that would result if a weight were heavier on the scales. It is
also in this sort of respect that a state whose numbers are not
scattered in villages, but are like the Arcadians, will differ from a
nation. But things from which a single thing must come, differ in
type. Hence, as was stated before in the *Ethics*, it is reciprocal ᵃ30
equality that preserves states, since this is essential even among
those who are free and equal; for they cannot all hold office simultaneously, but only for a year at a time or by some other temporal
arrangement. This procedure has the result that all rule: they act ᵃ35
just as shoemakers and carpenters would act if they changed places
with each other, instead of the same people being permanently
shoemakers and carpenters.

   3 (1261ᵃ37–ᵇ6)   But since it is better thus in relation also to the
association which is the state, it is clearly better that the same
people should rule permanently, if possible. But among those
among whom this is not possible, since they are all by nature equal,
and among whom it is also at the same time just that all should ᵇ1
share in the benefit or chore of ruling, then the principles (*a*) that
equals should yield place in turn, and (*b*) that out of office they
should be similar, approximate to that practice. Some rule while
others are ruled, by turns, just as they would if they had become
different persons. In the same way, among the rulers, some hold ᵇ5
one office, some another.

   4 (1261ᵇ6–15)   So it is clear from this that the state is not naturally one in the way some people think, and that what has been
alleged to be the greatest good in states destroys them, whereas the
good of each thing preserves it. And in yet another way it is clear ᵇ10
that to strive to impose extreme oneness on a state is not the better

policy: a household is a more self-sufficient thing than the single individual, the state than the household; and when an association comes to be self-sufficient in numbers, its tendency is to be a state then and there. So since the greater self-sufficiency is to be pre-
ᵇ15 ferred, the lesser oneness is also to be preferred.

II iii

LANGUAGE AND PSYCHOLOGY OF POSSESSION IN A SYSTEM OF ONENESS

1 (1261ᵇ16–32) Again, even if it is best that the association should as far as possible be one, this does not seem to have been shown to be so by the argument, 'if all say "mine" and "not mine" at the same time' (Socrates thinks this is an indication of the state's
ᵇ20 being completely one)—because 'all' is used in two senses. If all individually is meant, then this may perhaps be nearer to what Socrates wants to bring about; for each man will always refer to the same person as his son, and to the same woman as his wife; and he will speak in the same way of his possessions, and each thing that befalls him. But that is not in fact how people will speak who hold
ᵇ25 wives and children in common. They will *all* speak, but not individually, and the same with regard to possessions: all, but not individually. So then, 'all say' is clearly some sort of fallacy; for 'all' and 'both', and 'odd' and 'even', owing to their double senses,
ᵇ30 generate contentious syllogisms even in discussion. So, while in one way it is admirable, but impossible, that all should say the same thing, in another way it is not at all conducive to concord.

2 (1261ᵇ32–40) On top of this, there is other harm in the claim; for what belongs in common to the greatest number, receives the least looking after. People take particular care of their private property, less of the communal, or only in so far as it falls to the
ᵇ35 individual to do so. Other reasons apart, the thought that another person is looking after it makes them ignore it the more, just as in domestic duties a great number of attendants sometimes give worse service than a smaller. Each of the citizens acquires a thousand sons, but they do not belong to him as an individual: any one of them is equally the son of any one of them, and as a result will be
ᵇ40 neglected equally by them all.

1262 **3 (1262ᵃ1–14)** Moreover, a man says 'my' of a citizen who is faring well or ill, to this extent, that he is a certain fraction of the total number. In saying 'my', or 'X's', he is speaking of each indi-

vidually of the thousand (or whatever the number that makes up
the state), and even then he is not certain, since it is not clear who ᵃ5
has happened to have a child born to him, and one that once born
has survived. Yet really, which is the better use of 'mine', that by
each of two thousand or ten thousand persons, all with reference to
the same thing, or rather as people say 'mine' in states in practice?
For one man refers to as *his own* son the same person as he whom
another refers to as *his own* brother, and whom a third refers to as
cousin, or something in virtue of some other kinship or connection, ᵃ10
i.e. by marriage, his own in the first place, or of his own relatives;
and in addition to these terms another speaks of him as a phratry-
member or tribesman. It is better to be someone's personal cousin
than a son in the manner described.

4 (1262ᵃ14-24)   None the less, it is not even possible to prevent
people from assuming that certain persons are their own brothers, ᵃ15
sons, fathers, or mothers. For the resemblances which occur between parents and their offspring are bound to be interpreted as
sure signs about each other. And this is what actually happens,
according to reports of some who write up their travels round the
world, who tell us that certain of the Upper Libyans have commu- ᵃ20
nity of wives, but that they nevertheless distinguish by their resemblances the children born to them. And there are some females,
both human and non-human (like mares and cows), which have a
remarkable natural power of producing offspring resembling their
sires, like the mare at Pharsalus named 'Just'.

II iv

DRAWBACKS OF COMMUNITY OF WIVES AND CHILDREN IN PLATO'S *REPUBLIC*

1 (1262ᵃ25-32)   Here are examples of the other such disadvan- ᵃ25
tages which cannot easily be avoided by those who set up this form
of association: assault, homicide intentional and unintentional,
fights, and abuse. None of these are holy when they are committed
against father or mother or not far distant kin (as they are when
they are committed against those from outside this range). They
are bound to happen even more when people are not aware than ᵃ30
when they are aware. And when they have happened, and if people
are aware, the customary expiations of them can take place; if they
are not, none is possible.

2 (1262ᵃ32-40)   It is also curious that, while making sons com-

munal, he takes away only the sexual intercourse between lovers, but does not forbid the love, nor the other practices, between
ᵃ35 brothers or between father and son, whose occurrence is the most unseemly thing of all, since even the love on its own is. It is curious, too, that he takes away sexual intercourse for no other reason, on the ground of the excessively powerful pleasure that arises, and
ᵃ40 yet believes that it makes no difference that it is father or son, or brothers of each other.

3 (1262ᵃ40–ᵇ24)   The community of wives and children looks useful rather more for the farmers than for the Guardians. For
ᵇ1 where wives and children are held in common there will be less affection; but it is the ruled who ought to be disposed thus, in the interests of obedience and absence of revolt. And in general the results of such a law as this are bound to be the opposite of those
ᵇ5 which correctly enacted legislation ought to bring about, and of those that Socrates regards as the reason for ordering matters in this way as regards children and wives. For we believe that affection is the greatest of goods for states, because in those conditions they will least resort to faction. And Socrates is emphatic in his
ᵇ10 praise of the oneness of the state, which (as it seems, and as the man himself says) is a product of affection. In the discourses about love we know that Aristophanes said that lovers because of the warmth of their affection are eager to grow into each other and become both together one instead of two. In such circumstances both or one has necessarily perished. In a state, however, this sort of as-
ᵇ15 sociation is bound to make affection watery, in that a father inevitably says 'mine' of his son, or a son of his father, to a minimal extent. Just as a little sweetening mixed into a large amount of water makes the mixture undetectable, so too are the kinship-connections implied by these terms affected, since in such a con-
ᵇ20 stitution there is least obligation on a father to care for his son *qua* son, or a son for his father *qua* father, or brothers *qua* brothers for each other. There are two things which particularly cause human beings to cherish and feel affection: the private and the delectable. Neither of them can be present to people living under this kind of constitution.

4 (1262ᵇ24–36)   One further point, about the transfers of chil-
ᵇ25 dren at birth, some from the farmers and the skilled workers to the Guardians, and some from the latter to the former: there is great confusion as to how they will take place. Those who hand over and transfer the children are sure to be aware which children they are handing over to whom. Again, in these cases the results we men-
ᵇ30 tioned just now are bound to occur even more: assaults, homicides, love affairs; for those handed over to the other citizens will no

longer refer to the Guardians as brothers, children, fathers, mothers, nor in turn will those now among the Guardians so refer to the other citizens, so as to take precautions against any such act because of their kinship. So let these stand as our conclusions about the community of wives and children.   ᵇ35

II v

DRAWBACKS OF COMMUNITY OF PROPERTY IN PLATO'S *REPUBLIC*; THE CONSTITUTION

1 (1262ᵇ37–1263ᵃ8)   Connected with the foregoing is the investigation to be made of property. What arrangements should be made for it by people who are going to operate the best possible constitution? Should it be held in common, or not? One could consider ᵇ40 this question even in isolation from the legislation enacted about children and wives. In connection with property, I mean: even if *they* are separate, as is in fact the universal practice, would it be **1263** better for at any rate property to be communal, or its use? For instance, is it better for the plots of land to be separate, but their produce put into a common pool for consumption, as is done by some nations? Or the opposite, the land to be communally held and ᵃ5 communally farmed, but its produce distributed for private use? This too is a communal practice which is said to exist among certain non-Greek peoples. Or ought *both* the plots of land *and* its produce to be communal?

2 (1263ᵃ8–21)   A different system and an easier one would be if the land is worked by others; whereas if people themselves work hard for their own benefit, the arrangements about property will ᵃ10 give rise to greater ill-feeling. For if they become not equal but unequal in the work they do and the return they enjoy, charges will inevitably be brought against those who enjoy or take a lot without doing much work by those who do more work but take less. In general, to live together and share in any human concern is hard, ᵃ15 and particularly so in concerns such as these. That is evident in associations of people travelling together away from home. Most of them fall to quarrelling, because they annoy each other over ordinary and unimportant matters; and we also get especially annoyed with those servants whom we employ most regularly for routine ᵃ20 services.

3 (1263ᵃ21–30)   These then, and others, are the disadvantages of the common ownership of property. Present practice would be

not a little superior, provided it is enhanced by habits and a system
of correct laws, because it will then draw the benefit from both—
ᵃ25 and by 'benefit from both' I mean that from property's being communal, and from its being private. For, while property should in a
certain sense be communal, in general it should be private. The
responsibilities, if distributed, will not lead to those charges against
each other: rather they will be carried out more effectively, since
every man will apply himself to them as his private business; yet it
will be through virtue in respect of use that we shall find that
'common are the goods of friends', in the words of the proverb.

ᵃ30 **4 (1263ᵃ30–40)** Even now, this sort of arrangement exists in
some states in an outline form, which implies that it is not impossible; and in the well-run ones particularly it exists in part and in
part might come about. For although each individual does have his
own private property, he makes available some things to be used by
his friends, while he has the use of others communally. For exam-
ᵃ35 ple, in Lacedaimon they use each other's slaves practically as their
own, and horses and dogs too; and if they need food on a journey,
they turn to the fields across their territory. Clearly then it is better
for property to be private, but for its use to be communal. It is a
particular task of a lawgiver to see that people are so disposed.

ᵃ40 **5 (1263ᵃ40–ᵇ7)** Moreover, to regard something as one's own
makes an untold difference to one's pleasure. For it may well be no
ᵇ1 accident that each individual himself loves himself; on the contrary,
this is natural. But selfishness is condemned, justly; this is not to
love oneself, but to love more than one should—as in the case of
love of money, too (since of course practically everybody does love
ᵇ5 each of the things of that sort). And further, there is very great
pleasure both in helping and in doing favours to friends and
strangers and companions; and this happens when property is
private.

6 (1263ᵇ7–14) Those who make the state an excessive unity fail
to achieve these results; and in addition they openly suppress the
actions of two virtues: restraint with regard to women (for it is a
ᵇ10 fine action to keep off a woman if she belongs to another, through
restraint), and liberality with regard to property. For a man will
neither be seen to be liberal, nor do any liberal act; for it is in the
use made of possessions that liberality has its function.

ᵇ15 **7 (1263ᵇ15–29)** Such legislation may seem attractive and
benevolent: the hearer accepts it with pleasure, supposing that
everyone will have a wondrous affection for everyone, particularly
when someone charges that the evils at present current in constitu-
ᵇ20 tions arise from the fact that property is not communal. I refer to
suits against each other about contracts, trials for false witness, and

sucking up to the wealthy. But none of these things arises from the absence of communal ownership, but from depravity, since we see far more disputes between those who own and share property in common than we do among separate holders of possessions. (But we observe few quarrelling as a result of associations they enter, ᵇ25 because we compare them with the great multitude of private owners of property.) Again, it would be only fair to mention not merely how many suits they will be rid of when they have embarked on sharing, but also how many advantages. The life looks totally impossible.

8 (1263ᵇ29–1264ᵃ1) The cause of Socrates' blunder we must reckon to be his assumption, which is not correct. For both a ᵇ30 household and a state must be one up to a point, but not completely. The state will arrive at a point where in a sense it will not be a state, or at another at which in a sense it will be, but because it will be close to not being a state, it will be a worse one. It is as if you were to reduce concord to unison or rhythm to a single beat. ᵇ35 But as we have said before, a state is a plurality, and it is necessary to make it common and one through education. It is strange that the person who did intend to introduce education, and who believed that through this the state would be sound, should think to put it straight by such methods, and not by habits, philosophy, and ᵇ40 laws—as at Sparta and in Crete, where the lawgiver introduced common arrangements for property by means of the common meals.

9 (1264ᵃ1–11) Nor must we overlook this precise point, that we **1264** ought to pay attention to the immense period of time and many years during which it would not have remained unnoticed if these things had been good. Pretty well all things have been discovered, though some have not been collected, and others people know about but do not use. The point would become especially clear if ᵃ5 one could see such a constitution being put together in practice: for one will not be able to create the state without introducing the parts and dividing it up into messes, or into brotherhoods and tribes. Consequently, no legislation will have been enacted other than this, that the Guardians should not farm—which is exactly the practice that the Lacedaemonians are even today trying to follow. ᵃ10

10 (1264ᵃ11–22) Certainly, Socrates has not stated, nor is it easy to state, what the arrangements of the constitution as a whole will be for those who associate in it. Yet the bulk of the other citizens becomes almost the entire bulk of the state; but about them no decision has been taken as to whether the farmers too ought to have communal property or private, on an individual basis, nor yet ᵃ15 whether they ought to have wives and children privately or in

common. If in the same way everything is to be common to all, how will these differ from those, the Guardians? And what good will it do to these who submit to their rule, or what will possess them to
a20 submit to it—unless the Guardians resort to some such device as the Cretans use? For they allow their slaves the same things in general, and forbid them only the gymnasia and the possession of weapons.

11 (1264ᵃ22–40) If on the other hand they too are going to have such things, as in other states, how will the association be
a25 arranged? The inevitable result is two states within one, and these in some degree in opposition to each other. For he makes the Guardians like a garrison, but makes citizens of the farmers, the skilled workmen, and the rest; and charges and suits, and such other evils as he says are present in states, will be present to them too. And yet Socrates says that, thanks to education, there will be
a30 no need for a large number of regulations such as those governing the wardenship of the city and the market, and others of that kind—though he gives education only to the Guardians. Again, he gives the farmers, who pay a rent, control of their possessions; but they are likely to be much more difficult and full of their own ideas
a35 than the populations which some peoples have among them, of helots, serfs, and slaves. But no decision has been reached as to whether there is a similar necessity for these things, or not, nor about the related questions, namely what constitution they will have, and education and laws. The quality of these people is not easy to discover, and the difference it makes to the maintenance of
a40 the association of the Guardians is not small.
b1   **12 (1264ᵃ40–ᵇ6)** But if he is going to make wives common and property private, who will look after the household, just as their men look after the work of the fields? And who will if the property and the wives of the farmers are common? To draw a parallel with
b5 wild animals and say that women ought to engage in the same occupations as men is strange: animals have no household-management to do.

13 (1264ᵇ6–15) Risky too is Socrates' way of appointing the rulers: for he makes them the same people permanently. This is a source of faction even among those who have no standing, and all
b10 the more, of course, among the warlike and spirited. But clearly he finds it unavoidable to make the same persons rulers; for the gold from the god has not been mixed into the souls of some persons at one time and into those of others at another, but always in the same persons. He says the god, immediately at their birth, mixed gold into some, silver into others, and bronze and iron into those who
b15 are going to be skilled workers and farmers.

14 (1264ᵇ15–25) Again, though he deprives the Guardians of happiness, he says that the lawgiver ought to make the whole state happy. But it is impossible for the whole to be happy, unless all parts, or most of them, or some, possess happiness. For happiness is not made up of the same things as evenness, for this can be ᵇ20 present to the whole without being present to either of the parts, whereas happiness cannot. And if the Guardians are not happy, who is? Certainly not the skilled workers and the general mass of mechanics.

The constitution about which Socrates has spoken, then, contains both these puzzles and others no less great than these.   ᵇ25

II vi

CRITICISM OF PLATO'S SECOND-BEST STATE IN THE *LAWS*

1 (1264ᵇ26–1265ª1) The case of the *Laws*, which was written later, is largely similar; so we had better glance at the constitution there too. In the *Republic*, Socrates has come to definite conclusions about very few matters: (*a*) arrangements necessary for the common possession of wives and children, (*b*) property, and (*c*) the ᵇ30 organization of the constitution. For the bulk of the inhabitants is divided into two parts, the farmers and the part for defensive fighting; while out of the latter a third group is formed which deliberates and is in sovereign charge of the state. As for the farmers and skilled workers, whether they will have a share in some office, or in none, and whether they too must possess arms and join ᵇ35 the rest in fighting, or not, on none of these matters has Socrates come to a definite conclusion. But he thinks that the women ought to join in fighting and receive the same education as the Guardians; for the rest, he has filled up his account with extraneous matter, and with a description of the style of education which the Guardians are ᵇ40 to receive.

2 (1265ª1–10) The largest proportion of the *Laws* is in fact **1265** laws, and he has said little about the constitution, which in spite of his wish to make it more acceptable to states, he gradually brings back round to the other constitution. For, apart from the sharing of wives and property, in other matters he assigns the same practices ª5 to both constitutions—the same education, the life of freedom from essential tasks, and the common meals on the same lines— except that in this state women also are to have common meals, and whereas the former state consisted of 1,000 arms-bearers, this one consists of 5,000.

3 (1265[a]10–18) Now all the Socratic dialogues display extravagance, brilliance, originality, and a spirit of inquiry; but it is perhaps hard to succeed in everything—witness the number just
mentioned: we must not forget that so many people will require the
[a]15 territory of a Babylon or some other infinitely large territory to
support 5,000 in idleness, with a further crowd around them, many
times as great, of women and servants. We ought to postulate any
ideal conditions, but nothing that is impossible.

4 (1265[a]18–28) It is stated that the lawgiver ought to lay down
his laws with an eye on two things, the territory and the population.
[a]20 But also, it is as well to add the neighbouring territories too, if, first
of all, the state has to live the life of a state and not one of isolation;
for it must necessarily employ such arms for warfare as are useful
not merely within its own territory, but also against the regions
[a]25 outside it. And if one rejects such a life, both for the individual and
for the commonalty of the state, the need is just as great to be
formidable to enemies, both on their invasion and on their retreat.

5 (1265[a]28–38) The amount of property ought also to be
looked at: perhaps it would be better to determine it differently, on
[a]30 a clearer basis. He says that it ought to be enough for a 'moderate'
life, as if that were the same as saying for a good life, which is a
more comprehensive expression. Further, it is possible to live a
moderate life and yet a miserable one. A better definition is 'moderate and liberal'; for taken separately, the one leads to luxury, the
other to a life of toil—since these are the only desirable disposi-
[a]35 tions that bear on the use of resources. For instance, one cannot use
them gently or courageously, but one can moderately and liberally.
So the dispositions too relating to their use must be these.

6 (1265[a]38–[b]17) Furthermore, it is absurd to equalize property,
if one fails to regulate the matter of the citizens' numbers but
allows the production of children without limit, in the belief that it
[a]40 will be brought into balance at the same total through cases of
childlessness, however many births there are, because this appears
[b]1 to be the result in the case of actual states. But the precision with
which this ought to apply in the case of this state and in those is
dissimilar. For in them, thanks to the dividing of resources among
however great a number, no one is in want. But in this state property is indivisible, so excess children have to go without, whether
[b]5 there be few or many of them. One may well take the view that it
is the production of children that ought to be limited, rather than
property, so that no more than a certain number are born. One
ought to fix this number in the light of the chances that some births
[b]10 will not survive, and that other couples will be childless. To leave
the number unrestricted, as is done in most states, inevitably causes

poverty for the citizens, and poverty produces faction and crime. Pheidon of Corinth, one of the earliest of the lawgivers, held that the households and the number of citizens should be kept equal, even if to begin with they all had estates of unequal size. But in the ^{b}15 *Laws* it is the other way round. Our own view as to how these matters would be better regulated will have to be stated later.

7 (1265^{b}18–21) Another omission from this *Laws* concerns the rulers: how they are to be different from the ruled? He says that the warp comes from different wool from the weft, and that is what ^{b}20 the relation between ruler and ruled ought to be.

8 (1265^{b}21–6) Again, since he allows a man's total resources to be increased up to five times, why should this not be so up to a certain limit as regards land? One ought to examine also his division of the homesteads, in case it is disadvantageous for household-management. He distributed two of the separate homesteads created by the division to each man; but it is hard to run two houses. ^{b}25

9 (1265^{b}26–1266^{a}5) The tendency of the whole system is to be neither democracy nor oligarchy, but midway between them; people call it 'polity', because it consists of the heavy-armed troops. Now if he is framing this constitution as the one which of constitutions in general is the most acceptable to states, perhaps the pro- ^{b}30 posal he has made is good; but not if as the best after the primary constitution; for one may rather commend the Laconians', or even some other with a more aristocratic leaning. Indeed, some say that the best constitution is a mixture of all constitutions, which is why they include the Lacedaemonians' in their commendation. For ^{b}35 some of them say that it is made up out of oligarchy, monarchy, and democracy: its Kingship is monarchy, the authority of its Elders is oligarchy, and it is run democratically in virtue of the authority of the Ephors, because they come from the people. Others of them say that the Ephorate is a tyranny, and that the democratic running ^{b}40 exists in virtue of the common meals and the rest of their daily life. But in this *Laws* it is stated that the best constitution ought to be **1266** composed of democracy and tyranny, constitutions which one would either not count as constitutions at all, or as the worst of all. Therefore a better case is made by those who mingle a larger number, because the constitution which is constructed from a ^{a}5 larger number is better.

10 (1266^{a}5–14) Next, it clearly has nothing monarchical about it at all, but only oligarchical and democratic features; its tendency, however, is to lean rather towards oligarchy. This is obvious from the method of appointing the officials. The practice of choosing by lot from a number chosen by election is common to both; but the obligation on the richer people to attend the Assembly, to vote for ^{a}10 officials, or to do anything else within the province of a citizen, while others are exempted—that is· oligarchical. So also is the attempt to ensure that a majority of the officials come from among the wealthy, and that the highest offices should be filled by those from the highest property-classes.

11 (1266ᵃ14–22) He makes oligarchical also the election of the
ᵃ15 Council. All choose compulsorily, but from the highest property class, then again in the same way from the second, then from members of the third—except that there was no obligation on everyone to choose from members of the third or fourth class, and only members of the first and second were obliged to choose from members of the fourth. Then from these he says that an equal
ᵃ20 number is to be appointed from each property-class. The effect will be that those from the highest property-classes will be more numerous and of better quality, because some of the common people will not choose, since it is not compulsory.

12 (1266ᵃ22–30) That such a constitution ought not to be compounded out of monarchy and democracy is obvious from these considerations, and from what will be said when our investigation
ᵃ25 reaches this kind of constitution. And also, with regard to elections of officials, electing from the elected is dangerous. For if even a moderate number of persons decide to combine, the elections will always turn out as they wish. This, then, is the position in regard to
ᵃ30 the constitution of the *Laws*.

II vii

THE CONSTITUTION OF PHALEAS:
THE PROBLEMS OF EGALITARIANISM

1 (1266ᵃ31–ᵇ8) There are certain other constitutions also, their authors being sometimes statesmen and philosophers, sometimes private persons. They all come nearer than both of these to the established constitutions—those under which people do in fact run their state affairs; for no other person has ever made the innovation
ᵃ35 of sharing in children and wives, nor of women's sharing in the common meals. Rather, they start from necessities; to some it seems most vital to get the best possible regulation of resources, for they say it is about them that all men form factions. That is why Phaleas of Chalcedon took the initiative in proposing this; for he
ᵃ40 says that the property of the citizens should be equal. He thought
ᵇ1 that this was not difficult to do at the very foundation of states, and

that, although it was more troublesome to do it to states that were already up and running, still the levelling would quickly be imposed on them by means of the rich bestowing dowries but not receiving them, and the poor receiving but not bestowing them. (Plato, when writing the *Laws*, thought that there ought up to a certain point to ^{b}5 be no control, but that, as has been stated earlier, none of the citizens should be allowed to acquire property more than five times as great as the smallest.)

2 (1266^{b}8–14) But those who legislate along these lines must not forget this either, as indeed they do forget, that while fixing the total resources they ought to fix the total of children too; for if the ^{b}10 number of children exceeds the amount of resources, it becomes necessary to abrogate the law. And apart from the abrogation, it is undesirable that many should become poor after being rich; for it is a job to prevent such people from becoming revolutionaries.

3 (1266^{b}14–24) That levelness of resources has some power to affect the association which is the state has evidently been realized ^{b}15 by some even among those of long ago, for instance both by Solon in his legislation and in the law in force among others, which prohibits acquiring as much land as one may wish. Laws likewise prevent the sale of resources, as for example in Locri, where there is a law against their sale unless one can show that some conspicu- ^{b}20 ous misfortune has occurred. In yet other cases it is required that the ancient estates be maintained intact. It was the abolition of this requirement that rendered the constitution of Leucas (among others) over-democratic; for it no longer happened that men came to office from the specified property-classes.

4 (1266^{b}24–1267^{a}2) But equality of resources may exist and yet the amount may be either too great, with resultant luxury, or ^{b}25 too little, which leads to a life of penury. It is clear, therefore, that it is not enough for a lawgiver to equalize resources: he must aim at the midway point. Yet even if one were actually to fix moderate resources for all, that would be no use; for one should even out appetites rather than resources, and this is not possible for people ^{b}30 who are not being educated adequately by the laws. Perhaps, however, Phaleas would say that this is in fact what he himself means; for he reckons that in states there ought to exist equality of these two things, property and education. But one ought to say what the education is going to be, and it is useless for it to be one and the same. For it *can* be one and the same, but of such a kind that it will ^{b}35 produce men inclined by choice to get a larger share of money or distinctions or both. And men resort to faction because of in-equality not only of possessions but also of distinctions, though for opposite reasons in either case: the many do so because of the ^{b}40

inequality relating to property, the sophisticated with regard to
1267 honours, if *equal*—hence indeed 'both good and bad in equal
esteem'.

5 (1267ª2–17) It is not only on account of essentials that men
commit injustices (for which he supposes equality of resources to
be a cure, so that they will not steal clothes because of cold or
ª5 hunger), but also to gain enjoyment and not feel desire. For if they
have desire which is greater than for necessities, they will seek to
remedy this desire by committing injustice. Nor is that remedy the
only motive: even without desires, there is a purpose to enjoy the
pleasures that are without pain. What therefore is the cure for these
three? For the first, employment and modest resources; for the
ª10 second, restraint. Third, if any persons should wish to find enjoyment through themselves, they could hardly seek a cure except
from philosophy; for the other desires stand in need of people. In
fact, men commit the greatest injustices because of excesses, not on
account of necessities. For instance, men are not tyrants in order
ª15 not to feel cold. For this reason the honours are great if one slays
not a thief but a tyrant. So Phaleas' style of constitution would be
a help only against minor injustices.

6 (1267ª17–37) Moreover, he chiefly wishes to make arrangements on the basis of which they will run the state's affairs well as
between themselves, whereas they have also to look to neighbouring people and everyone outside. So it is essential that the constitu-
ª20 tion should have been constructed with regard to military strength,
about which the man has said nothing. The case is similar in the
matter of property too; for there has to be enough of it available
not merely for needs within the state but also to meet external
dangers. This is precisely why the total amount on hand ought to be
ª25 neither so large that more powerful neighbours will covet it, and
the owners will be unable to repel the invasion, nor so small that
they cannot sustain a war even against equal and similar people.
The man has fixed nothing; yet the amount of resources it is expedient to have is a point not to be overlooked. Perhaps, therefore,
the best limit is one which offers to the stronger side no profit in
ª30 going to war on account of the excess, but only what they would get
even if so many resources were not possessed. For example, when
Autophradates was about to lay siege to Atarneus, Eubulus told
him to consider how long it would take him to capture the place,
and then to count the cost of that period—since he was prepared
ª35 (he said) to abandon Atarneus forthwith in return for a smaller
sum than that. These words caused Autophradates to take thought,
and to abandon the siege.

7 (1267ª37–ᵇ9) So, while equality of resources for the citizens

is among the useful influences that discourage them from forming
factions against each other, it is certainly no great thing, so to
speak. For the sophisticated will feel discontent, on the grounds ^{a}40
that they do not deserve equality. This is the reason for the many
obvious instances of aggression and faction on their part. Next, the
depravity of mankind is an insatiable thing. At first, the mere two ^{b}1
obols suffice; but when once that is traditional they go on always
asking for more, until they go beyond all limit. For there is no
natural limit to desires, and most people spend their lives trying
to satisfy them. A start on such things would be, in preference to ^{b}5
the levelling of possessions, to contrive that naturally reasonable
people are such as not to wish to get a larger share, and that the
common people are not able to; and this is so if they are weaker and
are not treated unjustly.

8 (1267^{b}9–13) But he has not expressed even the equality of
resources aright. For it is only property in land that he makes equal; ^{b}10
but wealth exists also in the form of slaves, cattle, and coinage, and
when there is an immense stock of movable property, as it is called.
Equality, or at least a moderate degree of regulation, should be
sought in all these; otherwise, everything must go unregulated.

9 (1267^{b}13–21) To judge from his legislation Phaleas is obviously constructing his state on a small scale, at least if all the skilled
workers will be public slaves and will not serve to complete the full ^{b}15
membership of the state. But if those employed on common works
have to be public slaves, one should employ the system in force at
Epidamnus, for instance, which at one time Diophantus tried to
introduce at Athens. As for the constitution of Phaleas, then, these
points will enable one to consider whether he has in fact proposed ^{b}20
anything good or not.

II viii

THE CONSTITUTION OF HIPPODAMUS: PROBLEMS OF
PROPERTY, LAW, AND INNOVATION

1 (1267^{b}22–30) Hippodamus, son of Euryphon, came from
Miletus. It was he who invented the division of states and laid out
the streets of the Piraeus. His ambition caused him to adopt also a
rather extreme life-style in general, so that he appeared to some to
live somewhat affectedly, with his long hair and expensive orna- ^{b}25
ments, and wearing clothes that were cheap but warm, not only in
winter but in summertime too; and he wished to be considered

expert in the whole of nature also. He was the first of those not taking part in the running of a constitution to try to say something about the best one.

ᵇ30   **2 (1267ᵇ30–7)**   He set about designing a state of 10,000, divided into three parts. He intended to make one of skilled workers, one of farmers, and a third to bear arms and secure defence. The territory also he proposed to divide into three parts, a sacred, a public, and a private; that from which the customary worship of the ᵇ35 gods would be maintained would be sacred, that from which the defenders would live would be common, and the land belonging to the farmers would be private.

   3 (1267ᵇ37–1268ᵃ6)   He held the view that there were only three categories of laws too; for the matters about which lawsuits occur are three in number: outrage, damage, and death. He also proposed to legislate for a single sovereign court, to which all suits ᵇ40 that appeared to have been badly judged had to be referred; and he intended to form this court of certain selected elder persons. Ver-**1268** dicts in law-courts he thought ought not to be reached by the casting of votes; rather each member should present a tablet, on which he was to write the penalty if he simply found guilty, whereas if he simply acquitted he was to leave it blank; and if it was partly the one and partly the other, he was to specify that. For he thought ᵃ5 existing legislation badly drafted in this respect, that it forces men to commit perjury, by voting either one way or the other.

   4 (1268ᵃ6–14)   He next proposed to establish a law about discoverers of something useful to the state, providing that they should receive honours; and that the children of those who fell in war should be maintained at public expense (on the assumption that this had not hitherto been laid down by law among others— ᵃ10 but this law does actually exist both at Athens and in some other states). The officials were all to be elected by the people, and he intended the people to be made up of the three sections of the state. Those elected were to look after communal matters and those relating to foreigners and to orphans.

   5 (1268ᵃ14–29)   These, then, are most of the features of ᵃ15 Hippodamus' scheme, and those most deserving of comment. One's first difficulty would be with the division of the citizen body. For they all, skilled workers, farmers, and those who carry arms, take part in the constitution, though the farmers have no arms, and the craftsmen have neither arms nor land, so that they become ᵃ20 virtually the slaves of those who do possess arms. So the sharing of *all* offices is impossible. For it is inevitable that Generals, and Guardians of Citizens, and the most sovereign officials in general, should be appointed from those who possess arms. However, if

they do not share in the constitution, how can they feel affection for
it? On the contrary: those who possess arms have to be *stronger* ᵃ25
than both the other sections. Yet that is not easy unless they are
numerous; and if this is going to be so, what necessity is there for
the rest to share in the constitution and be sovereign over the
appointment of officials?

6 (1268ᵃ29–35) Again, what use are the farmers to the state?
Skilled workers are essential (every state needs them), and they ᵃ30
can support themselves from their skill, as in other states. The
farmers would reasonably have been some part of the state, if they
supplied provisions for those who possess weapons. But actually
they possess private land, and will farm it privately.

7 (1268ᵃ35–ᵇ4) And again, as for the common land which will ᵃ35
support the defenders, if they are to farm it themselves, there will
be no difference, as the legislator wishes there should be, between
the fighting element and the farming. And if there are going to be
certain others, different from the fighters and from those who farm
their own private property, this will be yet a fourth section of the
state, with no share in anything, but alien to the constitution. And ᵃ40
yet if one makes those who farm the private land and those who
farm the common land the same people, there will not be enough
produce for each man, who will be farming for two households, to ᵇ1
draw on. Why without further ado will they not *both* get maintenance for themselves *and* provide it for the fighters from the same
land and the same estates? All this contains much confusion.

8 (1268ᵇ4–11) The law relating to verdicts is no good either—
the requirement that in reaching them, though the charge is written ᵇ5
in simple terms, one should make distinctions, and that the juryman
should turn arbitrator. Certainly that is practicable in arbitrations,
even if there are several arbitrators, because they confer with each
other about their verdict. But it is not possible in a court of law, and
indeed most legislators take the opposite line and take steps to see ᵇ10
that jurymen do *not* confer with each other.

9 (1268ᵇ11–17) How, then, will the verdict fail to be confused,
when a juryman thinks the defendant owes something, but not as
much as the plaintiff thinks? If the latter thinks twenty minae, the
juryman will decide ten (or the former more, the latter less),
another five, another four (obviously this is just the kind of division ᵇ15
they will perform); and some will condemn in the full amount, and
others in nothing. How then will the votes be counted?

10 (1268ᵇ17–22) Again, since the indictment has been written
in simple terms, nothing forces a person who returns in a just
manner a simple verdict of condemnation or acquittal to commit
perjury. For he who acquits does not decide that the defendant

ᵇ20 owes nothing, but only not the twenty minae. But he who con-
demns the defendant in spite of not believing him to owe the
twenty minae, perjures himself immediately.

11 (1268ᵇ22–31) As for his suggestion that there should be
some honour for those who discover something advantageous to
the state, such legislation is not safe, but just pretty to listen to. It
ᵇ25 produces vexatious prosecutions, and, it may be, changes of constitution. The matter is part of another problem and a different
inquiry. For some people debate whether it is harmful or advantageous to states to change their ancestral laws, if some other is
better. Hence if indeed change is not advantageous, then it is not
easy to give ready assent to what was said; it is possible for certain
ᵇ30 people to bring in proposals for abrogating the laws or the constitution on the ground that it is for the common good.

12 (1268ᵇ31–1269ᵃ8) Now that we have mentioned the matter,
we had better treat it a little more expansively, since as I have said
it presents a difficulty, and alteration may seem better. In the other
fields of knowledge, at any rate, it has been beneficial, as for ex-
ᵇ35 ample in the changes made in traditional methods of medicine and
physical training, and generally in every skill and faculty. So since
we must regard the skill of a statesman as one of these, clearly
something similar necessarily applies there too. One could claim
that the very facts have supplied evidence, by showing that the old
ᵇ40 laws were excessively simple and uncivilized. The Greeks used
both to carry arms and buy their brides from one other; and such
traces as survive in places of the ancient observances are quite
1269 naïve—for instance, the law relating to homicide at Cyme, by
which, if the prosecutor of the murder produces a certain number
of witnesses from among members of his own kin, then the defendant is to be guilty of murder. But in general all men seek not the
traditional but the good, and it is probable that the first men,
ᵃ5 whether they were born from the earth or were survivors of some
catastrophe, were like ordinary, undiscerning people—and precisely this is, in fact, said of the earth-born. So it would be odd to
cling to their ideas.

13 (1269ᵃ8–12) In addition, even written laws are better not
left unchanged. For the same applies to the organization of the
ᵃ10 state as in the other skills: it is impossible for it to be written down
with precision in every detail: the general principle must be put into
writing, but the actions taken concern particular cases.

14 (1269ᵃ12–24) So from these considerations it is clear that
sometimes some laws need to be changed. But to those who consider the question from another perspective great caution will seem
ᵃ15 indicated. For when the improvement is small, whereas it is wrong

to accustom men to casual abrogation of the laws, obviously we must allow some errors on the part both of lawgiver and of rulers. A man will not get as much benefit from changing the law as he will harm from being made accustomed to disobey the rulers. Also, the model deriving from the skills is false: altering a skill is not like altering a law. The law has no power to secure obedience save habit, and this does not develop except over a length of time. Hence to change readily from established laws to other and new laws is to weaken the power of the law.

15 (1269ᵃ24–8) Again, if laws are indeed to be changed, are they all to be changed, and in every constitution, or not? And by anybody, or by certain persons? For these things make a considerable difference. Let us therefore give up this investigation for now: it is for other suitable occasions.

II ix

CRITICISM OF THE CONSTITUTION AND
SOCIAL SYSTEM OF SPARTA

1 (1269ᵃ29–34) About the constitution of the Lacedaemonians, about the Cretan, and in effect about the other constitutions also, there are two questions for consideration. One: is there anything in the legislation which has been enacted that is good, or bad, as compared with the best system? The other: is there anything in it that is contrary to the assumption and character of the constitution intended?

2 (1269ᵃ34–ᵇ7) Now it is agreed that a state which is going to operate a good constitution must be furnished with leisure from essential tasks; but the way it is to be so furnished is not easy to fathom. The Thessalians' serf class often attacked the Thessalians, just as the helots attacked the Laconians, for whose misfortunes they are for ever lying in wait, as it were. But nothing of the kind has so far occurred in the case of the Cretans. The reason is perhaps that the neighbouring states, though they fight each other, never ally, not one of them, with the rebels: it is not in their interest to do so, since they themselves also possess peripheral populations. The Laconians' neighbours, on the other hand, Argives, Messenians, Arcadians, were all hostile. The Thessalians are evidence too: they originally experienced revolts because they were still at war with their neighbours, Achaeans, Perrhaebians, and Magnesians.

3 (1269ᵇ7–12) And even if nothing else looks troublesome, at any rate the question of management does—the question of the way in which one ought to have dealings with them. For if they are given licence, they become arrogant, and claim they deserve ᵇ10 equality with those who are sovereign over them; if they live wretchedly, they plot and hate. It is clear therefore that those who experience this in regard to their helotry are failing to find the best way.

4 (1269ᵇ12–23)   Again, the licence in the matter of their women is detrimental both to the chosen aim of the constitution and to the ᵇ15 happiness of the state. For just as man and wife are part of a household, so clearly we should regard a state also as divided into two roughly equal bodies of people, one of men, one of women. So, in all constitutions in which the position of women is unsatisfactory, one half of the state must be regarded as unregulated by law. And that is just what has happened there. For the lawgiver, wishing the ᵇ20 whole state to be hardy, makes his wish evident as far as the men are concerned, but has been wholly negligent in the case of the women. For being under no constraint whatever they live unconstrainedly, and in luxury.

5 (1269ᵇ23–39)   An inevitable result under such a constitution is that esteem is given to wealth, particularly if they do in fact come ᵇ25 to be female-dominated; and this is a common state of affairs in military and warlike races, though not among the Celts and any others who have openly accorded esteem to male homosexuality. Indeed, it seems that the first person to relate the myth did not lack some rational basis when he coupled Ares with Aphrodite; for all ᵇ30 such people seem in thrall to sexual relations, either with males or with females. That is why this state of affairs prevailed among the Laconians, and in the days of their supremacy a great deal was managed by women. And yet what difference is there between women ruling and rulers ruled by women? The result is the same. ᵇ35 Over-boldness is not useful for any routine business, but only, if at all, for war. Yet even to those purposes the Laconians' women were very harmful. This they demonstrated at the time of the invasion by the Thebans: they were not at all useful, as in other states, but caused more confusion than the enemy.

6 (1269ᵇ39–1270ᵃ11)   So it seems that from the earliest times ᵇ40 licence in the matter of their women occurred among the Laconians, reasonably enough. For there were long periods when **1270** the men were absent from their own land because of the campaigns, when they were fighting the war against the Argives, or again the one against the Arcadians and Messenians. When they gained their leisure, they put themselves into the hands of their ᵃ5 legislator in a state of preparedness brought about by the military life, which embraces many parts of virtue. People say that Lycurgus endeavoured to bring the women under the control of his laws, but that when they resisted he backed off. These then are the causes of what took place, and clearly, therefore, of this mistake as well. But the subject of our inquiry is not whom we ought to excuse and ^a10 whom not, but what is correct and what is not.

7 (1270^a11–34) The poorness of the arrangements concerning women seems, as was said earlier, not only to create a sort of unseemliness in the constitution in itself on its own, but also to contribute something to the greed for money; for after the points just made one could assail practice in respect of the uneven levels ^a15 of property. For some of them have come to possess far too much, others very little indeed; and that is precisely why the land has fallen into the hands of a small number. This matter has been badly arranged through the laws too. For while he made it (and rightly made it) ignoble to buy and sell land already possessed, he left it ^a20 open to anyone, if they wished, to give it away or bequeath it—and yet the same result follows inevitably, both in this case and in the other. Moreover, something like two-fifths of all the land is possessed by women, both because of the many heiresses that appear, and because of the giving of large dowries. Now it would have been ^a25 better if it had been arranged that there should be no dowry, or a small or even a moderate one. But as it is one may give an heiress in marriage to any person one wishes; and if a man dies intestate, the person he leaves as heir gives her to whom he likes. As a result, although the land was sufficient to support 1,500 cavalry and 30,000 ^a30 heavy infantry, their number was not even 1,000. The sheer facts have shown that the provisions of this system served them badly: the state withstood not a single blow, but collapsed owing to the shortage of men.

8 (1270^a34–^b6) It is said that in the time of their early kings they used to give others a share in their constitution, so that in spite ^a35 of their being at war for a long time, a shortage of men did not then occur; and people say that at one time the Spartiatae actually had 10,000 members. None the less, whether these statements are true or not, it is better for a state to have plenty of males because possessions have been levelled out. But the law on the begetting of ^a40 children militates against this reform. For the lawgiver, intending ^b1 that the Spartiatae should be as numerous as possible, encourages the citizens to make their children as numerous as possible. For they have a law by which the father of three sons is exempt from military service, and the father of four from all taxes. But it is obvious that if many are born and the land has been divided ac- ^b5 cordingly, many inevitably become poor.

9 (1270ᵇ6–17) Moreover, the arrangements concerning the Ephorate too are in a sorry state. The office is sovereign in its own right over their most important business; but its holders are drawn from the entire people, with the result that often very poor men ᵃ10 intrude themselves on to the board, and their poverty used to leave them open to bribery. (They often showed this in the past too, and in our own day among the Andrians; for some, corrupted by money, wrecked the whole state, so far as it lay in them to do so.) And because the office was too great, and equal to that of a tyrant, ᵃ15 even the Kings were forced to court popularity among them. And this too brought along with it further damage to the constitution, for out of an aristocracy a democracy was emerging.

10 (1270ᵇ17–28) This board does indeed hold the constitution together: the people stay quiet because they share in the highest office. So whether it has fallen out thus thanks to the lawgiver or to ᵃ20 good fortune, it benefits their affairs. For if a constitution is going to be preserved, all sections of the state must want it to exist, and the same arrangements to continue. The Kings are so disposed because of the honour they receive; the men of quality are, because of the Board of Elders (for this office is a reward for virtue); and ᵃ25 the people, because of the Ephorate (appointments to it are made from among everyone). Necessary it was to elect to this office from among all—but not by this present method, which is utterly childish.

11 (1270ᵇ28–35) They are also sovereign in trials of importance, ordinary people though they are—which is precisely why it is better that they should not give verdicts on their own judgement, ᵃ30 but in accordance with written rules and the laws. And the life-style too of the Ephors is not consistent with the intention of the state. For it is too lax in itself, whereas that followed among the other people is extreme rather in its austerity, so that they cannot endure ᵃ35 it, but secretly evade the law and enjoy the pleasures of the body.

12 (1270ᵇ35–1271ᵃ8) Nor are they well served by the arrangements for the office of the Elders. One would probably say that provided they are respectable men, adequately educated with a view to manly virtue, the office is an asset to the state—yet their lifelong sovereignty in important trials is a point for debate; for the ᵃ40 intellect too has its old age, just like the body. But when they have **1271** been educated in such a way that even the lawgiver himself distrusts them, on the ground that they are not good men, the situation is not safe. Those who have taken on a share in this office obviously take bribes and show favouritism in a good deal of communal ᵃ5 business. This is precisely why it is better that they should not be, as they are at present, exempt from scrutiny. It may seem that the office of the Ephors scrutinizes all offices; but that is to give far too much to the Ephorate, and we say this is not the manner in which one ought to be subjected to scrutiny.

13 (1271ᵃ9–18) Next, the election of the Elders which they conduct is childish in the way the choice is made, and it is not right ᵃ10 that a person who is going to be deemed worthy of the office should himself solicit it; for he who is worthy of the office should exercise it whether he wants to or not. But the fact is that the lawgiver is obviously acting precisely as he does in regard to the rest of the constitution too: he makes the citizens ambitious, and then exploits the fact for the election of the Elders; for no one who is not ᵃ15 ambitious would ask to hold office. Yet pretty well the majority of deliberate acts of injustice are caused among men by ambition and love of money.

14 (1271ᵃ18–26) As to kingship, let us postpone considering whether or not it is better for states to have it; at any rate, it is ᵃ20 certainly better that each king should not be chosen in the present manner, but in the light of his own life. It is clear that even the Spartan lawgiver himself does not believe it possible to produce Kings of sterling quality; at all events, he distrusts them, on the ground that they are not sufficiently good men. This is precisely why they used to send out their enemies as fellow-ambassadors, and why they regarded faction between the Kings as constituting ᵃ25 stability for the state.

15 (1271ᵃ26–37) Unsatisfactory also are the rules about the common meals, the 'phiditia', made by the person who first established them. The gathering ought rather to be run at public expense, as in Crete. But among the Laconians every individual has to contribute, though some of them are very poor and unable to ᵃ30 meet this expenditure, so that the legislator finds the result is the opposite of his chosen aim. For he intends the arrangement of the common meals to be democratic; but under rules such as these it becomes very little democratic: it is not easy for the very poor to participate, yet this is their traditional way of delimiting the consti- ᵃ35 tution—to exclude from it anyone who in unable to pay this due.

16 (1271ᵃ37–41) Some others too have objected to the law about Naval Commanders. The objections are well taken, because the law becomes a cause of faction. For over against the Kings, who are permanent generals, the naval command has been established, ᵃ40 practically as another Kingship.

17 (1271ᵃ41–ᵇ6) And one could make the following criticism (which Plato too has made, in his *Laws*) of the legislator's assump- ᵇ1 tion: the whole system of their laws has in view a *part* of virtue—military virtue; for this is useful for conquering. Hence they were

stable enough while at war, but began to fall once they won control,
ᵇ5 because they did not understand how to be at leisure, and had
never undertaken any kind of training more sovereign than training for war.

18 (1271ᵇ6–10) There is an error no less great than that. For
they recognize, rightly, that the good things which men fight about
come more through virtue than through vice; however, in that they
suppose these things to be superior to virtue, they are not right.

ᵇ10 **19 (1271ᵇ10–19)** Public finance is another mess the Spartiatae
have on their hands. They are compelled to undertake major wars,
but the public treasury of the state is empty, and they are bad at
paying contributions; for as most of the land is the property of the
Spartiatae, they do not inquire into each other's contributions. For
ᵇ15 the legislator, the upshot has been the reverse of useful: he has
made the state into a pauper and the private individuals into lovers
of money.

So let that suffice as a discussion of the constitution of the
Lacedaemonians; for these are the points one could criticize most
strongly.

II x

CRITICISM OF THE CONSTITUTION AND
SOCIAL SYSTEM OF CRETE

ᵇ20 **1 (1271ᵇ20–32)** The Cretan constitution is similar to the foregoing; in details it is no worse, but for the most part it is less finished.
Indeed, appearances suggest—and it is in fact said—that the constitution of the Laconians is in most respects modelled on the Cretan;
and most old things are less fully elaborated than more recent ones.
ᵇ25 For they say that Lycurgus, after laying down his guardianship of
King Charillus, went abroad and then spent most of his time in
Crete, because of the kinship connection. For the Lyctians were
colonists of the Laconians, and those who went to the colony found
the system of laws already in place among the inhabitants of the
ᵇ30 time. Hence even to this day the peripheral people use them in the
same way, believing Minos first established the system of laws.

2 (1271ᵇ32–40) The island looks both naturally suited and well
situated to rule over the Greek world: it lies across the whole sea,
ᵇ35 and around the sea are settled nearly all the Greeks. For in the one
direction it is not far from the Peloponnese, and in the other from
Asia—the area round Triopium—and from Rhodes. Hence Minos

gained also control of the sea: he made some of the islands subject to himself, to others he sent settlers; in the end he attacked Sicily, where he met his death near Camicus.

3 (1271ᵇ40–1272ᵃ12) The Cretan system is analogous to the ᵇ40 Laconians'. The helots farm for the latter, the peripheral populations for the Cretans; both have common meals, which in 1272 ancient times the Laconians used to call not 'phiditia' but 'andreia', like the Cretans—a plain indication that they originated there. Next, the constitutional system: the Ephors have the same power as ᵃ5 the Cosmoi (as they are called) in Crete, except that the Ephors number five and the Cosmoi ten. The Elders, whom the Cretans call the Council, match the Elders. There was formerly a Kingship, but later the Cretans did away with it, and the Cosmoi exercise leadership in war. All share in the Assembly, but it has no final ᵃ10 power in anything except voting together for the decisions of the Elders and the Cosmoi.

4 (1272ᵃ12–27) Now then, the Cretans have better arrangements for the common meals than the Laconians. For in Lacedaimon each man contributes the specified *per capita* amount; if he does not, a law stops him sharing in the constitution, as has ᵃ15 been said earlier too. In Crete the arrangements are more communal: out of all the public produce and livestock, and the tributes paid by the peripheral populations, one part is allocated for the gods and for the communal public services, and another for the ᵃ20 common meals, so that all—men, women, and children—are maintained at the public expense. The lawgiver regarded frugality as beneficial and devoted a lot of thought to securing it, and also to the segregation of women, to prevent them from having numerous children, since he brought about sexual relations between males, in which connection there will be another occasion to examine ᵃ25 whether he acted ill or not. It is clear, then, that better arrangements for the communal meals have been made by the Cretans than by the Laconians.

5 (1272ᵃ27–ᵇ1) On the other hand the arrangements concerning the Cosmoi are still worse than those concerning the Ephors; for the defect possessed by the Board of Ephors, its being composed of ordinary people, is present in their case too; but the ᵃ30 benefit to the purposes of the constitution there is absent here. For there the people, because the election is from among all, have a share in the most powerful office and want the constitution to stay as it is. But here they choose the Cosmoi not from among everyone, but from certain families, and the Elders from among former Cosmoi. And about them one might make the same comments as ᵃ35 about those who become Elders in Lacedaimon: their exemption

from scrutiny and their life-tenure are a privilege in excess of their merits, and it is dangerous that they govern not in accordance with written rules but on their own judgement. The fact that the people
ᵃ40 make no fuss, in spite of not sharing, is no evidence of an arrangement soundly made. For there is no profit for the Cosmoi, as there is for the Ephors, in as much as they live on an island, a long way
ᵇ1 from those who will corrupt them.

6 (1272ᵇ1–15) The remedy they apply for this fault is outlandish, and more appropriate in a power-group than in a constitution. For often some of their fellow-rulers themselves, or some private persons, form a conspiracy and expel the Cosmoi; and it is also
ᵇ5 possible for the Cosmoi to resign office during their tenure. But it is better that all these things should take place according to law, and not by the will of men; for this criterion is not safe. Worst of all, however, is the absence of Cosmoi, of the powerful, which they often bring about when they want to escape punishment. From this it is in fact clear that the system does possess something by way of
ᵇ10 a constitution; yet it is not a constitution, but more of a power-group. Their habit is to sectionalize their friends and the people, bring about an absence of government, and form factions and fight each other. And yet is not such a situation tantamount to this: such a state is temporarily no longer a state, but the association which is dissolved?
ᵇ15 **7 (1272ᵇ15–23)** A state in this condition is at risk, since those who wish to attack it also have the power. However, as we have already remarked, Crete is kept stable thanks to its location; for its remoteness has served to drive foreigners away. That is also precisely why the institution of peripheral populations survives among the Cretans, while the helots are often in rebellion. For the Cretans
ᵇ20 do not participate in an external dominion—though a foreign war has recently crossed to the island, which has made the weakness of the laws there apparent. So much for this constitution.

II xi

CRITICISM OF THE CONSTITUTION AND SOCIAL SYSTEM OF CARTHAGE

1 (1272ᵇ24–33) The Carthaginians also are thought to manage their constitution successfully, and in many respects in a manner
ᵇ25 extraordinary as compared with other people, though in some particulars resembling the Laconians'. For these three constitutions,

the Cretan, the Laconian, and third among them the Carthaginian, are both in some sense close to each other and widely different from the others. Many of the arrangements that have been made work well among them, and it is an indication of a structured ᵇ30 constitution if the people abide by the constitutional system, and no faction even worth mentioning has developed, and no tyrant.

2 (1272ᵇ33–1273ᵃ2) Here are the resemblances to the Spartan constitution. The common meals of the clubs are like the phiditia, and the rule of the 104 like the Ephors—except that it is not worse; ᵇ35 for instead of a membership drawn from ordinary people, they elect to this office on merit. Their Kings and Board of Elders are the counterpart of the Spartan Kings and Elders; and it is an advantage that the Kings are neither a separate family nor an ordinary one at that, but if a family excels in some degree, then they ᵇ40 are chosen from *its* members, not on grounds of age; for they are appointed to supreme control of great affairs, and if they are non-entities they do a lot of harm, as they have already done to the state **1273** of the Lacedaemonians.

3 (1273ᵃ2–13) Most of the objections that would be brought because of the deviations in fact apply in common to all the constitutions mentioned. In relation to the assumption of aristocracy, or of polity, some features lean more towards democracy, others to- ᵃ5 wards oligarchy. For the Kings, in conjunction with the Elders, have sovereign power to bring or not to bring a matter before the people, provided they are all in agreement; failing that, the people have sovereign power in these matters too. Moreover, when these persons make proposals, not only do they allow the people to listen ᵃ10 to the resolutions of the officials, but the people have sovereign power to take decisions on them; and anyone who wishes is permitted to speak against the proposals being made. This practice does not exist in the other constitutions.

4 (1273ᵃ13–20) On the other hand it is oligarchic that the Boards of Five, which are sovereign over many important matters, (*a*) are elected by themselves, (*b*) elect to the office of the Hundred, ᵃ15 the highest, and moreover (*c*) have a longer period in office than the rest (for they rule before taking office and after they have left it). But we must treat as aristocratic the fact that (*d*) they receive no pay and (*e*) are not chosen by lot, and anything else of that kind; and also the fact that (*f*) *all* lawsuits are judged by the boards, and not, as in Lacedaimon, some by some persons, others by others. ᵃ20

5 (1273ᵃ21–30) The chief deviation of the Carthaginians' system from aristocracy towards oligarchy accords with a certain notion which is a popular view also; for they think that rulers should be chosen not merely on merit but also on grounds of

wealth, since it is impossible for a man without means to be a good
^a25 ruler—that is, to have the leisure. So if election according to wealth
is oligarchic, and on grounds of virtue aristocratic, a third system
will be this one which determines the constitutional structure set up
by the Carthaginians. For they have both these points in view when
they elect, and particularly when they elect the highest officials, the
^a30 Kings and the Generals.

6 (1273^a31–^b7) But this deviation from aristocracy must be regarded as a lawgiver's error. For from the start one of the most
essential things is to see that the best people have leisure and do
nothing unseemly, not only when in office but even when living as
^a35 private persons. But if we must look to wealth too, for the sake of
leisure, it is a bad thing that the highest offices, of King and
General, should be buyable. For this law makes wealth more
esteemed than virtue, and the whole state fond of money. Whatever it is that the sovereign authorities take to be valuable, the
^a40 opinion of the rest of the citizens too inevitably follows theirs; and
wherever virtue is not esteemed most highly, the constitution can-
^b1 not be run securely as an aristocracy. It is only to be expected that
those who purchase their position should grow used to making a
profit, when they rule by having spent money. If the poor but
respectable person will want his profit, it would be strange if the
more disreputable, having spent money, will not want his. Hence it
^b5 is those who are able to rule best that should rule. And even if the
lawgiver neglected the respectable persons' resources, one had
better look to their leisure, at least while they are in office.

7 (1273^b8–17) It would seem unsatisfactory also that one
man should hold several offices—precisely what is in high esteem
among the Carthaginians; for one task is best performed by one
^b10 person. The legislator ought to see that this is what happens, and
not require the same man to be a player on the pipes and a shoemaker. So where the state is not a small one, it is more statesmanlike, and more democratic, that several people should share in
the offices. For, as we said, this is a more communal practice, and
each task, as it belongs to the same persons, is performed better
^b15 and quicker. This is obvious in the case of military and naval affairs;
for in both these ruling and being ruled extend through practically
all personnel.

8 (1273^b18–26) But although their constitution is an oligarchy,
they are very successful in escaping faction, because from time to
time some section of the people grows rich on their sending it out
^b20 to the states. By this measure they cure the trouble and render their
constitution stable. But this is the work of Fortune, whereas they
ought to be free of faction thanks to the legislator. As it is, if any

mischance should occur and the mass of the ruled population should rebel, no remedy is available for restoring peace by means of the laws.

This, then, is the position with regard to the Lacedaemonian, Cretan, and Carthaginian constitutions, which are justly held in ᵇ25 high esteem.

II xii

DEFENCE OF THE CONSTITUTION OF SOLON; SIGNIFICANT MEASURES OF CERTAIN OTHER LAWGIVERS

1 (1273ᵇ27–34) Of those who have expressed some opinion about a constitution, some took no part in any state activities at all, but remained private persons all their lives. We have already spoken of nearly all of them, so far as there is anything worth mentioning. Others, after personal experience of state affairs, have become ᵇ30 lawgivers, some in their home states, some in certain foreign ones too. Some of these were framers of laws only, others, like both Lycurgus and Solon, of a constitution too; for these established both laws and a constitution.

2 (1273ᵇ35–1274ᵃ3) Well then, the constitution of the ᵇ35 Lacedaemonians has been discussed. As for Solon, some people think he was a sound lawgiver, because (a) he abolished the excessively undiluted oligarchy; (b) he ended the slavery of the people; and (c) he established the ancestral Athenian democracy by mixing the constitution well, on the grounds that the Council on the Areopagus is an oligarchical element, the practice of electing ᵇ40 officials an aristocratic one, and the courts a democratic one. But it seems that the first two, the Council and the election of the officials, existed already, and Solon refrained from abolishing 1274 them. On the other hand, by creating courts drawn from all it seems he did establish the democracy.

3 (1274ᵃ3–11) This is why some people in fact find Solon at fault: they say that by giving supreme power over all matters to the court, which was chosen by lot, he ruined the other things. For ᵃ5 when it became powerful, they converted the constitution into the present democracy, by courting the favour of the people like that of a tyrant. Ephialtes and Pericles clipped the power of the Council on the Areopagus, and Pericles established payment for service in the courts; in this way each popular leader increased the people's ᵃ10 power and led them on to the present democracy.

4 (1274ᵃ11–21) But it seems that this came about not in accordance with Solon's chosen purpose but by accident. For the people, having been responsible for the naval supremacy in the Persian wars, gave themselves airs, and adopted inferior men as popular leaders when respectable men pursued policies opposed to
ᵃ15 their own. But Solon, it seems, accorded the essential minimum power to the people: the practice of electing officials and of conducting scrutinies; for if they were not to have supreme power over even this, the people would be a slave and a foe; and he appointed all officials from the notables and men of substance—the Penta-
ᵃ20 cosiomedimnoi, the Zeugitae, and the third class, that of the 'Knights'; the fourth, the Thetes, had a share in no office.

5 (1274ᵃ22–31) Zaleucus became a lawgiver for the Epizephyrian Locrians, and Charondas of Catana for his own citizens and for the other Chalcidic states of Italy and Sicily. (Some try
ᵃ25 also to establish connections, on the grounds that Onomacritus was the first expert in lawmaking, a Locrian who trained in Crete during a visit there in pursuit of his art of soothsaying, that Thales was his comrade, and that Lycurgus and Zaleucus were pupils of Thales,
ᵃ30 and Charondas of Zaleucus. But when they say these things they speak with insufficient attention to chronology.)

6 (1274ᵃ31–ᵇ5) There was also Philolaus the Corinthian, who became a lawgiver for the Thebans. He was of the family of the Bacchiads, and became the lover of Diocles, the victor in the Olympic Games. This Diocles, in loathing of the amorous passion
ᵃ35 of his mother Alcyone, left the state for Thebes, where they both ended their days. Even now people point out their tombs, which are easily visible each from the other; but one is visible from the direction of the Corinthians' country, the other is not. The story is that they themselves planned their burial thus, Diocles out of
ᵃ40 bitterness at his suffering, so that the land of Corinth should not be visible from his mound, Philolaus that it might be visible from his.
ᵇ1 It was for this sort of reason, then, that they dwelt among the Thebans. Philolaus became lawgiver for them, both on certain other matters and on the adoption of children; these the Thebans call 'laws of placement'. And this legal enactment by him is peculiar
ᵇ5 to him, to keep the number of the estates constant.

7 (1274ᵇ5–18) There is nothing peculiar to Charondas except the suits for false witness, for he was the first to devise the denunciation; but in the precision of his laws he is more finished than even modern legislators. The feature peculiar to Phaleas is his levelling
ᵇ10 of resources; to Plato, community of resources, wives, and children, and common meals for women; also the law about intoxication, that the sober should preside at drinking parties, and about the

military training in which practice is intended to make people become ambidextrous, on the grounds that one hand of the two ought not to be useful and the other useless. There are laws of Draco, but his legislating was for an existing constitution. There is nothing peculiar to his laws worth any mention, except their severity, on account of their heavy punishments. ^b15

8 (1274^b18–28) Pittacus too was a framer of laws, but not of a constitution; and a law peculiar to him states that if the drunken commit some blunder they should pay a larger penalty than the sober. For since more drunken men than sober commit insolent offences, he paid attention not to the pardon—the view that they should have it all the more, since they are drunk—but to expediency. Androdamas of Rhegium became a lawgiver for the Chalcidians in the direction of Thrace, and to him belongs the material dealing with homicide and heiresses; still, one could not mention anything peculiar to him. ^b20 ^b25

So then, let our study of the questions relating to constitutions—both those realized and those described by certain people—stand completed thus.

COMMENTARY

I i

VARIETIES OF RULE IN STATE AND HOUSEHOLD

Introduction The chapter falls naturally into three parts; but the relationships between them are not immediately obvious. The theme that links them is outlined in **1**: the distinction between the 'most sovereign' association, the state, and the evidently less sovereign associations within it. Degrees of sovereignty imply differences in mode of rule; but (**2**) certain persons refuse to distinguish the various rulers in kind, recognizing only differences in point of numbers ruled. **3** then outlines a methodology for analysing the state into its constituent associations, in order to clarify the varieties of rule. Brief and allusive though it is, I i therefore raises some far-reaching issues about wholes and parts; it is more than a preliminary to I ii.

1 (1252ᵃ1–7) has implications which Aristotle does not spell out. The two key concepts are (*a*) association and (*b*) sovereignty.

(*a*) Several of Aristotle's works start with some almost platitudinous statement which one has to agree must be true in *some* sense, however basic. Here it is the whole of the first sentence (compare *EN init.*, on the good as the end of human activity). The procedure accords with his general wish to establish common opinion (*endoxa*) as the starting-point of inquiry (*EN* 1145ᵇ2–7); for 'a certain sort of' (association) casts a wide net. Yet at least after the first sentence Aristotle presumably intends a *koinōnia*, association, to be taken in his own strong sense: a *koinōnia* is of free men united by something in common (*koinon*), mutual friendship, and an agreement concerning the just (which is not necessarily the equal) distribution among themselves of the benefits accruing from their associating (1280ᵃ25 ff., 1281ᵃ2–10, 1295ᵇ23–5, 1328ᵃ21–ᵇ2, *EE* 1241ᵇ13–24, *EN* VIII ix, 1161ᵃ30–ᵇ15; cf. 1132ᵇ31–4, 1133ᵃ16–25). The good legislator has to see that state, tribe, and every other association attains the 'good life' and the measure of *eudaimonia*, 'happiness', open to it (1325ᵃ7–10, cf. *EN* 1129ᵇ17–19).

(*b*) The word *kurios*, 'sovereign' or 'supreme', conveys power, control, authority, and finality, in any sphere of conduct (cf. Mulgan (1970)). The 'most sovereign of all goods', i.e. happiness, is 'best' (1328ᵃ37); the most sovereign association, the state, is supreme in power; and indeed it makes sense to employ the most powerful association in attaining the highest good. But Aristotle is interested in more than power. The state is most *kurios* in the sense of most *authoritative*, in being the *locus* of *politikē epistēmē*, political knowledge, i.e. knowledge of how to *use* power. *EN* 1094ᵃ22 ff. (cf. 1141ᵇ23 ff.), though it only implies rather than mentions associations, tells us something of how political knowledge operates. It is 'architectonic', (i.e. 'of a master-craftsman', ᵃ27), and 'gives orders' (ᵇ2) about what should be learnt; its end 'embraces' (ᵇ6) those other branches of knowledge, which it 'uses' (ᵇ4); and these are employed in the *less* sovereign associations implied in 1, such as the home, *oikia* or *oikos* (note 'household [knowledge]', *EN* 1094ᵇ3).

The 'embracing', *periechein*, here seems parallel to that in I i: political knowledge embraces other branches of knowledge as the association which is the state embraces the other associations. In neither case is the relationship cumulative: the lesser branches of knowledge and associations are not bundles that *add up* to architectonic knowledge and the most sovereign association; for both these and the lesser branches of knowledge and associations are different. Rather, the point is that the superior one in each case 'embraces' the others in the sense of ranking them, of confining them to certain subordinate ends and ranges of activity, which subserve its own ultimate end, 'happiness'. A firm distinction in kind between 'architectonic' and subsidiary knowledge-and-rule is what lies behind 1, and is the immediate trigger for the criticism of Plato in 2.

In spite of its apparently objective opening, 1 is less factual than aspirational. Aristotle's ideal is sharply opposed to the vicious social and political strife common in Greek cities (1296ᵃ22–ᵇ2, 1318ᵇ1–5). In describing the state as 'the most sovereign association' he implies not a 'mixed' society but some co-operative and integrated structure, with a single ortho-doxy based on political knowledge. (Hence he here betrays no interest in the management of political *conflict*, important though the problem is to him elsewhere (Yack 1993).) His conception of the state is communitarian, in the sense that he sees the welfare and self-fulfilment of the individual as lying in the active membership of a network of associations founded and maintained for particular purposes (cf. 1325ᵇ23–32), and culminating in the state itself; he does not *oppose* state and individual in point of their rights, interests, powers, and obligations. The state has no interests other than those of its members; if it fails to subserve those interests, it is a state only in name, and forfeits its claim to authority (cf. comment on 1253ᵃ18–29). His political philosophy is neither confrontational (Thrasymachus in *Republic* I, Callicles in the *Gorgias*, Hobbes), nor contractualist (*Rep.* 358e ff.), nor minimalist (Lycophron, 1280ᵇ10–12; cf. Sorabji (1990) 273–6). Many details and problems are considered more fully in other books (e.g. VIII i, on education); but the general policy is clear.

'The association which takes the form of a state', *koinōnia politikē*: see note 3 to Glossaries. Possibly, 'association comprising citizens/statesmen' (citizens are 'statesmen' when, and in so far as, they engage in state affairs).

2 (1252ᵃ7–16) 'Those who suppose . . .': 'the Platos of this world'. At the start of his *Politicus* (258e ff.) Plato gives four examples of two persons who, in spite of being in different formal positions, may be said to have the same knowledge and so to deserve the same title as each other; and on this flimsy basis he asserts that the king (*basileus*), the statesman (*politikos*), the household-manager (*oikonomos*), and the master of slaves (*despotes*) are 'one', and possess 'one knowledge', which is *gnōstikē*, 'intellectual' or '*cognitive*', and *epitaktikē*, 'directive' (260a–261a, cf. *epistatikē*, 'controlling', 292b and 308e). (Much of the rest of the dialogue then relies on this thesis, and concentrates on the king and statesman, without distinction, as in total control of all policy in all areas of public and private life.)

Now if all these rulers have 'one', i.e. the same, knowledge, there has presumably to be some object of that knowledge, known by all of them. What is it? Perhaps one of the Forms, perfect exemplars imperfectly reflected in particular things (a theory prominent in the dialogues of Plato's 'middle' period). The Form of Ruling? The Form of Good? Forms in general? Or those supra-sensible entities, whatever they are, which Plato apparently supposes (285d–286b) to lie behind the 'divisions', i.e. categories, of objects of this world, and which fill so many pages of the *Politicus*? Plato does not tell us. Nor does he explain how knowledge of such entities enables the rulers to rule well in their various circumstances. Aristotle does not make that point here, but does so forcibly in his long criticisms in the two *Ethics* of Plato's doctrine of a single knowledge of the Good (*EE* I viii, esp. 1217ᵇ23–5, 33–5, 1218ª33–ᵇ7; *EN* I vi; cf. *Met.* I vi). What he fastens on is Plato's assertions in the *Politicus* that thanks to that single knowledge, all four rulers are 'one' (or 'the same person', as he puts it); for there are only *particular* 'goods' (*EE* 1217ª25 ff., *EN* 1096ª23 ff., ᵇ25–6), to which the four have to look, each in his own different special context, and in the light of his own different special knowledge, so that contrary to Plato, they do differ 'in kind', *eidei* (cf. 1325ª27–30); most crucially, each set of ruled persons differs from the others in point of rationality and virtue. Relationships betweeen rulers and ruled therefore vary widely.

The connection of 2 to 1 is therefore tight: for the Platonic statements reported in 2 depend on assumptions which seem to threaten (i) the 'sovereign good' of 1 as a co-ordinated set of *particular* goods, and (ii) the co-ordinated hierarchy of *particular* associations and branches of knowledge headed by the state and its overarching political knowledge. But it does not so threaten, at least in practical terms. Aristotle's 'architectonic' political knowledge is as all-controlling and directive as Plato's; but it is based not on Forms but on natural teleology combined with that distillation of practical experience presented in the *Politics* itself. There is no reason why Platonic political knowledge should not coexist with Aristotelian, provided we accept, as Plato seems to have done, that the latter is somehow a practical abatement or reflection of the full rigour of the former. For Plato himself in Magnesia, his practical utopia of the *Laws*, 'second-best' to that of the *Republic*, successfully articulates an impressive series of particular goods and particular styles of rule (see e.g. 776b ff., on how to rule slaves), with some references to nature as a norm of conduct (781b2, 839a6); and there are marked similarities between that utopia and Aristotle's own 'best' state in *Politics* VII and VIII. Plato is strongly encouraging of 'demotic' virtues, rather than metaphysical insight, in the citizens and rulers of the state. Yet at the end of the *Laws* he requires the supreme rulers of Magnesia (the Nocturnal Council) to study a curriculum which in part sounds as if it presupposes some version of the theory of Forms (961a ff., esp. 965b ff.). Precisely how he conceives the abating should be achieved is, however, obscure: we learn only that, in the absence of the genuine art of rule (*Pol.* 292d–293a), laws and constitutions are 'copies' of truth (300c–301a, cf. 297c). How Ruling may be applied to ruling remains a mystery.

Aristotle, of course, would not accept that political knowledge as he conceives it is an abatement of anything: it is intended to stand in its own right, independently of idealist metaphysics. In *EN* I vi he presents detailed arguments against Plato's view that goodness is a single simple property; yet he nowhere directly addresses Plato's fundamental point about the singleness of ruling: that *just as* the various things called good are so called not because they are 'homonymous by chance' (*EN* 1096ᵇ26–7) (but because there is some single Good in which they somehow partake), *so too* the various types of rule are all *rule*; *qua* rule, they are all the same and imply a single knowledge of Ruling—which aims at the Good. No doubt Aristotle would claim that the notion of a single art of Ruling would collapse by parity of reasoning; for who or what would be subject to it, and in what sphere of activity?

Though both Plato and Aristotle speak in sweeping terms of the powers of a good ruler (*Laws* 631d–632c, 780ab; *EN* I ii), neither envisages statesmen intervening in person in the individual's life from day to day—if only because law is a blunt instrument (*Laws* 925d ff., *Pol.* 294a–295b; 1269ª9–12, 1282ᵇ1–6, 1287ª23–7, *EN* V x). They are interested in prescribing ends and formulating policies; in the interests of efficiency, execution at the lower echelons is delegated to slaves, parents etc.; cf. I vii, *EN* 1180ª29–ᵇ28, *MA* 703ª30–4.

Why the lengthy ado about numbers? Aristotle grumbles that in so far as Plato differentiates rulers, it is not on the essential criterion of kind, but only on the trivial criterion of the number of the ruled. His evidence is *Pol.* 259b9–10, where it is claimed that there is no distinction between a large household and a small state 'for purposes of rule'; for the implication is that a state and a household do normally differ for these purposes, simply in point of numbers. However, this denial of a relevant numerical difference was *ad hominem*: it was intended to make it easy for 'Younger Socrates' to accept that the two rulers, in spite of their different formal positions, are the same; 'small household and large state' would have been hard to swallow by someone who assumes, as Younger Socrates evidently did, that numbers make an essential difference. Aristotle's point is that what was intended in the *Politicus* as support for the claim urged on the Younger Socrates, that all rulers are 'the same', is absurd; for any state and any household must be different in kind, irrespective of numbers.

'. . . that sort of knowledge' suggests a statesman's knowledge. In that case, the point is again numerical: not only the number of the ruled but of the rulers themselves is irrelevant to the latter's difference in kind. But 'ruling and being ruled by turn', which is characteristic of good statesmen (see e.g. 1261ª37 ff., 1277ᵇ7 ff., 1332ᵇ25–7), is barely mentioned in the *Politicus* (though it is integral to the state of the *Laws*, 643e, 942c). In so far as alternation of rule by statesmen is different from permanent rule by one man, the sentence has nothing with which Aristotle can disagree; so 'that sort of' may mean 'kingly', which would point up the paradox, as he sees it, of the assumption of a single political knowledge common to rulers as different as a king and statesman (contrast *Pol.* 259d3–4).

'Role of', see note 3 to Glossaries: I take the point of the *-ikos* endings to be that each ruler has a certain role or position *in relation to* his subjects—the theme of the paragraph.

3 (1252ᵃ17–23) The paragraph is rather foggily written. *What* 'point will become clear'? That each 'smallest part' (i.e. man/woman, master/slave, father/son, the smallest parts of a household and hence of a state, as in I ii and iii) is different, and requires a ruler different in kind. 'These' are the parts of the state; 'too' means 'as well as the parts of other composites'; 'roles', i.e. of the rulers of **2**, I insert to clarify what I take to be the point: the Greek has only 'of those mentioned'. A 'skilled', *technikon*, understanding, which is part of *politikē technē*, political skill, is of the general notion (cf. *EN* 1180ᵇ13 ff.), e.g. of 'king', of the essential features of kingly rule, and of the proper local contexts for it; for not only are there several particular kinds of king (III xiv), but kingly rule applies in one of the state's parts (1259ᵇ10–17; cf. comment on 1252ᵇ15–27).

Aristotle employs his 'mode of inquiry' (cf. *Phys.* 187ᵇ11–13) variously, e.g. in his analysis of tragedy (*Poet.* 1450ᵃ7–15); and in the *Politics* the state may be divided into 'parts' in several different ways (IV iii). In **3**, however, the parts in question are the 'smallest', by which he does not mean such pairings as buyer/seller, producer/consumer, much less the economic and occupational groupings of rich, poor, farmers, traders, etc. (e.g. 1290ᵇ38–91ᵃ8, 1321ᵃ5–7). By 'part' he means not merely something that contributes functionally to the state as a whole (those groupings certainly do that), but something with at least one ruler/ruled relationship internal to it, which in turn has some ruler/ruled relationship both to other such parts and to the sovereign whole, the state.

Functional analysis by part and whole is employed in the biological works also; for limbs contribute dynamically to the total functioning of the living body as a whole (e.g. *PA* 690ᵃ1–4). It readily suggests an analogy between animal and state: see intro. to I ii, and 1252ᵇ34.

I ii

ORIGIN, GROWTH, AND PURPOSE OF THE STATE

Introduction Nothing in I i has warned us that the analysis of the 'smallest parts' is to be historical, in their 'natural growth'; and the extreme selectivity of Aristotle's narration, laced with a certain amount of colour, may tempt us to regard it not as genuinely 'diachronic' but as 'synchronic', i.e. merely describing picturesquely what is the case *now*, or certain timeless truths about the human condition, but in an historical manner 'for the sake of teaching' (*Cael.* 280ᵃ1). This seems unlikely: such tender treatment is hardly needed by readers of an Aristotelian 'esoteric' work, as distinct from his more popular, 'exoteric' productions. Nevertheless, his historical anthropology has an effect characteristic of the genre: it makes the present seem natural and inevitable, or at least more intelligible; for one can see around one features of the present developing or surviving from the past (e.g. households). This continuity of institutions lends Aristotle's narration a great deal of its persuasive force. We should take it at face value, as history (*pace* Kullmann (1991) 96–9, 115–17). More importantly, it is in the state's history that we can discern its 'internal source of change' (see below on its 'naturalness').

Before approaching the problems in Aristotle's historical anthropology, it will be useful to summarize the salient features of his predecessors' work:

(*a*) They displayed a strong belief in historical progress, technological, moral, social, and legal, to the point where civilized life in a state became possible (e.g. Aes. *PV* 249 ff., 436–506, Plato *Prot.* 320c ff., esp. 322b).

(*b*) Such progress sometimes arose from human and communal trial and error, sometimes from outright 'gifts' of individual gods or legendary persons in the shape of particular resources or skills or virtues (e.g. Demeter gave grain); the two explanations were not thought to be mutually exclusive ('over-determination' of causation was characteristic of Greek thought); Plato, indeed, put them side by side in the same narration (*Prot.* 322a–d).

(*c*) However, some accounts were in whole or part pessimistic, dwelling on moral and social decay (Hesiod *WD* 109 ff., Plato *Laws* 678e–679e, 713a–714b); and some supposed periodical great floods or other disasters, from which mankind had had to recover on each occasion (*Laws* 677a).

(*d*) Some were written with an eye to the 5th- and 4th-century controversy about *nomos* (convention, law) and *phusis* (nature); for stories of human progress can be used to support *either* the thesis that morality and law are natural (*Rhet.* 1373ᵇ1 ff.), *or* the thesis that moral and legal standards and institutions, which have developed in all their conflicting variety, are entirely conventional and without special validity (Plato summarizes this view, which he represents as prevalent in the mid-4th century, at *Laws* 888e–890b; cf. *EN* V vii).

Aristotle's view of what he calls 'usual' history was not a high one, for he thinks it merely relates particular facts, whereas poetry is 'more philosophical and more serious', since it deals with general patterns of conduct (*Poet.* 1451ᵃ36 ff., 1459ᵃ21–4). Now in I ii there are no particular facts at all, except perhaps the action of the 'first' founder of a *polis*, 1253ᵃ30). What we are given is something we may suppose to be 'Aristotelian' history, a schematic account of the successive trends: the formation of households, from them villages, from them states. This would preclude neither different rates of development in different places and at different times, nor development in one place in imitation of that in an other. Aristotle is interested in a sequential pattern of development, a pattern he could have arrived at *a priori*, by intelligent retrospection, or by wide reading in Greek literature, particularly the historians, or by noticing it repeatedly in the historical parts of the 158 'Constitutions' compiled in the Lyceum (for what happens 'always or for the most part' is for him significant (see de Ste Croix (1975)); or from any combination of these three. Almost certainly he would have read the several (and very various) accounts by Plato: *Rep.* 369a ff., *Prot.* 320c ff., *Pol.* 268d ff., *Tim.* 22a ff., *Crit.* 109d–110a, *Laws* 676a ff., 713a–714b; some verbal and thematic echoes are detectable, especially of the *Laws*.

Aristotle both cleaves to, and sits apart from, the anthropological tradition:

(i) The growth of technological competence, and its motivation in material need and comfort, are entirely ignored, or rather just assumed (cf. 1329^{b}27–30), in the concept 'for the sake of living'; moral and social progress, which leads to the 'good life', is however marked increasing strongly as the chapter goes on. In general, his account falls into the optimistic category (cf. 1264^{a}1–5, 1268^{b}31 ff., 1331^{a}1–2); for he is no admirer of the primitive as such: 1268^{b}39–1269^{a}8, 1329^{b}30–5; cf. *EN* 1098^{a}20–6.

(ii) The narration has other conspicuous absences. No god appears, and the only individual benefactor is the first founder of a state, who is 'responsible for very great benefits'.

(iii) The exclusion of distracting technological detail focuses attention on other kinds of progress, and the virtual exclusion of individual benefactors clears the ground for the extreme stress on *nature* as the cause (in some sense) of moral and social progress, achieved by everyone communally (even, minimally, by slaves).

(iv) Aristotle's version of the pessimism of some earlier accounts is in *this* chapter neither recurrent cataclysms etc. (but see 1269^{a}5, 1329^{b}25–7, and the implications of *Cael.* 270^{b}19–21, *Met.* 1074^{b}8–14), nor human miscalculation in framing constitutions for states (see later books *passim*), nor angry gods: it is arrested development. For some peoples, non-Greeks, remain stuck at the kingly stage of development, and do not achieve states; and for this, climate and environment may be to blame (to judge from 1285^{a}16 ff., 1327^{b}18 ff.; cf. Hipp. *AWP* 16).

In short, Aristotle exploits, with significant modifications, a tradition of progressive and optimistic anthropological speculation for the purposes of his own natural teleology, for which it is ready-made.

The naturalness of the polis. In *Phys.* II i (cf. *Met.* 1015^{a}13–19) Aristotle distinguishes natural objects from 'artificial' ones. The former are the simple bodies (such as earth, air, fire, water), and plants and animals. They have a 'nature', *phusis*, in virtue of: (*a*) the possession of an internal source of change and rest, the former embracing movement and growth, (*b*) the attainment of some identifiable and definable form, which was somehow inherent in and determined the direction of the growth until complete. For example, an embryo, given the right conditions (nourishment etc.), and in the absence of impediment, develops of its own accord into its adult form.

Artificial objects, by contrast, such as beds and coats, are of material without such built-in directive power: they have change and form imposed on them by an external agent, the craftsman.

Aristotle is apparently thinking chiefly of plants and animals, and the application of (*a*) and (*b*) to the simple bodies raises special problems, which we may leave aside. But their application to the *polis* is not free of difficulty either. For clearly the state is neither a plant nor an animal (though animals and states are in some respects functionally and structurally comparable: 1290ᵇ21 ff., *MA* 703ª23 ff.). But presumably (*a*) is in some sense on display throughout the anthropology of our present chapter (note 'natural growth', 1252ª24). Man is an 'animal' naturally fitted to live in a *polis* (1253ª2–3); he has a natural 'impulse' (1253ª29–30) towards that kind of association. This impulse generates partly instinctive and partly calculated choices and actions over a long period of history; it thus constitutes an inner source of change and development from primitive beginnings (the 'pairings', household, village) into (*b*), the *polis*. This is the complete and developed form of association, in that it is 'self-sufficient' (**5**); it caters for all man's needs (not merely physical ones), and so enables him to fulfil his nature as a man. In a word, it maximizes his happiness, *eudaimonia*. And even after the state is formed, the nature of man remains as an inner cause of change in the state, in determining how men maintain and adapt it in response to circumstances.

Aristotle's assumption throughout is that a man's needs, flowing as they do from his nature as a *man*, are objectively determinable; so too is the best means of meeting them, the *polis*. Nevertheless, just as one member of an animal species may be better than another (i.e. instantiate its form more fully or perfectly), so too one state may meet those needs better than some other. That is, the merits of states (*poleis*) and their constitutions (*politeiai*) are subject to normative evaluation; and this is the subject matter of political skill (*politikē epistēmē*). Yet although Aristotle thinks that an individual man may be 'in the best condition, both of soul and of body' (1254ª37–9), he cannot point to any perfect *polis*, only to more or less close approximations. Evidently the political facts do not quite fit the biological model. For given facilitating conditions, the development of the individual infant animal into the adult simply happens: there is an inbuilt blueprint. But where lies the blueprint in the development of the state, which is not a single animal body but an aggregation of animals in complex and variable relationships? Presumably in men's calculations of the purpose of the *polis*, and of how to achieve it. But this introduces scope for error (which it is the aim of the *Politics* to dispel). Even given a high level of facilitating conditions (abundant food, territory, etc., see intro. to II i), the degree of automaticity in the end product is less than in animal growth.

Other doubts too begin to gnaw, notably:

(i) There is a sense in which a *polis* seems much more an artificial thing than a natural one. For just as men contrive tools, by using their intelligence and skills, so too they contrive constitutional arrangements: laws, voting systems etc. Such things may be congruent with men's nature, and in a sense spring from it; but they do not develop and mature spontaneously. Nevertheless, Aristotle ascribes naturalness to good constitutions (1287^{b}36–41, cf. 1295^{b}27–8, *EN* 1135^{a}5, cf. *EE* 1248^{b}26 ff., and indeed the nests which birds construct from natural purpose at *Phys.* 199^{a}26–31). In I viii–x he attempts to distinguish between natural and unnatural modes of acquisition. It seem we have to recognize a category of 'natural artefacts'. 'Natural' is used doubly, (*a*) in a primary sense, to describe the impulse men have to seek and adopt efficient means to meet their natural needs (cf. F. D. Miller (1995) 40–6), then (*b*) to denote those means themselves, whether actions, objects, or institutions. Clearly this is to extend the notion of 'natural' very widely indeed. But the fact that those means may be *contrived*, by human ingenuity, is not a licence to regard them globally as not natural (as Keyt (1991) does); rather, we should seek to distinguish the more efficient and therefore more natural from the less efficient and therefore less natural; for efficiency and naturalness are on a sliding scale (for which see intro. to II i).

(ii) Is it not open to the Callicleses of this world to claim that what is natural in man is to seek mastery over others by any means (Plato *Gorg.*, 483e–484a, cf. 1324^{b}22 ff.)? Such a view need not deny natural teleology: it would simply deny *Aristotle's* natural teleology, by construing the 'end', *telos*, of man differently; and empirical evidence would not, to say the least, be lacking; for many men do thus seek. More generally, relativists, brushing aside claims of objectivity and normativeness, can easily claim that determining what is natural is an essentially arbitrary exercise, and that therefore human institutions are a matter of mere local convention.

The thesis that the *polis* exists by nature may then be accommodated to the analysis of nature in *Phys.* II i, but not without some difficulties. Aristotle does not address them, perhaps because they have not occurred to him, or because he regarded the broader use of 'natural' as implicit in *Phys.* II i. Yet in *Pol.* I ii he is conscious of applying natural teleology to major new subject-matter, as the length and elaboration of the chapter suggest; and he makes some allusive attempts to marry *Politics* and *Physics* (see e.g. comment on 1252^{b}31–4). However that may be, there is no reason to allow the *Physics* or any other of his works to be a straitjacket for the *Politics*.

Recent attempts to tackle the issue are: F. D. Miller (1989/1995), an excellent statement of the teleological explanation adopted here, Kullmann (1991), Chan (1992), and especially Keyt (1991), an exhaustive analysis of the logic of the chapter, arguing that Aristotle fails in the terms of *Phys.* II i and other works to establish his thesis; here and in the comments that follow I can do no more than take some swift account of his salient points.

1 (1252^{a}24–34) is limited to the first two of the three pairs of which the household is composed: man/wife; master/slave; parent/child (for the last, see **4**, 1253^{b}10–11 and I xii). Both are presented as examples of cases in which one member of a pair cannot 'exist' without the other (presumably the third pair is another example), given that each member of each pair has a certain aim, preservation in the case of master and slave, in that of man and woman 'to leave behind another such as one is oneself'. The latter is the means by which (i) they hope to fulfil their desire for immortality, so far as it is open to them, (ii) the human species is itself eternal. Aristotle is silent on these two wider matters, but presumably thinks that conscious aims are limited to (i), and (ii) simply follows. See *Anim.* 415ᵃ26–ᵇ7, *GA* 731ᵇ18–732ᵃ25, *Symp.* 207c ff., *Laws* 721b ff. For further and certainly conscious purposes, of daily living, that human beings have in procreation, see *EN* 1162ᵃ19 ff.

'Not from choice', which according to the official doctrine of *EN* 1112ᵇ11 ff., 1113ᵃ11 ff., is of means, not ends. But here the lack of choice seems more naturally to be of the end, i.e. leaving behind one like oneself, i.e. 'immortality', which is adopted instinctively.

The first thing Aristotle says of the slave is that that status is advantageous to him; cf. on 1244ᵃ17–28, and 1255ᵇ4–15. For the main discussion of slavery, see I iii–vii, xiii.

2 (1252ᵃ34–ᵇ9) The disapproval of treating women as if they were slaves has a fine ring, but it is not in the least feminist in inspiration. On the basis of what he supposes to be the mental and physical characteristics of women and slaves, Aristotle argues that there is some one particular type of work for which each is uniquely or specially suited (domestic and manual respectively)—but then apparently slides into the rather different proposition that each has or ought to have only that one function. When Plato in the *Laws* (780a–781d, 804e–806d) decries treating women as slaves, it is in the course of advocating that they should not be confined to the home, but encouraged to live a full public life like men, because their talents, though in general less than men's, are too great to be wasted; and the state will be the richer for their participation. Aristotle has no such radical intentions (for fuller discussions, see comment on I xii and xiii, on 1269ᵇ12–23). As for the slave, what appears here just as part of a dictum about specialization, 'tool', turns into reality in I iv, where Aristotle argues that the slave is precisely that. On function, cf. **8**.

No one knows what exactly the Delphic knife was; the implication of 'stingily' is presumably that the manufacturer supplied material inadequate in type or shape, so that the knife was not fully efficient in any of the different cutting functions it was intended to perform. Aristotle likes to see one tool or bodily organ (*PA* 683ᵃ20–6) or office-holder (1273ᵇ8–17, 1299ᵃ31–ᵇ13) devoted to one function only; for there is a danger that two or more functions will impede each other. Nature employs 'economy' of provision only when specialization of function is impossible; and art should imitate nature as far as it can. Aristotle gives no synoptic account of the conditions under which the impossibility arises; presumably there is some refractoriness in the material or structure of the artefact or organism (e.g. *PA* 659ᵃ21–37, where, interestingly, one double use replaces another). Today we should be inclined to *admire* multi-purpose tools—provided they are efficient. However that may be, the principle of specialization of

function seems to Aristotle to require that slaves be confined to a single activity: manual labour.

The naturally ruling element lacking among non-Greeks (*barbaroi*) is one rational enough to distinguish the natural roles of women and slave (cf. the confounding of roles complained of in I i); hence non-Greek authorities (heads of households? kings?) are effectively, by stunted development, themselves slaves—a harsh judgement, though Aristotle in quoting Euripides implies (*IA* 1400) it would command some popular support (but presumably on broader grounds than this). When at *Met.* 995ᵃ7–8 Aristotle mentions speakers who adduce a poet as a 'witness', *martus*, he does not mean *eye*-witness, only (following the usage of forensic oratory) someone who can offer reasonable support to an argument. That is in general the function of his quotations and references: they supply generally received views (see on 1252ᵃ1–7) but they prove nothing, and given good reasons he is quite prepared to contradict them (see penult. para. of introd. to I ix).

3 (1252ᵇ9–15) Since Aristotle assumes that species are eternal, we might suppose that at any rate the association which is the household must always have existed, and that when he parenthetically says the first association was the household (1257ᵃ19–20) he means just that. But this remark is not part of a systematic history, and our present paragraph seems to tell a different story. The Greek of the opening statement has no verb: it has simply 'a household first'. 'First' presumably means that village and state come second and third. Whether 'a' implies only one household, which was then followed by others (by imitation?), is obscure. But we are told that the household was formed 'from these two associations' (i.e. man/woman, master/slave). Now when 'from' (*ek*) is used in **4** and **5** of the later emergence of the village and state, it is clear that the associations 'from' which they were formed existed antecedently. Aristotle may then have envisaged a genuinely historical pre-household period in which a man might have, on the showing of **1**, either or both of a woman (or several) 'for breeding', and a slave (or several) 'for preservation'; and that he operated these two associations more or less independently, perhaps only occasionally (cf. the casual sexual unions of primitive mankind in Lucretius V 962–5, which may have some Greek source; *EE* 1242ᵃ24–5 describes only practice in Aristotle's day). When however he combines the associations he has a household (he is an *oikonomikon* animal, 'fit for a household': *EE* 1242ᵃ23), in which a much wider and more constant range of cooperative activities than breeding and preservation can be pursued; and that, I take it, is the point of 'the needs of *every* day'. On relationships within the household, see Price (1989) ch. 6.

In the household, these two associations and their two purposes are obviously not overtaken or replaced. As *EN* 1162ᵃ17–22 explains, human beings live together not just for procreation, which we share with animals (as in **1**), but for the purposes of life. Breeding and preservation are the basis for the household's enlarged range of activity, which enables them to be achieved in greater security and comfort; and security and comfort are steps on the way to happiness. This pattern, of *core* and *accretion*, is the model for the other transitions, from household to village and from village to state; see further on **5**.

Life in an early household may nevertheless have been rather grim. *EE* 1242ª19–ᵇ2 and *EN* 1160ᵇ22–1162ª33 explore the varieties of justice and friendship that exist within households as Aristotle knew them much later, in the economic, social, and ethical context of the state—and that would make a considerable difference. At any rate, in the household of his day he saw 'the origins and founts of friendship, of a constitution (*politeia*: perhaps 'citizenship'?), and of justice' (*EE* 1242ª40–ᵇ12, cf. 1253ª15–18, and comment on I xii). On friendship according to Aristotle, see also on 1263ª40–ᵇ14, and Cooper (1990), arguing for a specifically *civic* friendship, beyond familial etc. friendships, with Annas's (1990) sceptical response.

The quotation from Hesiod (*fl. c.*700) is *WD* 405; to make it embrace slaves, Aristotle has to give it some exegesis.

4 (1252ᵇ15–27) Aristotle's villages are mysterious things; his account is brief, allusive, and ambiguous; and translation is at two places unavoidably tendentious. The one firm point is that a village is made up from several households. Presumably a son of one household takes a wife from another (even when households were isolated, this must always have been the practice, short of inbreeding); but instead of eventually taking over his own household (some other son does that) on the death of his father, he sets up his own; and then one or more of his sons in turn acts similarly. The result is a group of households, not necessarily situated close to each other, but related by blood in virtue of descent from the same original mother: they are 'sucklings of the same milk', *homogalactic*. Aristotle, relying on (or misled by) the jingle *oikia/apoikia*, says the village is a colony, *apoikia*, of the *oikia*, household; but this is a figure of speech (cf. Plato, *Laws* 776b), since colonies are normally a group of familially non-related persons sent off from one state to found another. Aristotle ignores the possibility that the village might (and surely would?) contain households *not* related by blood; contrast Plato, who acutely conjectures that such a situation generates conflicts of practices and interests, and hence the first legislation, to reconcile them (*Laws* 680e–681d). The narrower focus of Aristotle's account enables him to represent the village as natural 'in the highest degree', in virtue of the kinship, which lends colour to his claim in **5** that the state in turn is natural. On the other hand the words at ᵇ16–17 rendered 'the village . . . household' could be translated to imply that by nature the village is more an *apoikia* than it is anything else, or is an *apoikia* more than anything else (e.g. a tribe) is an *apoikia*. And there is some further bother with the idea of 'first', in the opening sentence. The point could be that the village is the first association of *households* for more than daily needs (the second being the state—or tribe?). But as the state is an association of households only at one remove, by containing villages, I prefer the translation printed.

What then can one achieve in a village but not in a household? More secure defence, no doubt. Friendship with a wider range of persons, certainly (cf. *EN* 1162ᵃ1–4). A more assured supply of material goods, acquired by (non-monetary) exchange: see on 1257ᵃ19–28. Such things probably represent the *accretions*; the *core* appears to be kingly rule, i.e. rule by one man, *monarchia*, in the interest of his subjects (1279ᵃ32–4). This is exercised (i) by father over children in the household (I xii), (ii) by 'the eldest' in the colony which is the village, and (iii) in early states, which later did not tolerate it (1286ᵇ8 ff.). Though (i)–(iii) are different types of association, Aristotle seems not to feel that the notion that kingly rule applies in all of them falls foul of his censure of Plato in I i, for failing to distinguish e.g. the household-association from the state-association in point of rule. In (iii) and perhaps (ii) kingly rule is no doubt a merely historical practice, now (except among foreign nations) replaced by mature 'political' rule; but then, as for (i), what becomes of the insistence in I i that a household-manager's rule is *different* from that of a king? Presumably the former subsumes, in the same person, (*a*) a household-manager's rule in a narrow sense, in economic matters (cf. 1253ᵇ11–14, I viii, x); (*b*) 'despotic' rule over his slaves; (*c*) aristocratic (*EE* 1241ᵇ30) or political (1259ᵇ1) rule over his wife; (*d*) a king's rule over children (ibid.). At any rate, the male head of the household seems to have to be a versatile fellow; see further on 1254ᵇ2–16 and 1259ᵃ37–ᵇ10.

As for the excursus in the rest of the paragraph, the Homeric quotation (*Od.* ix 114–15) describes rule over scattered households (the Cyclopes), not village-rule. 'Lays down the law' is *themisteuein*, to give *themistes*, judgements in particular situations about right and proper conduct, *themis*. It had long been noticed that men conceive of gods in their own image (Xenophanes DK B14–16).

5 (1252ᵇ27–1253ᵃ1) In the account of the formation of the state from several villages (cf. 1280ᵇ40–1281ᵃ1) there is an irritating lack of hard information. Are the villages the villages of **4**, those based on blood relationships? If so, how do such simple structures, when aggregated, fuse into something as complex as a state (cf. 1303ᵃ25–8)? What are the implications of 'at once'? In particular, how do the two forms of government differ? How is 'the good life' of the state related to the 'other than daily needs' of the village? And can we conclude, from the tense-distinction 'came into existence'/'exists', that the 'good life' was discovered only *after* the establishment of the state, having been no part of the conscious intentions of the founder?

But Aristotle has bigger fish to fry. At first sight, in arguing for the naturalness of the state he cannot rely wholly on parity of reasoning ('since the first associations did so too', i.e. exist by nature). Clearly the early associations, as he represents them, emerged to satisfy natural, physical, and everyday needs; so too does the state (cf. *EE* 1242ᵇ22–3, *EN* 1160ᵃ8 ff.); so far, a reference to the naturalness of the early associations will suffice for the state too. But 'the good life' (= happiness), while requiring and incorporating the satisfaction of such needs, is something over and above them; for as 'so to say' hints, much more is meant than *economic* self-sufficiency or independence (1278ᵇ15 ff., 1280ᵃ31 ff., ᵇ29 ff., 1291ᵃ22 ff.,

1326ᵇ2 ff., *EN* 1297ᵇ14–16), and even in that sense the word should not be taken narrowly: Aristotle does not imply that states do not or should not trade with each other: 1257ᵃ28–41, 1327ᵃ25–8. How then can the natural-ness of the state, in so far as it includes the good life, *depend* on ('since') the naturalness of the earlier associations, which did not include it?

The answer emerges from the thrust of the rest of the paragraph, which implies that the state is the final stage of a continuous linear development (cf. *Phys.* 194ᵃ29), whereby each association is not separately 'natural', but connectedly. As 1334ᵇ13–14 remarks generally, 'coming into being is from a beginning, and the end which is from some beginning is the beginning of another end'. Consider again the cores and the accretions. Each of the five associations (the two pairs, household, village, state) satisfies certain natu-ral needs; the next in line continues to satisfy those, probably better than before; and that was indeed its immediate purpose. But it also provides an economic or social framework which awakens certain other needs and potentialities in the members; the new structure allows and indeed stimu-lates what had never happened before, because the opportunities had not been there; it is natural not only in satisfying existing and felt natural impulses, but in calling forth existing and so far unfelt ones; and these in turn, when actualized, become part of the core of the next development. Here then is some sensible content for the principle of 'the transitivity of naturalness', which Keyt (1991) 129–30 rightly suggests Aristotle in some sense entertained. It is like the naturalness that passes continuously from the embryo to the child to the youth to the adult; we do not say 'the embryo was natural, the child was natural, etc., therefore the adult is too', as if we were enumerating separate things inductively.

Nor is Aristotle's argument one of mere aggregation; the naturalness of the state does not rest on its containing the other associations, or on being constituted by them; for a collection of natural objects does not necessarily produce a natural object.

The fourth sentence (ᵇ31–4), on ends, is apparently offered in elucida-tion of 'since . . .'. When a thing's process of coming to be is completed, *telestheises*, we have the *telos*, end, i.e. the thing towards which the process moved, e.g. man, horse, house; and the 'sort of thing' (*hoion*) we have we call its 'nature', *phusis*, e.g. 'it is in this thing's nature to be a horse', as a result of that process. This usage certainly links the word *phusis* to the state, which is the 'end' of the process of historical growth; but since not all ends of all processes are natural, it hardly shows that the state is by nature, or natural. For even if we allow that objects do have 'a' nature (as the 'house' has, cf. 1342ᵇ16, *Poet.* 1449ᵃ15), that does not confer natural*ness* on them or in their process of creation, at least in the terms of *Phys.* II i (note also the house at 199a12). Cf. Keyt (1991) 130.

The final sentence (1252ᵇ34–1253ᵃ1) seems prompted by the notion of 'end' in its predecessor: it claims that the aim, i.e. the end(s) of a process ('that for the sake of which'), is 'best', i.e. better than the stages that led up to it; they are 'for' it. The total self-sufficiency offered by the state clearly qualifies as both end and best. Why say this? Presumably to suggest that since bestness of end is a characteristic of natural processes, self-sufficiency, which is best, is a natural end; and since the *polis* is part of the process leading to that end, the *polis* must be natural. However, bestness of end is characteristic of 'artificial' processes too, so the argument fails; it could be rescued by treating the *polis* as a 'natural artefact', subserving the 'best' (see introd. to this chapter).

6 (1253ᵃ1–7) The translation of *politikon*, 'fit for a state', does not imply that a man is born already endowed with the appropriate virtues, but only that he is born with the capacity or faculty (*dunamis*, *EN* II i) for developing them by education. It is then something of a surprise to learn that one could be 'naturally' stateless, i.e. by nature without even the capacity, or 'impulse' (see **9** and cf. *EN* 1169ᵇ18–19), to live in a state. Aristotle assigns no reason for the deficiency, but would presumably allege some physiological defect that affects psychology (cf. 1254ᵃ37–1254ᵇ2). Such a person is a 'wretch', or perhaps 'impaired', *phaulos*, because the co-operative virtues are essential to life in a state, which is in turn essential to happiness; for without co-operators, he has to fight to live, and therefore lacks leisure (cf. *EN* 1177ᵇ4 ff.). The inference seems extreme: hermits may have only minimal happiness (*EN* 1169ᵇ16 ff.), but why do they have to be bellicose? Perhaps *EN* 1170ᵃ5 implies he has to steal what he does not get by co-operation; cf. Nussbaum (1986) 363–4. *Pettoi*: a board game called *polis*.

7 (1253ᵃ7–18) 'Fit for a state' renders *politikon*, as in **6**; cf. 1278ᵇ15 ff., *EN* 1162ᵃ17 ff. But no animal lives as a member of a state, so the sentence sounds absurd. The point is that animals have two characteristics which are necessary but not sufficient for life in a state: the sensations (*aesthēsis*) of pleasure and pain, and 'voice', *phōnē*, with which to 'indicate' them to each other. The same is true of men (cf. *HA* 536ᵃ33–ᵇ3); but men have also a sense/perception (*aisthēsis*) of benefit and harm etc., as listed, and 'speech', *logos*, to express them. A further distinction emerges from *HA* 488ᵃ2 ff.: some animals are solitary, some 'herding' (*agelaia*); among the latter some—e.g. men, bees, wasps—are *politika*, that is to say, in each case the activity/task/function (*ergon*) of all members of the herd is single and common (*koinon*). In sum, to pursue their common task (whatever that is), bees etc. have sensations of pleasure and pain, plus voice; to pursue theirs, men have in addition a sense of good and bad, just and unjust, plus speech. Men are thus 'fit for a state to a fuller extent': they are better *equipped*, in such a way as to be able to live in the complex association, *koinōnia*, which is the *state*. Detailed discussion of the implications of the biological dimension in Mulgan (1974), Miller (1989) 198 ff., Cooper (1990) 222 ff., Kullmann (1991), Depew (1995).

There are implausibilities. (i) At *HA* 488ᵃ9 Aristotle says that not all herding animals have a common function, *koinon ergon*. When there is no such function, what is the purpose of the herding, and of indicating feelings of pleasure and pain? (ii) Common observation suggests that animals do more than feel, and then express, pleasure and pain: they are able to identify and indicate in advance what is likely to be beneficial or harmful; and elsewhere Aristotle recognizes in some animals a certain *phronēsis* (practical wisdom), mutual communication, teaching and learning (from each other and from men), care, and the faculty of looking ahead (*EN* 1141ª26–8, *HA* 536ᵇ17–18, 608ª14–19, *GA* 753ª8 ff., *PA* 660ª35–ᵇ2). Moreover, there must be a high correlation between what any animal finds pleasurable and what it finds beneficial. Aristotle has over-sharpened the distinction, which is *perhaps* why 'beneficial and harmful' disappear from the second list, at ª16–17, being replaced by 'good and bad', which have moral implications inappropriate to animals. (iii) The implication of 1253ª15–18 seems to be that man has a moral sense by nature, and is thus able to live in a state. But clearly moral sense is acquired only *by* living in a state (*EN* II i); it is not present from birth. Presumably 'man alone has perception of good and evil, just and unjust' is shorthand for 'man alone has by nature a capacity to acquire that perception', whereas animals do not. See Miller (1989) 201–5.

'And so also': why are the just and the unjust entailed? Presumably because the benefits and burdens of living in a state have to be distributed in some principled manner (cf. *EE* 1242ᵇ27–31), and that is a matter of justice (see e.g. V i). The use of *logos* to 'make clear' the just and the unjust implies deliberation and persuasion. Aristotle may wish to imply that whereas animals merely act and react automatically, treating pleasurable as beneficial without reflection (cf. *Anim.* 414ᵇ4–6), men consider, debate, and choose alternatives, by *distinguishing* pleasurable and beneficial (neither is necessarily the other: *EN* 1113ª33–ᵇ2). Again, observation suggests this is over-simplification.

'In these matters', ª18: perhaps 'of these', i.e. animals with that sense.

8 (1253ª18–29) A restatement of **6**, in more elaborate terms, and embracing the household too. Though the state is of course chronologically later than its parts, it is 'prior by nature' to them in having been immanent in them as the structured unity, the end or form, to which they naturally developed historically (cf. *Phys.* 261ª13–14). But in this chapter Aristotle is thinking of another use, connected but different, of that expression. For *why* did the parts so develop? To satisfy certain 'natural' needs, to enable men to fulfil 'natural' functions; for all this is necessary to happiness. Therefore a man cut off from a state suffers functional impairment, and his happiness diminishes. He can indeed exist outside a state (the analogy of the severed and therefore dead hand does not imply he would be dead, but not in his complete functional fulfilment (cf. Miller (1995) 47–53). To that extent, his condition is *un*natural: it is not one of simple primitive felicity, a 'natural life' that may be thought *preferable* to life in a state, with all its complexities and troubles. It is in this functional sense that the whole which is the state is prior by nature: it can continue to exist if any individual is withdrawn; but he cannot exist in that sense without it (cf. *Met.* 1019ª1–4).

The paragraph limits itself to the argument from function; but it is not clear whether the claim that the state exists by nature is supposed to follow from its being prior by nature (see Keyt (1991) 127, 136), or whether it merely draws a conclusion from **1–7**. Very wide questions arise (cf. on **2**). (i) Does it follow that, since a man functions (if not, he is dead), he has a specific *function to perform*; if so, why must it be the practical life of the part of him that has reason (*EN* 1098ᵃ3–5), i.e. that faculty which is peculiar to him? Why is 'peculiarity' so crucial for happiness? Presumably, and plausibly, because the criteria for being a good *x* depend on what it is to be an *x*, i.e. its definition, as opposed to what it is to be something else; 'peculiarities' (rationality in the case of man) mark the essential differences. But then, is being a good *x* good *for it*, i.e. does it make a happy *x*? Certainly Aristotle thinks so (cf. *EN* 1177ᵇ24 ff.). Yet many men have seen the satisfaction of our other faculties besides reason as at least equally important to happiness. See *EN* 1097ᵇ2 ff., a general account of human function (discussed by Ackrill (1981) 14–16). At any rate, **1, 2,** and **8** offer some description of what Aristotle sees as the function of three particular categories: woman, slave, free man. (ii) Even if Aristotle has identified correctly those of our functions that are natural, ought not our nature to be transcended? There are plenty of reasons for mistrusting our natural endowments, however rational, and concluding that 'the proper business of mankind' is (e.g.) to worship God. (iii) What are the implications of the 'whole and part' thesis for the autonomy of the individual? (In the case of slaves, it is employed in I iv with extreme rigour.) Cf. 1337ᵃ27–30, Allan (1965), and Barnes (1990), esp. 262–3, with Sorabji's comments; the latter suggests Aristotle moves away from Plato's 'totalitarianism'; also Everson (1988) and Taylor (1995) 239–41. 'Beast or god': cf. *EN* 1145ᵃ15 ff.

9 (1253ᵃ29–39) Finally, the whole and part argument is driven home by resort to a *topos* of historical anthropology (see introduction to this chapter), the moral improvement of men achieved by founding states, and in particular systems of law and justice. The shadowy first founder exploited men's 'impulse' or 'drive' (*hormē*, cf. the natural urge at 1252ᵃ29) to form such an association, others being founded by imitation (see *Poet.* 1448ᵇ5–9 on man as an imitative animal). Aristotle may have supposed him to have been one of the early lawgivers, *nomothetai*; that would bring the history down to the 7th/6th centuries.

The identity of the 'weapons' is obscure: probably a man's total natural capacities, both mental and physical. 'Justice' (*dikē*) I take to be a *system* of some kind: a code, courts, and especially a political constitution (cf. V i); these rely for their operation on the *virtue* of justice (*dikaiosunē*), i.e. a judgement of what is just, *dikaion*. 'The association which takes the form of a state': see comment on 1252ᵃ7.

I iii

PRELIMINARY ANALYSIS OF THE HOUSEHOLD

Introduction Programmatic of the rest of book I. The household was centrally important in Greek life, and indeed in Aristotle's own social, political, and ethical thought (see e.g. I xii, xiii, and *EN* 1160ᵇ22 ff.) The household-manager, *oikonomos*, is the first member of each of the three 'parts' of the household:

1. Husband/wife ⎫
2. Father/children ⎬   Discussed in I xii and xiii.
3. Master/slave   Discussed in I iv–vii and xiii.

But we have to add that part of household-management which is:

4. The art of acquiring   Adumbrated in **2**, and discussed in viii–xi.
   property

1 (1253ᵇ1–11) The villages of I ii disappear, and the two pairs of 1252ᵃ24–34 are expanded into three. Why no *oikia* is 'complete' without slaves emerges from I iv–vii; on this showing, a good many ancient Greek households were incomplete: see 1252ᵇ9–15, 1323ᵃ5–6.

The sharp focus on the three 'parts' of the household sounds businesslike: we ask (*a*) 'what' each is, and (*b*) 'what qualities it ought to have'. The distinction between 'what' and 'what sort of thing' is frequent in Aristotle (see e.g. 1274ᵇ32–3, *EE* 1216ᵃ30–1). For (*a*), he seems to require some kind of handy definition, as several times elsewhere (e.g. 'a state's constitution is an arrangement of its offices', 1278ᵇ8–10; the good or bad qualities of the arrangement are another matter). What would such a definition of (e.g.) husband/wife be? Perhaps, 'a union of a man and a woman for *x* purposes and with *y* stipulations (such as minimum age)'. That would no doubt be theory-laden, but it would be something one could work with.

The answer Aristotle gives ('They are . . .') is not like that at all. Indeed, it is not clear whether he is answering (*a*) or (*b*) or both. The linguistic difficulties are secondary: evidently Greek had no word for the marriage state, only for the wedding (*gamos*), nor any for the relationship between father and children (Aristotle makes do with 'procreation', *teknopoiēsis*). But it seems that even if he had had suitable words, he would have given them not as such but as adjectives of the *-ikos* form (see note 3 to Glossaries), and in the feminine singular at that, implying a noun, standardly *technē* ('art', 'skill') or *epistēmē* ('knowledge'), or possibly *archē* ('rule'); we are in fact given here *despotikē* and (for the want of better terms) *gamikē* and *teknopoiētikē*. He seems to define the pairs in terms of the manner in which they are directed, and therefore function; for this makes them *what* they are (or should be). As in i and ii, *rule* is still his central concern.

2 (1253ᵇ11–14) The art of goods-getting, which does not involve rule, is provisionally adopted here (and again at the start of I iv) as a 'part' of the manager's duties, in deference to a reasonable opinion. But Aristotle's heart is not in it: see I viii and x.

3 (1253ᵇ14–23) Theory and practice go hand in hand: cf. e.g. *EN* X i. 'Some . . .' refers to 1252ᵃ7–16 and I vii; 'others . . .' looks ahead to the important debate in I vi. If there is a link to be made, it is presumably this: if mastership is the same as the other four forms of rule, it must be just—precisely what is denied by the 'others'. But the report of the opinion of 'some' could be independent, and relate only to the two points debated in

I vii: the difference between mastership and other forms of rule, and its status as a 'knowledge'.

I iv

THE SLAVE AS THE TOOL OF HIS MASTER

Introduction Apparently an attempt to answer in plainer terms than in I iii the questions 'what is it?' and 'what sort of thing should it be?' in respect of the master/slave pair. At any rate, we are offered several statements of what a slave is (though not what a master is), and we learn something of their relationship, a peculiarly tight form of functional (not merely legal) ownership of the one by the other.

1 ($1253^{b}23-1254^{a}1$) 'Essentials' picks up 'essential needs' in $1253^{b}16$. The point is not that the slave is himself one of the essentials (one *can* live without slaves), but that he is to assist his master in acquiring and using them (cf. $1277^{a}33$ ff.). This, and the exclusion of the slave from productive labour in **2** and **3**, amount to a sharp diminution of his economic role as compared with historical practice; for many were put to work, often in bad conditions, in craft-workshops and mines; and Aristotle himself proposes to have them work on farms ($1330^{a}25-6$). His confining of them here to a domestic role is however ideological rather than humanitarian.

The household-manager will need other men as his 'tools' in various contexts and to varying degrees; that sounds offensive, but even friends can use each other 'like tools' ($1099^{a}34-^{b}1$). Aristotle is not claiming that, since a possession is a tool for living, all (animate) tools must be possessions, i.e. slaves—only that some of them should be, if the household is to be 'complete' ($1253^{b}4$). Since the slave is a possession, he is a tool, and a living one, which makes him doubly useful, since non-living tools are not robots (if one may summarize the long bracket thus). The implication is perhaps that the slave has some degree of rationality (see further $1254^{b}20-3$).

'Plucker': an instrument used by players of the lyre; the poet is Homer, at *Il.* XVIII 376.

2 ($1254^{a}1-8$) Aristotle draws himself up: he has seemed to suggest that slaves are concerned, as shuttles are, with production, *poiēsis*; but he believes that they are concerned with action, *praxis* (so presumably we should still need them for that purpose, even if we did possess robots for production). According to *EN* ($1139^{a}35-^{b}4$, VI iv, $1140^{b}3-8$), production has an aim beyond itself, whereas doing *well*, *eupraxia*, is itself 'an' end— part of *the* end, in that acting well is happiness, which can have no end beyond itself.

In the first sentence Aristotle does not mean that tools are never possessions and that possessions are never tools. The distinction between possessions for action and tools for production may rest on the principle of 'one job, one tool' (cf. 1252ᵃ34–ᵇ5); but why should not the same tool be used for both, given efficiency? Aristotle has over-sharpened the distinction, in order to put the slave firmly under the heading of action.

The action–production antithesis is dubious, since production always entails activity and all activity can be represented as production in *some* sense. As employed in this chapter, it is open to the objection, 'But I find part of my happiness in the activity of productive carpentry, making tables, and I use my slave to help me'. Aristotle would presumably see more happiness in the exercise of one's more rational capacities, in office-holding, social intercourse, etc.

The point of confining the slave to action emerges from **3**, where slave is argued to be in effect an intimate extension of his master. The master's aim is of course acting, i.e. living, well; to employ the slave for production would therefore be a misuse of him—except, presumably, when it is unavoidable; for at any rate production subserves doing well. The slave 'shares his master's life' (1260ᵃ39–40); and the master is concerned with action, not production. And there is probably an ancillary reason: Aristotle believes that production all too easily becomes over-production, to yield excessive wealth (cf. I ix and x); masters should avoid the temptation of using slaves to increase their wealth beyond due bounds. Cf. in general Plato, *Laws* 846ᵈ–847ᵃ.

3 (1254ᵃ8–17) The nub of the argument is:

(i) a part is *holōs*, wholly or absolutely or unqualifiedly, 'of' something else (e.g. this leg is of this chair, not of that chair).
(ii) a possession is wholly 'of' something else.
(iii) a slave, *qua* possession, is wholly 'of' his master.
(iv) a slave is not 'of' himself (entailed by (iii)).

Clearly in (i) 'wholly' is structural, but in (ii) and (iii) legal, one of ownership. Therefore Aristotle, rather as he sometimes says a state is *like* an animal, but never says that it *is* an animal (see introduction to I ii), here claims only that a possession 'is spoken of in the same way as a part', not that a possession *is* a part of its owner (on the contrary, it is 'separate'); accordingly, he does not say that the slave is a part of his master; nor does he say it at 1255ᵇ11–12, *EN* 1134ᵇ12, and *EE* 1241ᵇ23–4. Nevertheless, he plainly wishes to establish the tightest possible connection of continuity: the slave is not 'of' himself, but like a limb (cf. 1255ᵇ11–12 and Democritus DK B270), wholly 'of' his master; but in the end the argument has to depend on language only, i.e. two uses of the genitive case, 'of'. Aristotle might have done better to drop the argument from ownership, and argue simply that the slave is 'part' of a functional relationship, as indeed he does in the next chapter in an attempt to *justify* slavery. Meanwhile, this description of status and function of the slave as practically a part of the master amounts to an explanation of 'what sort of thing' the master/slave relationship 'ought' (ideally?) to be (1253ᵇ4–8). As when he says the slave 'is' a tool for action only, he is using the indicative to state what he thinks ought to be the case.

In the last sentence, he is careful to stipulate that the slave should be a 'natural' slave. This point is central to the next two chapters.

I v

NATURAL PATTERNS OF RULE AS A JUSTIFICATION OF SLAVERY

Introduction An airy start: in asking whether natural slaves exist, and whether it is beneficial and just for someone to be a slave, Aristotle claims that neither 'theoretical examination' nor 'learning from what occurs' is difficult; clearly he expects both to point to the same conclusion (cf. *EN* 1098ᵇ9–12). The former is hard to find in *this* chapter, unless it is merely the methodology (induction, and large generalization at the start of 2 and 4). It should rather be sought in I vi, where Aristotle reconstructs and arbitrates between the assumptions made by attackers and defenders of slavery.

Our present chapter is devoted to 'what occurs'. It rambles around somewhat, but its logical shape seems to be:

A. Master/slave is a ruler/ruled relationship.
B. Man/animal, soul/body, mind/desire, mind/emotion, male/female, are ruler/ruled relationships.
C. All B's confer benefit on the ruled [and on the ruler].
D. This benefit is conferred because in each case the ruler is by nature rational, the ruled by nature either non-rational or partly-rational.

By applying what is (alleged to be) true of the B's to A (for induction, cf. 1268ᵇ31 ff.), Aristotle can plausibly suggest that there are such persons as natural slaves, and that they benefit from their status (on 'just' see commentary on 1); slavery is one item in a frequently repeated pattern of natural relationships. That the induction (like all induction) is inconclusive is quite acceptable to him; it is enough that it should point to the truth in *some* instances of A (see 'any one', 1 *init*, and 'some people', 6 *fin.*; cf. 'in some cases', 1255ᵇ6). He is fully aware that some slaves are not natural slaves and do not benefit from their status, and that some masters are inadequate (1255ᵇ9); but in the relationship between a natural master and a natural slave he sees benefit to both (cf. 1252ᵃ34); if benefit is absent, the relationship is presumably not a natural one, as the incompetent master is not a 'natural' ruler, or at least is a natural ruler only potentially (he may need experience and/or instruction). As in more directly political matters (see introd. to I ii), 'natural' is very widely conceived, being applied to any human contrivance that helps natural impulses and relationships.

Aristotle has often been accused of merely seeking to justify, in a conservative spirit, an undesirable but entrenched institution that subserved a divisively hierarchical ideology, and of arguing essentially from what is to what ought to be. He would surely have riposted that what is, is *because* it is what ought to be: *because* it is natural, it *is* what generally 'occurs' (though of course he offers no evidence that natural slavery is more common than conventional); and that his position neither justifies nor entails repression and exploitation. Nevertheless, even if we grant the force of his induction, the dependency of the ruled need not take the form of chattel slavery, much less the tight chattel slavery advocated in I iv. But in a world where slavery was prevalent and largely unchallenged, and the employed/employee relationship far less developed than now, how else could Aristotle seek to express institutionally his pessimism about the intellectual capacities of a certain proportion of the population? No doubt he was historically conditioned; but his attitude to slavery is a notably independent one, as is clear from I vi.

One wishes he had tried to tackle two further issues. (i) Suppose a man is born naturally free, but becomes slavish in habits and demeanour as a result of a long period of slavery (cf. Homer, *Od.* xvii 322–3). What is his 'nature' then? (ii) Ought the state to determine who is to be a slave, perhaps in response to changing social needs, and if so, on what criteria and by what practical measures? Aristotle seems to assume that existing slaves will go on producing roughly the right number of naturally slave offspring indefinitely. But when free parents produce a natural slave, what is to be done?

1 (1254ª17–28) How are 'better and just' (cf. **6** *fin.*) linked? The slave derives benefit, certainly (1252ª34); but 1278ᵇ32–7 argues that slavery is more for the benefit of the master, and that the slave benefits only incidentally, in virtue of the master's having an interest in his safety and welfare (cf. 1333ª3–6, *EN* 1161ª32 ff., *EN* 1241ᵇ12–24). The master treats the slave instrumentally (cf. Plato, *Laws* 777d), and keeps him in good order like the tool he is. The slave does not get much from the relationship; but without a master, it seems, he would be even less well off. The slightness of the benefit is 'just' on grounds of desert, or 'proportionate equality' (for this important concept, see 1261ª22 ff., 1329ª13–16, V i and ii, and Harvey 1965 and 1966); for the slave contributes only lowly services. This is the relevance of the remark that the quality of rule varies according to the quality of the ruled: better 'ruleds' do better work. 'Better' presumably means 'more rational', and so more effective and useful; hence rule over a slave is less good than that over a free man, but better than over an animal. (On the justice due to slaves, see further on 1260ª36–ᵇ7, 4th para.) However, perhaps this is on the wrong tack: 'just' may refer not to the justice of the scale of benefits, but to that of the status itself (the theme of I vi). But it is not easy to separate the two.

'Differentiated right from birth': male/female etc. What 'things', then, are *not* so differentiated? Perhaps free men who in a political context *later* prove better at one activity or the other; or slaves who prove to be in soul or body deserving of free status, or *vice versa* (see **5**); for genetic traits may take time to become obvious (cf. 1334ᵇ22–5). In general, however, Aristotle seems to assume that natural slaves will produce natural slaves. Strictly, late development would not make natural traits *less* natural; but he is happiest, when arguing for the naturalness of something, if that something appears *early*, and hence unaffected by social and environmental influences; cf. 1256ᵇ7 ff., *EN* 1144ᵇ4 ff., *EE* 1247ᵃ9–13.

2 (1254ᵃ28–ᵇ2) 'Continuous', e.g. soul/body; 'discontinuous', e.g. master/ slave (cf. 1254ᵃ17). **2** deals with the first kind, **3** with both.

'In common', *koinon*: the statement is very wide, apparently covering not only human and animal associations (the state, herds), but physical things with some principled structure (not mere aggregations of various contents). Are there then no *purely* co-operative enterprises, no associations, in which no one rules? And what would constitute 'rule' in a physical compound? Cf. 1261ᵃ22 ff., on the structure of a *polis*. As for rule 'over a musical mode', the note *mesē*, the highest in the tetrachord, was called the 'leader' ([Aristotle] *Problems* 920ᵃ22; for technical detail, see Schütrumpf i. 252–3). The reference to rule in non-living things is tantalizing: Aristotle refrains from discussion, but clearly his synoptic mind has discerned some sort of parallel.

At the end, the wretched person and the person in a wretched condition evidently differ—but how? Perhaps the former is (e.g.) corpulent from self-indulgence, the latter because of bodily malfunction. In neither case, just by looking at the body, can we make a sure inference that it rules the soul. We ought 'rather' to take as models (for use in the induction) persons who obviously do have the two in their natural and correct relationship. Aristotle confidently assumes we recognize it as natural when we see it.

3 (1254ᵇ2–16) Aristotle offers three examples of the ruled/ruled relationships *within* living beings, then two *between* them.

He speaks of (i) the rule of the soul (*psuchē*) over the body (cf. **2**), then of (ii) the rule of one part of the soul (mind, *nous*) over another (appetition, *orexis*). We are not told how the two models are related. (i) looks like simple dualism, Plato-style (e.g. *Phaedo* 80a, *Laws* 726 ff.), in which the (rational) soul is somehow distinct from the (irrational) body but within it and (ideally) in control of it. As a model for the relation of master to slave, this has obvious attractions; but it is hard to see how it is to be reconciled with Aristotle's official psychology, according to which the soul is a structured set of actualized faculties of the body, where the language of *rule* of the one by the other seems inappropriate. (ii) is perhaps more in accordance with that psychology: the soul has various faculties (here 'parts', as sometimes in the *de Anima* itself), of which the highest is reason (see in general *EN* I xiii). But even on this model Aristotle is ever apt to talk of the parts as though they were in some sense independent agencies, almost mini-persons (e.g. *EN* 1102ᵇ30–2: the desiring and appetitive part is amenable and obedient to reason). He is keen to build up his inductive list, by finding the rule of master, statesman, and king *within* the individual; he has therefore to find there counterparts to the rulers and ruled of real life; and that dictates a rather crude psychology.

In what respect is the rule of mind over desire 'of a statesman or king'? Both these rules are over free and willing persons, and are for their good (1255ᵇ20, 1277ᵇ7–9, 1333ᵃ3–6); and statesmen and kings are rational rulers of rational subjects. So perhaps part of the point is that mind has to *persuade* desire (see above on *EN* 1102ᵇ30, and further references in **4**). But *alternation* of rule, characteristic of a statesman's rule (1252ᵃ15–16), is obviously excluded as between the parts of the soul, and indeed as between the parts of the household. For Aristotle talks of certain forms of rule in a state as existing there too (e.g. 1255ᵇ19, *EE* 1241ᵇ27–32); but in this case he is alive to the qualifications to be made (1259ᵇ4 ff.) Perhaps *-ikè* in such contexts should be translated, (rule) 'like' that of a king etc.: cf. on 1259ᵃ37–ᵇ10, and see note 3 to Glossaries.

4 (1254ᵇ16–26) 'Can and therefore does belong to another': 'can' is *dunamenos*, normally 'able', but here apparently 'with the capacity or potentiality, *dunamis*, to . . .'. A natural slave in the natural course of events *is* a slave, the property of another (see I iv).

'Apprehend but not possess reason': a good description of Lennie's intellectual range in Steinbeck's *Of Mice and Men*, who can comprehend a train of reasoning but not institute one and work it out for himself. Initiative and independence in reasoning are crucial. The slave's complete lack of deliberative capacity (1260ᵃ12) calls for 'despotic' rule, i.e. of a master; but the reason possessed by the soul's faculty of desire, which has it not 'in the sovereign sense', *kuriōs*, but 'as a child listens to its father' (*EN* 1098ᵃ3–5, 1103ᵃ1–3; cf. 1333a16–18), evidently to the father's *advice*, requires 'political or kingly rule' by reason (**3**). It is not clear how this squares with 1260ᵇ5–7, where slaves are probably implied to have *more* reason, of the kind requiring advice and admonition, than children.

'Obey . . . feelings': said also of 'the many' at *EN* 1179ᵇ13; cf. 1281ᵇ19–20.

5 (1254ᵇ27–34) 'Erect bodies': contrast the scheming clergyman in Trollope's *Barchester Towers*, Mr Slope. Aristotle thinks that physiology, sensation, and reason are assisted by upright posture, which he claims is possessed by man alone among the animals: *PA* 653ᵃ28 ff., 656ᵃ11–14, 686ᵃ27–32; cf. 1258ᵇ35–9, Theognis 535–6, Plato *Laws* 734d. The 'opposite' of nature's purpose occurs when 'some people' (presumably *natural* slaves) have the body of a free man, but not the soul, while 'others', presumably free men, though having the soul of a free man, have the body of a slave. In this case, would the inferior body actually impede or override the rational activities of the soul? **2** *fin.* says that that 'impression' can be given. On the failures of nature, cf. *GA* 778ᵃ4–9.

6 (1254ᵇ34–1255ᵃ3) Presumably Aristotle does not agree with what would be the popular inference from extreme excellence of body; but the second sentence nevertheless utilizes the inference in an argument *a fortiori* in favour of the soul as the factor determining natural status.

The final sentence answers the question posed at the start of the chapter, whether there is 'anyone' who is a natural slave; it reads literally: 'there are by nature some, some free, some slaves . . .'. The claim seems carefully restricted: not all people are *either* natural slaves *or* naturally free—only some. What then of the rest? Are they in some intermediate position, and may they go either way as a result of education and social conditions? Or does Aristotle mean only that *some* people do in fact occupy their 'natural' position, while others do not (some natural slaves are *de facto* free, some naturally free are *de facto* slaves)? These latter possibilities are the theme of the next chapter.

I vi

THE CONTROVERSY ABOUT THE JUSTIFICATION OF SLAVERY

Introduction   In ancient Greece slavery was in general taken for granted. This exceptionally difficult chapter is (with I iii *fin.*) our main evidence for the existence of some measure of controversy about it, legal, popular, and philosophical (see 1 *fin.*). If the rival schools of thought had identifiable spokesmen, Aristotle does not name them. Other evidence is threefold: (i) claims or implications, especially in drama, that some slaves (notably former free men) are morally and socially as good as if not better than free men; (ii) a statement (*c*.360) of the rhetorician Alcidamas, reported by a scholiast on *Rhet.* 1373ᵇ18: 'God has left all men free; nature has made no one a slave' (on its context and uncertain status as evidence, see Guthrie (1962–81) iii. 159 n. 2, Cambiano (1987) 24–5); (iii) a statement in a fragment of the comic dramatist Philemon (late 4th–early 3rd century): 'Even if someone is a slave, he has the same flesh; no one was ever born a slave by nature, but chance enslaves the body' (fr. 95 Kock (1880–8)). The common tendency of (i)–(iii) is to call attention to important features that slave and free have in common, and to play them off against the slave's formal status, which is, or at least implied to be, unnatural, and therefore, one supposes, to be deprecated as unjust, though neither (ii) or (iii) infers this explicitly, much less that slavery should be abolished. (Plato, however, recommended abolition of enslavement of *Greeks*: *Rep.* 469bc, 471a.) Further discussion in Newman i. 139 ff. Cambiano (1987) has a wide-ranging review of the arguments that may have been deployed.

Now it is presumably to this kind of view that Aristotle is referring at the end of I iii: 'Others think that it is contrary to nature to be a master, because the fact that one man is a slave and another free is by convention, whereas in nature they do not differ at all, which is why it is not just either; for it is the result of force.' It is important, but hard, to know how far this is report/summary, how far reconstruction, and how far supplementation, in terms of Aristotelian concepts, of the reasoning of slavery's attackers. At any rate, *two* reasons are given for slavery's being unjust: (i) it is contrary to nature, (ii) it is the result of force. (i) The justice is presumably *distributive* justice (see *EN* V iii): slave and free being equal by nature, they have an equal claim to freedom (just as, by 'numerical' rather than 'pro-portionate' equality, democrats claim equal political power for each man, since each is equally free: see V i, and cf. *EN* 1131ᵃ24–32). (ii) 'For it is the result of force' implies 'if forcible, then unjust': in Aristotelian terms, 'a slave has been forcibly moved from his natural place as a free man'

(Cambiano (1987) 38, citing *inter alia EN* 1110[a]1–4, *GC* 333[b]26–30); this robs him of the moral choice and freedom of action naturally belonging to him (cf. Keyt (1993) 138–9). If all this fairly represents the views of the attackers of slavery, their claim would amount, at least by implication, to a doctrine of natural justice—of the natural right of all persons not to be enslaved.

Is I vi intended to address *this* controversy? Perhaps not, or not quite in those terms. For until the summing-up in **4**, nature appears (apart from an implied contrast between it and law ('law too') in the second sentence of **1**), only as an objection brought by Aristotle himself against the defenders of enforced slavery as just in **3**. In the tangled analysis of the controversy of **1** and **2** it has no role at all: the discussion is wholly in terms of law, good, virtue, justice, and force. The attackers of slavery are allowed to express only outrage and scorn (**1** 'dreadful,' **2** 'nonsense'); it is not *they* who appeal to nature; and the equality thesis in Alcidamas and Philemon is not confronted, at least directly.

The debate in **1** and **2**, between the defenders of slavery and its attackers, is written hazily, and generates sharp conflicts of interpretation. The most detailed analysis is by myself (1984), which I now summarize; there are briefer ones by Goldschmidt (1973) esp. 153–6, and Schofield (1990) esp. 23–7. On the role of force in this chapter, and the 'anticoercion principle' in Aristotle's political thought, see Keyt (1993).

1. The *defenders* ('others', [a]11 and [a]18) of forcibly imposed slavery notice that all conquerors conquer by dint of superiority in some 'good'; that virtue when equipped with resources is best able to use force; and that virtue is a good. They argue, from cases of forcible enslavement where that 'good' is virtue, that it *always* is ('force is not without virtue'); and, by a short step from virtue to justice, that forcible enslavement is always just.

2. The *attackers* ('some', [a]11 and [a]17) of forcibly imposed slavery argue, from occasions when that 'good' is *not* virtue, that the step from virtue to justice can *never* be taken—indeed talk of 'justice' in regard to forcibly imposed slavery is a 'nonsense'. Both sides illegitimately infer a general rule from particular instances.

3. *The 'overlap'.* The defender wrongly extends his own thesis to embrace those cases in which the 'good' is *not* virtue; such cases are legitimate 'territory' to be exploited by the attackers. The attacker wrongly extends his own thesis to embrace those cases in which the 'good' *is* virtue; such cases are legitimate 'territory' to be exploited by the defender.

4. The 'disentanglement' (literally the 'separation' or 'standing apart') of the arguments is when each side pulls back to its legitimate territory. Thus *neither* 'the use of force to enslave is always accompanied by virtue', *nor* 'the use of force to enslave is always *not* accompanied by virtue', conflicts with 'the superior in virtue ought to rule and be master' (**2** *fin.*)— precisely Aristotle's own position, who is quite prepared to sanction the acquisition of *natural* slaves by force (1255[b]37–9, 1256[b]20–6, cf. 1324[b]32–41). The 'other arguments' are presumably the unqualified positions set out in **1**, *before* their disentanglement.

Thus so long as each side confines itself to its proper territory, Aristotle agrees with both. He is not prepared to let the defenders (Thrasymachus, Callicles, in Plato *Rep.* 338c ff. and *Gorg.* 483d) get away with 'justice is the rule of the stronger'; for that would prevent his saying 'this man is ruling, but ought not to' (he is *not* superior in virtue). Nor will he let the attackers say 'justice is a nonsense' as applied to forcibly imposed slavery; for he holds that it *is* 'just' to impose it on natural slaves.

If this reconstruction is correct, it is a nice example of Aristotle's procedure (cf. *EN* 1145^{b}2–8, 1146^{b}6–8): he sets out opposing views, reconstructs the reasoning which he either knows or supposes to lie behind them, eliminates error, and leaves what he conceives to be the truth holding the field. In the present case, it is not a truth that would satisfy either side completely.

1 (1255^{a}3–12) 'The law ...' There was of course no such law. Aristotle, or the school of thought he is reporting, means that law in general recognizes slaves as chattels, and pays no regard to the justice of the institution itself: it accepted a common 'agreement' that what is conquered becomes the property of the conquerors. Since law and justice were commonly thought to be antithetical to force, the attackers of slavery can refer paradoxically and disparagingly to 'this "justice" (or "right")', *dikaion*. The bringer of a charge of illegality, *graphē paranomōn*, claims a (proposed) legal rule is *il*legal; the attackers of slavery claim the justice of the law about slaves is *un*just; they attempt in effect to redefine the concept of justice. They use a familiar technique: to reproach something for insufficiently maintaining its own standards (humanists sometimes claim to be more Christian than Christians).

2 (1255^{a}12–21) '... the dispute is only about what is just.' Difficult words: for justice is the central issue. A conceivable alternative to my own view (see introduction to this chapter, (1), 'short step') would be (the defenders speaking): 'Our point that force entails virtue answers your reproach that we sanction the former; that leaves only the question of justice; but the *law* is just, and the law sanctions slavery, in virtue of what is after all an *agreement* (^{a}6) about the rights of the stronger; so slavery is just.' In that case, why all the song and dance about 'good' and virtue? Can that really have been an independent argument? Surely not; and those who rely on law exclusively seem to be dealt with separately, in the next paragraph ('Some cleave ...').

'Nonsense' renders *anoia* in the Oxford text; Richards' *euētheia*, 'naïvety', is possible (cf. *Rep.* 348c). The MSS have *eunoia*, 'goodwill'; if there is sense to be made of that, it is elusive (see Schofield (1990) 24 n. 1, but cf. Brunt (1993) 353).

3 (1255^{a}21–^{b}4) The paragraph deals with an apparent subset of defenders, those who do not have the courage of their convictions. In spite of doggedly sticking to 'law is justice' (i.e. by legal agreement enslavement in war is just, cf. *Soph. Ref.* 173^{a}11–12), they import the criterion of desert (cf. **4** *fin.*), which is fatal to their position. Aristotle pounces, and claims that they are in effect seeking *natural* slaves. But that is true only on his own assumption, which he claims the defenders share, that virtue and vice are determined genetically (though for his vacillation on this point, see comment on 1271ᵃ18–26). Yet to speak of someone's 'deserving' to be a slave does not commit one to believing that he so deserves on grounds on nature; for he may deserve it as a punishment, for *acquired* depravity. Aristotle's final remark is a careful *caveat*; cf. 1286ᵇ22 ff. Theodectes: 4th-cent. tragedian, fr. 3 Snell (1971).

4 (1255ᵇ4–15) Largely a *résumé* of the chief conclusions of chs. iii–vi, until the casual and startling announcement at the end, that friendship, *philia*, is possible between such masters and slaves as are 'deemed to deserve' their condition by nature, but not in cases of enforced 'legal' slavery, when the (non-natural) slaves' resentments at the injustice would prevent it (but could not a 'natural' slave, once free but now enslaved, also be resentful?). I postpone consideration of friendship between master and slave until I xiii, which deals *inter alia* with the slave's moral character.

I vii

THE SKILL NEEDED TO RULE SLAVES

Introduction This chapter raises, in miniature, the question of the scope and nature of the knowledge to be possessed by the various rulers. On the principle of 1254ᵃ24–7, the better the ruled the better the work produced; and that makes the works of slaves, though good, the least good in terms of the contribution they make to the life of their master and his household; for their role is only menial. Now if the master's knowledge of how to rule a slave is knowledge of how to specify the ends of the slave's work, how far need he himself be knowledgeable about the detailed technical processes? Not at all, Aristotle hopes; apparently his role is to give orders, stating policies and goals (cf. I xiii). The slave's role is actually to do the job; this is apparently in virtue of *his own* knowledge; and presumably he follows his master's reasoning, since he has none of his own to exercise independently (1254ᵇ20–3). But how is the master, especially if he has no (slave or free) overseer, to give reliable orders if he is insouciant or ignorant of the correct procedures and methods? There is a tension in Aristotle's thought: the slave is to be virtually an extension of his master's body (I iv), and is to be taught a degree of virtue by him (1260ᵇ3–4); yet the master is to distance himself from his activities (cf. 1277ᵃ33 ff.).

A similar tension is manifest throughout. The same man is to be master, household-manager, husband, father, and statesman. If he is to deliberate and prescribe ends in all these areas of conduct, how wide and deep will his technical knowledge of means in each of them have to be? Aristotle is anxious to insist that political knowledge, i.e. the knowledge possessed by a statesman, should be all-embracing (see I i introd.); yet its practitioners are to seek leisure and philosophy.

1 (1255ᵇ16–20)   Rule over slaves is distinguished from other forms of rule, in familiar fashion (see 1252ᵃ7–16: 'some' = Plato again), especially from rule (normally alternating) over fellow-citizens. The thought that each rule, including that of the master, demands a body of *knowledge*, prompts the worries of 2.

2 (1255ᵇ20–30)   Aristotle nevertheless seems reluctant to recognize a master's knowledge; certainly he will have no truck with the Platonic notion that it is the same as the knowledge the master will exercise when acting as other 'rulers' in the same household (cf. 1253ᵇ8–14, 18–20). But even if we admit that master, freeman, and slaves are so styled in virtue of the kind of persons they are (i.e. by the degree of virtue they possess), the implications are unclear. Does the statement apply only to them, and not to household-manager, statesman, etc.? Character is hardly an *alternative* to knowledge appropriate to the rule one exercises in one's station, as Aristotle grudgingly admits ('there *could* be').

3 (1255ᵇ30–40)   There may be mild humour in the description of the overseer's job (who himself might be a slave: Xen. *Oec.* XII 3) as an 'office' (*timē*, honour, status). Capture of *natural* slaves is just: 1256ᵇ20–6. 'Both these' are not statesmanship and philosophy, but the master's knowledge and the slave's knowledge. The discussion now passes from the use of slaves to their acquisition, and thence to all other property and acquisition in general, a topic already broached at 1253ᵇ11–14 but held back in favour of the discussion of slavery in iv–vii.

I viii

HOUSEHOLD-MANAGEMENT AND NATURAL ACQUISITION

Introduction   The subject of this and the following three chapters is the art of acquiring goods or wealth, *chrēmatistikē (technē)* in a wide sense (sometimes *ktētikē (technē)*, 'art of acquiring property'). Aristotle distinguishes 10 sources, and an early conspectus may be useful:

Food
  1. Milk etc., for newly-born animals, including human.
  2. Plants, animals, for later stages of life.
  3. Human beings (1324ᵇ36–41).
Property
  4. Plants and animals, other than for eating; mining.
  5. Plunder.
  6. Slaves, servants.
  7. Exchange: goods for goods.
  8. Exchange: goods for money.
  9. Trade: maximization of profit from 8.
  10. Usury.

From some to others of these, when arguing for naturalness, Aristotle argues by induction; in other cases, when arguing against naturalness, he halts induction. How good is his reasoning?

1 (1256ᵃ1–10) 'Guiding method': analysis into parts; see 1252ᵃ17–23 (parts of state) and 1253ᵇ1–8 (parts of household). In those cases the parts went to form a structured whole; but it is a little hard to see how that could be true of the parts (i.e. methods) of acquisition, because they vary sharply from community to community (**3–6**). Perhaps Aristotle thinks there is some ideal combination of some of them (cf. 1318ᵇ9 ff. for a hint of this).

'Part or subsidiary?' is not a merely academic question: as in vii, Aristotle is concerned about the life-style of household-managers, who need time to be statesmen. Contrary to popular belief (see e.g. 1257ᵇ24–31, Xen. *Oec.* III 15), he thinks they should not have to bother with acquiring goods, but only with directing their use (see **2** and, on specialization of function, 1252ᵃ35–ᵇ5, 1273ᵇ8–17). 'Part' would imply that acquisition was part of his duty, 'subsidiary' would allow him to delegate it. If acquisition is subsidiary, then it is not clear whether it is so as providing tools, or materials; but what would hinge on the difference? However, the essential point is that skill in acquisition supplies resources to the household-manager, who is conceived on the analogy of a craftsman with tools and a product, i.e. happiness (1253ᵇ23 ff., 1256ᵇ36–7); and it is characteristic of craftsmen not to need *unlimited* resources: 1257ᵇ24–31.

2 (1256ᵃ10–19) The paragraph is awkward. (i) 'The skill of acquisition' is not in the Greek; but nothing else seems to make sense. (ii) The alternative to 'part', i.e. 'subsidiary', is replaced by 'different kind of thing', probably implying only 'different (from household-management), *but subsidiary to it*'. (iii) But a similar question is then, according to the Oxford text, asked of farming: is it a part of the skill of *acquisition* or a different type of thing? The answer 'part' is so obviously correct that any alternative seems merely mysterious. Sense can be neatly restored by the conjecture 'skill of household-management', *oikonomikēs*, for 'skill of acquisition', *chrēmatistikēs* (in ᵃ17–18; cf. **8** *init.*). That is, Aristotle asks (ii) if the skill of acquisition in general is part of household-management, (iii) whether a particular form (farming) of the skill of acquisition is part of household-management, perhaps thinking that the answer to (iii) might point to an answer to (ii). In **8**, (iii) is indeed answered affirmatively: see comment there.

Aristotle is not asking *whether* household-managers engage in farming or any other form of acquisition (clearly they do), but whether they ought to, rather than delegate it, because of their higher commitments (1255ᵇ30–40); the answer is, at least ideally, 'delegate it' (VII ix in general, but cf. **8** *fin.*). But as viii–xi progress, another preoccupation emerges: farming is one of those forms of acquisition that ought to be engaged in, because it is eminently natural; and unnatural forms ought not to be engaged in by anyone. So he turns to farming 'first'; he will then move on to forms of acquisition whose naturalness has to be argued for. *Mutatis mutandis*, he used the same technique in arguing for the naturalness of the state: he tackled the *obviously* natural forms of organization first.

3 (1256ª19–29), 4 (1256ª29–40), 5 (1256ª40–ᵇ7) Accordingly, Aristotle embarks on a long review of the very many varieties of what looks to be the most *natural* mode of acquisition, that of taking food directly from the *natural* environment. His argument is however more elaborate than that jingle would suggest. It is fundamental to his biology that animal bodies are in structure and formation such as to be viable, given their special environment; nature has so contrived them that they can take food and other resources from it (e.g. *PA* 658ᵇ33–659ª9). Necessarily, therefore, their ways of life will differ widely, in accordance with (*inter alia*) the type and availability of various kinds of food (*HA* 588ª17–19, cf. 487ª14 ff.). Moreover, each species of animal has a physical affinity with its environment, having been formed from it; the food on offer there is 'sweet' to it; and thus it thrives, having food cognate to it (*HA* 589ª6–10, 590ª8–12, 595ᵇ23–7; see 'convenience' (ª26) and 'tasty' (ª27) in **3**, and cf. 'agreeably' (ᵇ3) in **5**). However, we should beware of concluding that Aristotle believed animals evolved historically into their present forms, under *pressure* of the environment: species are eternal and were ever thus; for nature has made them so. Nor does the quasi-personification of nature necessarily imply some cosmic intellect that designed the whole world as we know it, in all its detail (see on **6**). Aristotle means only that animals are (somehow) fitted *for* living in their respective environments. It is in this sense that certain foods, the modes of acquiring them, and the consequential life-styles, are 'natural' to certain animals—including, he claims in **4**, human beings.

4 (1256ª29–40) 'Raiding' (cf. **5**) appears unexpectedly, palliate it as one may (discussions in Newman and Schütrumpf); for it involves robbery of some kind, and one wonders how an immoral action can be natural. However, Aristotle may intend only to list facts; if challenged, he would perhaps say that while hunting itself is natural and virtuous, it needs to be brought under rational control (cf. the 'natural' as opposed to the rationally directed virtues at *EN* VI xiii *init.*, also 1338ᵇ23–4)—and that would entail the elimination of that 'kind' of it which is raiding.

The fullness of Aristotle's enumeration tempts us to forget that the food-supply is not the only determinant of life-style: he omits e.g. climate, terrain, and the need for housing and defence. But perhaps food, being essential and urgent, is the *primary* determinant: it dictates where one lives, and therefore the climate one experiences, the building materials available, etc.

5 (1256ª40–ᵇ7) 'Self-engendered', *autophuton*, 'by natural growth' (*phuton*) 'from within/among themselves' (*auto(i)*). The absence even of exchange betokens a primitive economy (cf. 1257ª19–21). 'Need joins in compelling . . .': joins *nature*, presumably, because some life-styles, though natural, are inadequate singly. Nature 'compels' in the sense that if a creature fails to adopt the life-style marked out for it by nature, it dies. But that is truer of animals than of men. A man does not *have* to live as a nomad rather than as a raider. His capacity of deliberating and choosing equips him to respond to need, in particular by the use of tools.

6 (1256ᵇ7–20) contains a significant shift in the argument. In **3–5**, (*a*) food-supply determined the various life-styles of the animals; but now we learn (*b*) that the various animals determine what food nature supplies *for* them. The accommodating of the one to the other has been inverted. No doubt (*b*) enables Aristotle to garner some support from the kind of popular teleology found in e.g. Xen. *Mem.* I iv 5 ff., IV iii, esp. 10 (divine care for mankind). But the real reason is that in arguing for the legitimacy of certain kinds of acquisition on grounds of naturalness, it is not enough to show the naturalness of the *methods* of acquisition answering to the available supplies; for some sources of supply are not natural. Aristotle has to show also the naturalness of (some) *sources*, as being 'there' by nature, for the animals. The full picture is of a reciprocal determining of the methods *of acquisition* by available sources, and of sources by the methods available to, i.e. within the natural capacities of, the various animals. And that some but not other sources are *natural* might be important in arguing against those who deprecate the killing of animals (see e.g. *Laws* 782b–d); it certainly is in the argument (in **7**) against opponents of slavery. On 'material causes' as essential to the 'final cause' or 'end', see *Phys.* 200ᵃ34–ᵇ8.

It is important that the argument is not from what animal behaviour is to what human behaviour ought to be or may legitimately be. Aristotle is not claiming that men should adopt the same sources and methods as animals. Natural animal behaviour and natural human behaviour are arrived at by reasoning that since nature 'gives' food in some form at birth to all animals, men included, she must do so later in their lives too. In spite of the confident 'so similarly', the inference from childhood to adulthood is weak, because sweeping. It would be perverse to deny that a mother's milk is by nature 'for' her child; but it is not evident that sheep or poison mushrooms are 'for' anything at all, or at any rate in the same way as the milk; for effort, skill, and choices are involved (as he admits: 'most but not all wild animals').

In fact, there are all sorts of restrictions Aristotle himself wishes to impose. He confines animals to the use of plants, but knows perfectly well that some animals eat each other (*HA* 592ᵃ24–5); even some men do so (1338ᵇ19–21), but ought not (1324ᵇ39–41). And are we 'given' by nature for animals to eat? The principles controlling the restrictions are not made clear.

One way of tackling the problem may be to pray in aid the 'ladder of nature' found in Aristotle's biological works (e.g. *HA* 588ᵇ4 ff.); then lower forms of life might be supposed to exist, by natural teleology, 'for' the higher, i.e. the more rational. Then the eating of men by animals could be deemed *un*natural (cf. F. D. Miller (1991) 235, on the implications of 1333ᵃ21–4).

But how far such a natural ecology is indicative of, and part of, a grand universal anthropocentric teleology is unclear. A good case can be made for such a world-vision in Aristotle (e.g. Sedley (1991), with Wardy's reply (1993)); but some deny it, and find in **6** and **7** a merely factual or reportative sense of 'for the sake of': animals do subserve men's interests, and are indeed essential to them; but only thus are they 'for' them (cf. Wieland (1975) 158 ff., Balme (1987) 278–9).

'Such acquisition', *ktēsis*, ᵇ7–8, i.e. the sort that consists in taking food from the environment, the mode Aristotle regards as natural; or possibly in a concrete sense, 'such property, goods'. 'At the start' (birth): cf. 1254ᵃ23 and comment, on the significance of earliness. On the biology, cf. *GA* 732ᵃ29–32, 752ᵇ15–28.

7 (1256ᵇ20–6) The restriction of warfare (fighting in defence apart, presumably) to forcible enslavement of 'natural' slaves is partly explicable on the principles of I iii–vii; yet Aristotle does not say why one set of men should not regard another as instrumentally 'for' themselves, and so attack and kill and even eat them. No doubt it would not be just: the victims would morally deserve to live. (But since animals are not moral agents, they cannot claim that defence: they cannot be *owed* anything.) But the matter is obscure: Aristotle excludes everything that does not serve his immediate purpose. Certainly he has not the faintest conception of animal 'rights'.

8 (1256ᵇ26–39) In spite of Aristotle's wish that the household-manager should confine himself to the *use* of property (**2**, 1255ᵇ30–40, 1277ᵃ33 ff.), here at any rate is a plain statement that one part of the art of acquisition (*ktētikē*), i.e. farming and fishing etc., is part of the skill of household-management (cf. 1253ᵇ23–5, 1257ᵇ19–20). In 1258ᵃ34, however, he backtracks somewhat, and talks again of the 'subsidiary' skill. The tension in his thought is obvious once again: he regards each skill as having a separate and distinct function and goal (cf. Plato *Rep.* 345e–347a), and wishes them therefore to be practised by different people—which is too neat and tidy for the facts of life.

In **6–8** the discussion is broadened, in three ways: (i) From food to objects and tools, but apparently only those derived from organic sources (**6** *fin.*): there is a silent contrast with mining (and, oddly, lumbering): see 1258ᵇ31. (ii) From household to state: some economic role is recognized for the authorities of the state—but precisely what, is unclear; cf. 1259ᵃ33–6, 1299ᵃ23, *EN* 1094ᵃ26–ᵇ7. (iii) From evaluation on the criterion of naturalness of source (cf. 1257ᵇ19–20) to evaluation on the criteria of sufficiency and excess in possession: cf. *EN* 1179ᵃ1–19. The polemic against unlimited accumulation of wealth is developed later, 1257ᵇ24–1258ᵃ14. The reference to Solon is to fr. 13.71.

By analogy and induction, we have moved far and fast from mother's milk. Compare I ii, which started with isolated individuals and ended with the state. Such ease of travel is characteristic of arguments based on considerations of what is natural.

I ix

ORIGIN, DEVELOPMENT, AND VARIETIES OF EXCHANGE

Introduction The clearest and most convincing work on Aristotle's economic theory, to which my own owes a good deal, is by Meikle (1991*a*,

1991*b*, 1994, 1995); but Soudek (1952), and Finley's challenging account (1970), are still well worth reading. See Meikle (1991*a*) 170 ff. for a review of modern, especially Marxist, interpretations, and R. W. Miller (1981) for a direct comparison of Marx and Aristotle in this and cognate matters.

In discussions of this chapter and the next it is vital to keep distinct four varieties of *chrēmatistikē*, 'skill of acquiring goods':

- (*a*) Direct from nature, i.e. plants, animals.
- (*b*) By direct exchange of goods between two parties, without money: barter.
- (*c*) As (*b*), but with money as a plain stand-in for goods.
- (*d*) Trade, with the aim of maximizing profit.

In *EN* V v Aristotle seeks to define justice in 'associations involving exchange', *koinōniais allaktikais* (on the characteristics of *koinōniai* in general, see comment on 1252^a1–7). The chapter presumably antedates I ix (see Introduction), and is notoriously difficult; nevertheless, it is essential to the full understanding of the remarkable economic doctrine that now confronts us.

Aristotle maintains in *EN* V v that (i) equality is essential to exchange, *allagē*, and (ii) commensurability is essential to equality. (i) By 'equality' he means 'proportional' equality (e.g. 100 shoes are equal to one house), not 'arithmetical' equality (e.g. one shoe = one house). That is, until the parties agree on the ratio of value between shoes and houses, no exchange is possible. (ii) How then are shoes and houses to be made commensurable? Money, though invented as a middle term, as a measure by which commensurability may conveniently be expressed (1133^a19 ff., $^b16$–17, cf. 1164^a1–2), is not the instrument of its achievement: for exchange on the basis of proportionate equality antedates money (1133^b26–8). What money does is to guarantee a *later* exchange: I take money for my goods, in the confidence that since its value remains roughly constant, I may present it later for goods of equivalent value from someone else; and that is why everything ought to have a monetary value put upon it, presumably once and for all (1133^b10–13; but on inflation cf. 1306^b9–16, 1308^a35–$^b10$). But, 'in reality, things so different cannot be commensurable, but they can be sufficiently so to answer need, *chreia*' (1133^b18–20, cf. $^b6$–10, $^a25$–8). In effect, Aristotle despairs of establishing general principles of commensurability, and settles for a proportionate equality of a pragmatic kind: the two parties to an exchange have different goods of their own, varying needs (cf. 1156^a21–2) for those of others, and no doubt different temperaments and bargaining skills; nevertheless what they *agree* to be equal *is* equal, for the purpose of the exchange they carry out (cf. 1164^b6–21).

'Need' then, is Aristotle's nearest approximation to a basis for commensurability. He presumably conceives it narrowly; for what I need (to live a 'happy' life) is different from, and commonly less than, what I misguidedly desire (cf. 1257^b40 ff., *EN* 1178^b33 ff.). It is not to be confused with the modern term 'demand'; for the individual consumer's 'demand' for a good is determined by the interaction of his tastes and preferences with prevailing prices and his level of income and wealth. That is a more complex notion, with a psychological but not a moral dimension.

In Aristotle's eyes, agreement about equality is central. For in other contexts of proportionate reciprocity, men resent coming off worse, i.e. unequal; for instance, they regard it as slavery if they cannot return ill for ill: 'by proportionate reciprocity the state endures' (1132^{b}33 ff., cf. 1126^{a}4–8). In 'associations for exchange', therefore, in the interests of civic harmony, the objects of the exchange must be (at least thought to be) equal. When they are not so, when e.g. strong demand leaves needs unsatisfied because of high prices, or a monopoly exists, there can be social strife (cf. 1259^{a}6–23). It is true that Aristotle ignores many factors which bear on prices, e.g. competition, and which to a modern economist are of crucial interest; nevertheless, he is writing economic theory of a kind: he is interested in how the market works, as a consequence of (what he alleges to be) men's moral perceptions; and in this he anticipates the view of many economists today, that the study of economics cannot properly be conducted without reference to the psychology of economic agents. The stress on reciprocal *equality* in *EN* V v is the conceptual basis of the vigorous prescriptive political and ethical thrust developed in I ix–xi.

EN V v says nothing about the naturalness of the various forms of exchange, nor anything about (*a*) and (*d*): it concentrates on the proportionate equality and justice of direct exchanges between the two parties in (*b*), and probably by implication in (*c*). Conversely, *Pol.* I ix says nothing of equality and justice: it is not in *this* connection that Aristotle here denounces (*d*). Further, I ix seems to assume that the desire to maximize gain is invariably absent from (*b*) and (*c*), and that it is invariably present in trade, (*d*). This is unconvincing. Moderate profit is possible in trade; conversely, in barter-with-money, (*c*), there is a standing temptation to maximize the financial exchange-value of a commodity, rather that its simple use-value; and in plain barter too, (*b*), the desire to 'win' the exchange is notorious. So (*b*), (*c*), and (*d*) tend to collapse into each other, and Aristotle's account of their historical development looks to that extent implausible (cf. Meikle (1994) 29 ff.). The question therefore becomes this: is there a principled distinction to be made between exchange and trade, even if they are blurred in practice? For if in exchange what the parties decide is (proportionately) equal and just, why should the decisions of the parties in trade not be also?

The only evidence seems to be a very brief remark at the end of the next chapter, I x, at 1258^{a}37–^{b}4 (cf. *Rhet.* 1381^{a}20–3). Aristotle censures that variety of the art of getting goods which is to do with trade and changing-round: it is 'not in accordance with nature, but is from each other'. The point seems to be that men naturally treat crops and animals as 'for' them (see I viii), as exploitable; we benefit from them, they lose from us. Trading, Aristotle seems to claim, requires men to regard each other in the same light, and to import non-equality, which he regards as exploitative and unjust (cf. *EN* 1132^{b}11–20, 1133^{a}31–^{b}6), into their exchange-relationships (cf. 'living "from" others/each other', in [*Oec.*] 1343^{a}26 ff., Xen. *Mem.* III v 16). Here then is the link we need with *EN* V v. We no longer

89

have plain exchange at agreed rate x, between A and B, because B, the eventual buyer from the trader, who had bought from A at x, has to pay price x plus profit—and the profit will typically be as large as the trader can make it. The proportionate equality between A and B has been unjustly distorted, at B's expense—albeit by agreement. Meanwhile the goods in question have not been improved; for apparently Aristotle has no conception of value added by distribution and availability. But he knows use-value and exchange-value, and *perhaps* even recognizes (*pace* Soudek (1952) 64 ff., Meikle (1991b) 193–4) that the value of a thing is affected by the time, labour, and costs that have gone into it. (On this point cf. *Rep.* 369^{e}4–5, 1258^{b}25–7, [*MM*] 1194^{a}2–6; it is probably implicit in *EN* V v, esp. 1133^{a}5–10, provided that there *ergon* means 'labour', not 'product'.) A further, or alternative, implication of 'not in accordance with nature' may be that resources are taken which, as F. D. Miller (1991) 237 puts it, 'others need in order to attain their natural ends'.

Plato admired trade within a state (not foreign trade) in principle, as ensuring the proper distribution of goods, but disliked the greed and tricksiness with which it was carried on (*Laws* 918a ff.). He proposed in the *Laws* to permit it only to non-citizens (919c ff.), and to allow them their profit, but to restrict their margins to specified levels (920c, cf. 918cd). Aristotle seems committed to eliminating trade altogether; yet in all realism he knows his ideal state (in VII and VIII) cannot do without it: 1291^{a}4–6, VII vi; 1331^{b}1–4, 10–13. At 1321^{b}12 ff. he says that buying and selling 'for essential needs' is beneficial to a state's self-sufficiency and constitutional cohesion. So is the state, a natural thing, kept going by unnatural activities?

If in fact Aristotle too wished to confine trade to non-citizens, it is strange that he never said so outright (cf. 1278^{a}25–6, 1291^{a}25–6, 1319^{a}24 ff.). It would not have been a huge step, for a large proportion of Athens' trade was in the hands of non-citizens (Peǎrka (1967)), and he could have relied on a certain long-standing prejudice against the occupation (Humphreys (1978) 144; cf. 1258^{a}38–^{b}8). Perhaps one can insulate citizens as persons from the corrupting effects of actually engaging in trade; it is harder to see how their households could be cocooned against its purely economic effects; no doubt Plato's limiting of profits is intended to achieve that. At all events, in the matter of trade, Aristotle can do little to buttress himself by an appeal to common opinion: here, if anywhere, because of his fundamental postulate, equality, he is *contra mundum*. For it was traders' greed and tricksiness that attracted popular censure, not the bare principle of profit.

Aristotle knows nothing of the notion that property beyond the needs of modest consumption is a guarantee of a man's personal autonomy, particularly against encroachments by the state. Ideally at least, he would see no conflict (see comment on 1252^{a}1–7). Further, property is at best a secondary claim to political power (e.g. 1280^{a}21 ff., 1301^{a}25–^{b}6); nor is it to be used for conspicuous public display, to gain the favour of the people, with a view to personal advancement (1309^{a}17–20, 1321^{a}31–^{b}1). And he would be as scornful as Marx of 'commodity fetishism'; he would have called it by a simpler name: greed (cf. and *EN* 1122^{a}1–2).

1 (1256ᵇ40–1257ᵃ5) The 'closeness' of the two kinds of skill in acquiring goods, (1) those employed by household-managers, embracing farming etc. (see viii), and presumably the two kinds of exchange explained in this chapter, and (2) trade for profit, is explained in 7–11; so too 'limit'. On 'skill', cf. 5 *init.*, and comment on 1252ᵃ17–23. Presumably trade requires more experience and skill than (say) hunting, because animals are simply and naturally 'there', as it were ready-made, to be taken by us, who are by nature already at least partly equipped to take them (see on viii 3–6); but nature has not equipped us with the skills of trade, which had to be developed from scratch, either by individuals or by the race over a period of history (Aristotle does not make it clear which he means). Yet he can hardly be denying that mankind had to learn the skills of hunting too. So the difference between the two modes of acquisition, in so far as they both require *some* skill, will be one of degree rather than of kind, and could hardly be the ground for claiming the one is natural and the other not; rather, the inference runs the other way.

2 (1257ᵃ5–19) The second use of the shoe is proper to it because even after exchange the shoe is still meant to be used as a shoe. *EE* 1231ᵇ38–1232ᵃ4 more strictly calls its use in sale, for eventual use as a shoe, 'incidental' use. (Meikle (1991a) 165 n. 11 and (1994) 29 ff. refers to the Delphic knife of 1252ᵇ2; but the point there is merely that it has several proper uses, not that it has a proper use and an incidental use, cheap sale, which influenced the shoddy construction.) *EE* 1246ᵃ26–31 adds the possibility of *misuse* of something (of an eye *qua* eye); would a counterpart in the case of the shoe be its use in (*d*), *trade* (as distinct from (*b*) and (*c*), exchange), even if for eventual use as a shoe? Cf. comment on 1258ᵃ38–ᵇ8.

'Changing-round': Aristotle in this chapter seems to use *metablētikē* and its cognates as wider terms than *allagē*, to embrace trade for profit as well as direct exchange by barter or direct non-commercial exchange in the form of buying and selling as between two parties. But in 1258ᵇ1 the term seems restricted to trade for profit.

3 (1257ᵃ19–28) The paragraph interestingly supplements the meagre information about the village in 1252ᵇ15 ff. The original basis of sharing was a common pool of goods in each isolated household, drawn on by its own members exclusively. But the proximity of household to household in a village encouraged a development from *intra*-household sharing to *inter*-household sharing. Presumably exchange was 'forced' on the villagers because a common pool to meet the 'needs' of the village as a whole was ruled out, since they shill persisted in living in individual households. Yet the difference between sharing and exchanging is not great: if I have an exchange with you, we each in a sense share each other's property; and indeed 'make exchanges' renders *metadosis*, which is ambiguous as between sharing and exchanging. Here then is another example of core (sharing) and accretion (exchange) (see comment on I ii); and exchange obviously encourages specialization of production and so a more complex society (compare the specialization of the people who 'live apart' at 1280ᵇ12 ff., and Xen. *Cyr.* VIII ii 5).

4 (1257ᵃ28–41)   This clear and convincing paragraph has been extremely influential. ('It is the basis of the bulk of all analytic work in the field of money', Schumpeter (1954) 63.) Aristotle attempts to explain how money's three functions arose ('a medium of exchange, a unit of account and a store of value', Soudek (1952) 70). As in **3**, the necessity imposed by distance is crucial; cf. *EN* 1133ᵇ10–13, on money as a 'guarantee of exchange in the future'—presumably within states too, not just in foreign transactions. 'In its own right': slightly louder than the Greek (merely 'itself'), but conveying the point that, being valuable themselves (as material for tools, ornaments, etc.), iron and silver inspired confidence when used in exchange; for even before 'stamped' money, there must have been proportionate equality between other goods and the 'size and weight' of iron etc., and between goods and goods even earlier (cf. Homer, *Il.* VI 234–6). Aristotle does not say how the crucial step to a token amount (cf. Plato *Rep.* 371b) of silver etc., i.e. coinage, was taken. It is this step that can make money seem 'trumpery' (**6**).

5 (1257ᵃ41–ᵇ10)   In effect an attempt to elucidate a confusion of means and ends. In trade, profits are only a means to produce the real end, a supply of goods. People mistake the means, a subsidiary end, for the real end; confusion is easy, since trade is 'productive of' money, i.e. profit (cf. **7**); naturally, therefore, money is thought of as a form of 'produced' wealth as real as the supply of goods which trade aims to produce, and as an end as real as the real end.

6 (1257ᵇ10–17)   Coinage: nom*isma*; convention: nom*os*; cf. *EN* 1133ᵃ30–1. The identity of the sceptics is not known; on the controversy about the 'real' and 'sham' value of money, see Soudek (1952) 70. Nor it is clear what is meant by the 'alteration' of money (cf. *EN* 1133ᵇ13–15): replacement of one currency by another? Inflation? Manipulation of demand for goods? By creating monopoly (see I xi)? The argument seems to be: if natural, then *un*changeable in value or validity (just as the non-naturalness of laws is inferred from their changeability: Plato *Laws* 889a–890a). At *EN* 1133ᵃ30 Aristotle himself says coinage is not 'by nature', presumably in the primary sense discussed in the introduction to I ii; yet he sanctions its use in non-commercial exchange (type (*c*)), presumably because it is natural in the extended sense. So he would probably say that the sceptics go too far in claiming it is not natural 'at all', while conceding ('Yet . . .') their point about the rich but starving.

7 (1257ᵇ17–24)   In **5, 6**, and **7** Aristotle follows essentially the same procedure as in I vi: he describes two extreme positions, tries to isolate the reasoning on which they are based, and then establishes his own position—here evidently by sharply distinguishing trade, type (*d*), from types (*a*)–(*c*). His point seems to be that although trade 'produces' goods in the sense of providing them for the trader in the form of profit, the appearance that profit gives of being *new* wealth, generated over and above what is already in circulation, is an illusion. Trade is a zero-sum game of exchanges, in which the trader is parasitic: he does not produce goods 'in the full sense'; only (*a*) can do that.

It is not clear in what sense coinage is the 'limit' of exchange. Is the point merely that exchange which is not barter is limited by the amount *in coin* the buyer is prepared to pay and the seller to accept? That would give the impression that trade is 'concerned with' coinage.

8 (1257^{b}24–31)   The theme of 'limit' is from **7** and 1256^{b}30–7 (cf. 'enough' in 1257^{a}18); but it is deployed confusingly. A thing may (i) have a limit in the sense of being finite, or (ii) impose a limit on something else. The end of a doctor is (i) unlimited health; but that end (ii) imposes a limit on his means: he needs a scalpel, not a spade, and only one at that. The trader's end is similarly unlimited (i): wealth; but in this case sense (ii) does not apply; on the contrary, the greater the means, the greater his ability to gain unlimited wealth. (If that is right, there is here the germ of the notions of capital and investment; but it is not developed.) The household-manager, by contrast, does not have 'this' (i.e. acquisition of unlimited wealth) as his end: he aims to acquire *limited* wealth, enough to serve as a means for living; so in his case (ii) does apply. Compare 1256^{b}26–39, where this wealth is called 'true' wealth (^{b}30–1), because it is limited, and (by implication) money is 'false' wealth, because it is unlimited. But, (*a*) why is the money with which I shall buy tomorrow's loaf not equally 'true' wealth? (*b*) what of the trader who is content with limited money, enough to live on but no more?

This analysis may seem inconsequential. But Aristotle does not believe, with Dr Johnson, that 'there are few ways in which a man can be more innocently employed than in getting money'. By its pursuit of unlimited gain, trade breaks free of the controlling and limiting functions of political knowledge (see on 1252^{a}1–7); not only does it become an independent sphere of activity 'disembedded' from the social and political structure, to use Polanyi's term ((1957) 68), but it infects the attitudes of household-managers with commercial assumptions, as Aristotle now explains in **9** and **10**.

9 (1257^{b}32–40)   'Overlap': Aristotle employs the same means of unravelling a confusion as in I vi, though in a much simpler matter. There, the overlap was of arguments, in illegitimate generalizations from a narrow range of cases to a wider; here, it lies in the double use of a single thing, money, which generates the illegitimate generalization that the essential characteristic (unlimited gain) of the one use (in trade) ought to apply to the other use (in exchange) also. 'Something different' means presumably 'having enough'. It is a little odd that he deprecates the mere maintaining of one's wealth, which seems only prudent; perhaps he has in mind stinginess in its use, or unnecessarily *great* wealth (cf. 1326^{b}36–9); or perhaps even an obsession with coin, as distinct from goods.

10 (1257^{b}40–1258^{a}14)   The attempt to reconstruct the psychology of the misguided continues. The first group have 'an infinite desire for (mere) life', i.e. either to busy themselves with the ordinary business of living, or to live as long as possible (it is hard to tell which, cf. 1278^{b}24–30). In either case, they have an infinite desire for the means of life: property; we might say their basic motive is anxiety (cf. *EN* 1096^{a}5–6, and Lewis (1978)). The second group are more ambitious. They do set their sights on the good life, but suffer from two misapprehensions: (i) that since bodily pleasure is a legitimate part of it, or contribution to it (but a lowly one: *EE* 1215ᵇ30–6; cf. Woods (1982, 1992) on *EE* 1216ᵃ28–37), they may pursue that pleasure without limit—which demands property in excess of need, and therefore the use of the skill of goods-getting for excess gain; they fail to strike the mean (*EN* II vi). (ii) If their employment of that skill is not successful, they fall into the error of thinking that *all* their faculties and skills must or may have the same aim as the skill of goods-getting (e.g. one might misuse one's courage, which is intended to lead to bold conduct in war, to pursue and acquire goods by aggression; cf. *EE* 1249ᵃ14–16). But this is not to deny that private property can have a good effect on the exercise of our virtues, which are legitimately employed in obtaining it: see II v, and esp. comment on 1263ᵃ40–ᵇ14.

11 (1258ᵃ14–18) 'Food'; we are tugged back to I viii; add 'and other supplies taken direct from nature'. 'This one', i.e. the non-necessary kind.

I x

HOUSEHOLD-MANAGEMENT IN RELATION TO ACQUISITION, TRADE, AND MONEY-LENDING

Introduction   Chiefly *résumé* of viii and ix: Aristotle takes a leisurely canter up to the climax of the chapter, his condemnation of usury. On the central dilemma of **1** and **2**, see comment on 1256ᵃ1–19, ᵇ26–39.

1 (1258ᵃ19–27) 'At the start': 1256ᵃ3, cf. 1253ᵇ11–14. 'This' in the first sentence is presumably 'goods'. On the relationship between animals and their food-supply, see comment on 1256ᵃ19–ᵇ20.

2 (1258ᵃ27–38) 'Earlier, this' (ᵇ34): goods again, as in **1**.

3 (1258ᵃ38–ᵇ8) 'As we have said': 1256ᵇ26–39, 1257ᵇ17–23. On the importance of 'from each other', see introduction to I ix. On changing-round, see on 1257ᵃ5–19. The point of the 'name' is that interest is *tokos*, 'offspring', from *tiktein*, to give birth, cf. Plato *Rep.* 507a. On usury in the *Laws*, see 742c, 842d.

Aristotle's thesis that money ought not to be used for purposes other than its original function, for which it was invented, i.e. for natural exchange, does not rest on a claim that a thing ought not to be used for purposes other than those for which it was invented. The decisive point is the quality, i.e. naturalness or unnaturalness, of the aim: cf. the shoes at 1257ᵃ5–13, and the state at 1252ᵇ27–1253ᵃ1. Money has been perverted to serve an unnatural end (cf. 1257ᵇ35–40, where wealth is said to be treated as an end in itself); the state, by contrast, founded for one natural purpose, now serves another and better end.

How shall we assess Aristotle's economics? He believes that natural teleology is supported by empirical observation, in that the further one moves from natural sources of supply of goods the less satisfactory the outcome. He attempts, like any modern economist or indeed practitioner of any other science, to match theory and facts (or facts as he sees them; he may well be exaggerating e.g. the ill-repute of usury: Natali (1990) 318 n. 47). His theory is perhaps less economic than ideological, i.e. inspired by natural teleology; but a theory does not have to be strictly economic to have economic explanatory power; indeed, an evaluative theory can be more valuable than a merely descriptive one. In spite of his lack of systematic data, his indifference to cost and labour value, and to the operation of the market as a whole (so far as one had developed in his day: Meikle (1979) 66 ff., (1991a) 170 ff.), his over-confident 'economic psychology', and perhaps some *parti pris* against trade (1258ᵇ1), his purpose is nevertheless 'to *understand* economic phenomena' (Schumpeter (1954) 1, his italics). It is both inaccurate and harsh to say 'of economic analysis there is not a trace' (Finley (1970 (1977 repr.)) 152, controverted by Meikle (1979), esp. 68–9). If economics is now the 'dismal science', it had a stimulating start.

I xi

MODES OF AQUISITION, INCLUDING MONOPOLY: ANALYSIS AND ASSESSMENT

Introduction Aristotle now turns from the economic theory of viii–x, and distinguishes two levels of practical study: (*a*) more fully analytical lists of wealth-winning occupations (**1** and **2**), (*b*) the detail of their technical procedures (**3**). He declines to spend much time on (*b*), however useful it is in practice, since it is 'a low thing'; so it is a paradox that he devotes nearly half the chapter (**4** and **5**) to relating two examples of it. On the other hand, he lavishes some attention on the lists and comments of (*a*); but to whom is this sort of material useful?

1 (1258ᵇ9–21) On *natural* acquisition. 'Speculation . . . needs', or possibly, 'there is free scope for speculation, but we cannot avoid (practical) experience' (though of course the household-manager does his best to). 'Most authentic', literally 'most proper' (to men), the same word, *oikeios*, being applied to the use of a shoe as a shoe in 1257ᵃ12.

2 (1258ᵇ21–33) On *unnatural* acquisition, exchange for profit and cognate activities. The major addition is working for pay; no doubt in viii–x it would have been a complication, as labour is not a good that can be handed over directly like other goods; but on the implicit recognition of labour as a commodity see introduction to I ix (p. 90). Usury, not just petty usury as at 1258ᵇ2–8, is mentioned without censure. 'Things from the earth': e.g. trees for timber; 'barren but useful', e.g. stone.

3 (1258ᵇ33–1259ᵃ6)   Aristotle is extremely selective about what to study in detail. Here he dismisses the detail of wealth-getting, an essentially ancillary activity carried on by men who are only necessary to, rather than part of, the state (1328ᵇ33–1329ᵃ2, 17–26). But he was soaked in biological detail, in the interests of theoretical knowledge (see *PA* I v); and he took very seriously the pixilating complexities of the voting-systems employed by statesmen (1300ᵃ8 ff.), obviously because they had political and consti-tutional implications. Cf. 1260ᵃ24–31, 1269ᵃ9–12, and especially 1337ᵇ4–23.

The remark about skill and chance may mean merely (*a*) that occupa-tions not subject to much hazard allow skill its widest play (cf. *EE* 1247ᵃ3–7), or, possibly and more pointedly, (*b*) that the greater the skill, the less the scope for hazard; for skill guards against it, in a way in which simple experience could not. On the body, cf. 1337ᵇ11–14. 'Virtue too': in the form of practical wisdom.

4 (1259ᵃ6–23) and **5 (1259ᵃ23–36)**   The stories are told at length, possibly by way of relief after the hard work of viii–x. They are intended to be useful, but the principle they embody can hardly have been news to Aris-totle's readers, for he twice implies that it is in common use. No doubt he took particular pleasure in the exploit of a fellow-philosopher.

I xii

RULE IN THE HOUSEHOLD: HUSBANDS AND FATHERS

Introduction   A brief and in many ways incomplete chapter, best studied in close conjunction with xiii. The reference at the start is to 1253ᵇ1–14, where Aristotle distinguished as 'parts' of household-management: (*a*) master/slave, (*b*) husband/wife, (*c*) father/children, (*d*) the acquiring of goods. I iv–vii dealt with (*a*), viii–xi with (*d*): (*b*) and (*c*) now remain.

1 (1259ᵃ37–ᵇ10)   The treatment of women is original and important. Else-where Aristotle without hesitation labels a man's rule over his wife as either 'kingly' or 'aristocratic', broadly on grounds of substantially super-ior virtue and therefore of fitness to rule (1252ᵇ20–1, 1254ᵇ13–14, 1255ᵇ19, cf. *EN* 1158ᵇ11 ff., 1160ᵇ32–5, 1161ᵃ22–5). Here, however, he says that a man rules his wife 'in a statesmanlike manner', elsewhere defined as rule by and over free and equal persons, by turns (1252ᵃ13–16, 1255ᵇ20, 1261ᵃ32 ff., 1279ᵃ8 ff., 1332ᵇ12 ff.). The reason for this change of emphasis seems to lie in 1260ᵃ12–14: the woman has the deliberative element, though it 'has no authority' (see comment there); nevertheless, Aristotle sees sufficient similarity to a statesman's rule over his fellow-statesmen to jus-tify calling marital rule 'statesmanlike'. By this he does not mean that a woman deserves political rights in the public arena, nor that there are periods when she will in turn rule her husband (Aristotle is careful to rule that out). But she is nearer to being the natural equal of her husband in rationality and deliberative power than she is to being as sharply different from him as would be implied by the kingly and aristocratic models (cf. 1288ᵃ15 ff.). Her deliberative faculty requires consultation, argument, and persuasion (cf. mind's 'statesmanlike' rule over appetition, 1254ᵇ5–6); to that extent, she has to be treated as one statesman treats another. Aristotle saw advantage in this continuity between domestic and political practice; for he regarded the virtues practised in the home as the 'origins and founts' of those practised in the state itself (*EE* 1242ᵃ40–ᵇ1, cf. 1260ᵇ13–18, *EN* 1160ᵇ22 ff.; on this topic in general see Swanson (1992)). There is no violation of his position that all forms of rule are different (I i); for a statesman's rule in the home can only be a 'likeness' of a statesman's rule in a state: see the terminology at *EN* 1160ᵇ22 and comment on 1252ᵇ15–27, 1254ᵇ2–16. Nevertheless, this paragraph is the nearest he gets to treating women on an equality with men. At least some Greek men would have been surprised or even outraged by the description of their authority over their wives as '(like) a *states*man's'; for women were not thought to be concerned with the state. Aristotle marries to a deep conservatism a strongly independent initiative; but he still does not go as far as Plato (see on 1252ᵃ34–ᵇ9 and 1269ᵇ12–23). Nor is he a crypto-feminist: for a rebuttal of such revisionist views, see Mulgan (1994). On the physiological and other reasons Aristotle supposes himself to have for insisting on some inferiority, see Horowitz (1976), Fortenbaugh (1977), Morsink (1979), Clark (1982), and comment on 1260ᵃ2–14.

On the vocabulary of the first sentence, see on 1253ᵇ1–11. Aristotle now substitutes 'paternal' for 'procreative'. 'Most' cases of rule by statesmen implies there are some exceptions: see 1261ᵃ37 ff., 1318ᵇ27 ff., cf. 1281ᵇ21 ff. The parenthesis is donnish satire on the inequality between the ruler's normal condition and his airs and graces when ruling; cf. *EN* 1134ᵇ6–7. Amasis' humble foot-basin was refashioned into a statue of a god, and then worshipped (Her. II 172).

2 (1259ᵇ10–17) is very swift, and assumes ideal conditions; for the elder is not necessarily superior (1332ᵇ35–41 assumes superiority as a natural norm, but cf. 1272ᵇ40–1). The quotation is from Hom. *Il.* I 544.

I xiii

THE MORAL VIRTUES OF MEMBERS OF THE HOUSEHOLD

Introduction By a kind of 'ring-composition' the beginning and end of this important chapter, **1** *init.* and **7**, raise the question of the virtues of the 'parts' of the household: husband, wife, children, slaves; and **7** further links that topic to the constitution of the state in which they live. Four intervening sections, **2–5**, provide a map of their respective mental and moral conditions; **6** extends the discussion to artisans.

Apparently prompted by an assumption implicit in I xii, that in order to rule and be ruled in certain ways, the members of the household must have certain virtues, Aristotle talks mostly of virtues and rule; but in **3** he embraces also (i) the parts of the soul, (ii) the virtues attached to those parts, and (iii) the mental states of the various categories of persons. There is also (iv) a distinction between a general and a particular level of discussion (**2** and **5**). The chapter is therefore rather complex; and it is not always obvious what he wishes to argue. However, he himself claims no fewer than seven times that matters are 'clear'. What *is* clear is that the chapter is a systematic attempt to ground the structure of the household and the state in the psychology and moral condition of their categories of members.

1 (1259ᵇ18–32)   Wealth is the 'virtue' of acquisition in that it is the end-product of acquisition's function: cf. *Rhet.* 1362ᵇ18. The sudden reversion to the question of property is unexpected. Up to a point, Aristotle is simply clearing the ground; for although inanimate things can have virtue/excellence (*aretē*) in Greek (as indeed in English), it is not the virtues of these that concern household-management (they are merely facilitating conditions for the 'good life': see e.g. 1253ᵇ23–5, 1256ᵇ31–3). But his real purpose is to use the point to clarify a serious problem. If the slave is a 'living tool' (see I iv), is his virtue merely that of a tool, or of a something living, a man?

A man's virtue is 'a condition/disposition, *hexis*, to do with choice, *prohairesis*, lying in the mean relative to us, which is determined by reason, and as the man of practical wisdom would fix it' (*EN* 1106ᵇ36–1107ª2). Hence when Aristotle asks if a slave has virtue (note 'condition' *hexis*, in ᵇ25), he seems to be asking whether the slave can make a rational choice of action, i.e. goals; for after all, we are told, he is a human being and shares in reason. If not, he can offer only bodily services (cf. 1254ᵇ16–20), and is controlled totally at the discretion of another, as a tool. Aristotle then broadens the problem to include women and children, who, while obviously not tools, have rational faculties less than those of the free adult male.

2 (1259ᵇ32–1260ª2)   The dilemma now emerges starkly, with obvious relevance to I xii. The ruled need virtue to be ruled properly; but if they do have virtue, why should they be *ruled*? There may be slender humour in the prospect of slaves etc. attaining 'high moral character', *kalokagathia*, roughly, 'fine, complete moral goodness' (for detail, see *EE* 1248ᵇ8–1249ª17). But why does Aristotle scout the notion of a sliding scale of virtue ('more and less'), on which man, woman, child, and slave might appear in that order, a higher point indicating a greater claim to rule? Because such claims, except in the case of the free adult male, are precisely what he cannot tolerate: the male's rule must be 'unqualified'—that is, the virtues of the other three persons must not appear on a scale implying any entitlement to rule at all. (He ignores here the extent, if any, to which a woman rules in her home.) *Their* virtues have to be defined in terms not of fitness to *rule*, but of fitness to be *ruled*.

The polemic against the sliding scale is strange, since Aristotle himself seems to think in terms of more and less, e.g. 'as much as pertains' (1260ª19), 'little' (1260ª35); and *EN* 1173ª15–22 recognizes an opinion that one may be more or less virtuous than someone else (contrast *EN* 1107ª22–

7). But Aristotle's intention is not to contest that, but to argue that he who has (in whatever degree) the virtue of being ruled has a virtue *distinct* from that of ruling. Of the latter he has no share at all; for the two virtues are, it seems, incompatible in the same person (if they were not, other persons than the free adult male could sometimes claim to rule). It is not clear how this is reconcilable with the alternation of ruling and being ruled elsewhere required of citizens: do they switch on and switch off the two virtues from time to time? Aristotle discusses this crucial problem at length in III iv, but concludes merely, and obscurely, that 'a good man's virtue . . . takes [different] forms, *eidē*, according to whether he is going to rule or be ruled, just as moderation and courage vary as between men and women' (1277ᵇ18–21). 'Just as' papers over the fact that the virtues of a man and a woman are in permanent play, whereas the virtues of ruling and being ruled are sometimes exercised and sometimes held in suspense. However, it is consistent with this passage that in **4** and **5** we are told that the individual virtues, e.g. courage, vary according to whether they exist in a man or a woman. Evidently what makes the difference is the ruling and being ruled (1260ᵃ23).

3 (1260ᵃ2–14) In the first sentence, 'just as' is a little obscure; but the point seems to be that not only do the virtue of the ruled and that of the ruler differ (as explained in **2**), but there are 'differences' also between the virtues of the various categories of the ruled—though this can hardly be said to be 'clear' (ᵃ2) from **2**. Likewise, what is 'clear' (ᵃ7) from the analogy (which is highly reminiscent of those in I v, cf. 1333ᵃ16–18) of the virtues of the two parts of the soul is—if anything—only that 'most' instances of ruling and being ruled are 'natural', being of the irrational by the rational. ('Most' is presumably intended to exclude *un*natural forms of rule, e.g. tyrannies.) The analogy cannot show that *each* relationship (master/slave, men/woman etc.) between ruler and ruled is different; to achieve that result, Aristotle has in effect to resort to a sliding scale of the type he has rejected in **2**: of the rational deliberative faculty the slave has more, the child has some but in an undeveloped form, a woman some (more than a child, surely), but in non-authoritative form, the adult male all of it (presumably). Aristotle generalizes by speaking of their having 'the parts of the soul present in them in different ways' (he presumably intends 'ways' here and 'fashion' in **4** to be pointedly different from 'extents').

A woman's deliberative capacity is perhaps 'without authority', *akuron*, in the sense that it is less than complete and therefore not *final*: its decisions can be overridden by her husband; see on *kurios*, 1252ᵃ5. But in what would the incompleteness consist? In (*a*) a weakness intrinsic to itself, leaving it capable of discerning means but not ends (see comment on **4**), or in (*b*) domination by the emotions arising in the irrational part of the soul? In that case it may be 'without authority' in not being able to override them (see Fortenbaugh (1977)). Are then the natural virtues (*EN* 1144ᵇ1–8) weaker in her from birth, so that the natural vices (*EN* 1150ᵇ12–16) are *relatively* stronger? Or is the irrational part of the soul in a woman simply stronger *than in a man*? If so, the incompleteness of her deliberative capacity might not be original or intrinsic to her but induced: (*b*) might *cause* incapacity during her lifetime. But why should such an induced weakness be peculiarly and invariably such as to undermine the ability to determine ends but not the ability to determine means? Cf. Mulgan (1994) 196 ff.

4 (1260ª14–24) What is the connection between 3 and 4? Are the varying intellectual states of 3, i.e. the varying ways the parts of the soul are present, merely a persuasive model for the varying virtues of 4? Or is there some tighter link between virtue and deliberative power? Aristotle presumably means, '*if* this person, say a child, who has a given level of capacity to deliberate, does have moral virtue, it *must* be a moral virtue different from the moral virtue of someone, say an adult, who has some other (a higher) capacity to deliberate'; for their *functions* are different. In that case, a person's virtue, apart from the adult male's, is now to be described or defined not in terms of the adoption of the right end, but in terms of the ability to excogitate the means of achieving it (on deliberation as the discovery and choice of means, see *EN* 1112ᵇ11 ff., 1113ª9 ff., 1141ᵇ9 ff.). If so, the implication seems to be that only adult males, not women, children, and slaves (the latter lack choice, 1280ª33–4), are expected to set the actual goals; and slaves, having *no* deliberative capacity, have no virtue either, not even a 'little' (1260ª35); cf. *EN* 1111ᵇ9. But that is *not* a palatable conclusion (**2** *fin.*).

It is not quite easy to see how the courage of a ruler and the courage of a servant would differ. There may be a clue in *EN* 1117ª4–9: the most natural courage is 'because of' spirit (*thumos*) and 'the fine' (*kalon*); it has choice and purpose. Another kind, close to it but apparently not identical, is 'because of' the emotions, *pathos*. Could one generalize, and say that the virtues will be 'different' from person to person in accordance with the *ratio* between intellect and emotion (cf. *EN* 1144ᵇ8 ff.)?

The reference to Socrates is almost certainly to Plato *Meno* 70a ff., where Meno enumerates the virtues, i.e. the virtue of a man, of a woman, of a slave, etc., and Socrates argues that in so far as they are all virtues they must in some sense—i.e. in so far as they are *virtue*—be the same. Aristotle, somewhat tendentiously, here omits to specify that sense; for his response to Plato's general line of argument, see comment on 1252ª7–16. Master-craftsman': cf. on 1252ª1–7.

5 (1260ª24–36) 'In detail', literally 'part by part', i.e. by individual virtues, parts of virtue in general. 'Gorgias': Meno's inspiration for his account of the virtues, *Meno* 71cd. Enumerations of the virtue of man, of women, etc. tend quickly to diminish in conceptual or psychological content: they become lists of prescribed functions, e.g. a woman's keeping silent (cf. *Meno* 71a). For persons other than the adult male, the prescribing arises not from an independent judgement of theirs, but from him, their superior in point of reason, who both chooses goals and guides their exercise of their deliberative capacity, if any, in the attaining of them (cf. *EE* 1249ᵇ6–9); and the disposition to habitual obedience constitutes virtue. The child's 'end' is the fully developed choice of moral goals, the choice exercised by the free adult male, towards which his father guides him; unlike his mother, he has that natural potentiality in full. (For a list of natural differences between male and female, see *HA* 608ª22 ff.) The natural slave needs only 'little' virtue, because not only his goals but his means of attaining them are prescribed totally—as they have to be, since he has *no* deliberative capacity.

6 (1260ª36–ᵇ7) contains an important problem with a radical solution. Craftsmen, presumably to the extent that they work for another, are in a state of limited slavery; yet this is not 'natural' slavery, as they are free men, and do not share like slaves in the life of a master. At first sight, '[moral] virtue pertains to them to the precise extent that slavery does' seems silly; for slaves have only 'little' virtue, and one might expect free persons to have much more, in all sorts of ways unconnected with their profession. For would not the power of deliberation they will undoubtedly need professionally (*EN* III iii, VI iv) generate a certain corresponding moral character also, by some kind of transference? After all, their work is not simply bodily but skilled (1258ᵇ25–7). So perhaps a 'not' has dropped out somewhere? 'They do not have virtue, in so far as they have slavery', or 'they have virtue, in so far as they do not have slavery'. But Aristotle probably does mean exactly what the text says; he sees a close connection between the professional and the moral virtue of a craftsman. The former determines the latter: by reason of his function in mere mechanical matters (cf. 1258ᵇ35–9) a craftsman just *is* a certain sort of person in point of moral virtue: such virtue as he has, has to be imparted to him precisely to the extent that he is controlled, like a slave, by his employer/master—a control which is exercised at some remove. Hence Aristotle's doubts about the wisdom of allowing craftsmen to be citizens (III v); for as far as moral virtue is concerned, they are in the same bag as slaves. This consideration may render more intelligible Aristotle's proposal (1330ª31–3) that all slaves should have the prospect of being freed 'as a reward'; for at first sight to deprive a (natural) slave of a natural master's rational moral guidance (cf. 1252ª32, 1255ᵇ4–14) would do him no service. But if he became a free craftsman, his position, though not fitting him to be a citizen, would be perfectly viable. Indeed, Smith (1991) 153–4 suggests that perhaps in Aristotle's eyes natural slavery helps the natural slave to realize his 'psychological potential', until the point where he may be freed.

Who is the instructor of slaves? The 'overseer' of 1255ᵇ35–7? If so, his duties are presumably limited to technical instruction of slaves, while the master imparts the moral admonition. But, (i) how can this be, if the overseer has, as craftsman, only the deliberative capacity of a slave, i.e. none? What if the overseer is himself a slave (Xen. *Oec.* XII iii)? (ii) What of when a craftsman is himself a master of slaves? What moral instruction can *he* impart?

Aristotle now ticks off 'those' (i.e. probably Plato, *Laws* 777e) who refuse to allow slaves any reason. But if they do have some, how is that to be squared with their lack of deliberative power? Presumably he is thinking of the slave's 'apprehension' of reason, as distinct from its possession

(1254ᵇ22–3 and comment there). But his advice is ambiguous. Admonishment implies, as orders do not, a degree of rational persuasion (cf. Fortenbaugh (1977) 137, citing *Rhet.* 1380ᵇ16–20, 1391ᵇ10–11). So are we to give admonishment to slaves more than to children, (i) because slaves are capable of rationally and usefully *receiving* more of it, or (ii) because they are nearly incapable of receiving any and therefore *need* more, i.e. emphatically and constantly? The positive tone of the insistence on reason suggests (i).

This paragraph, and *EN* 1161ᵃ31–ᵇ11, are what lies behind the remark 1255ᵇ12–14, 'there is actually a certain advantage for master and slave, and mutual friendship, for those of them deemed to deserve their condition by nature'. Our relationship with our inanimate tools raises no question of justice, for such a tool can have no 'claim' to any particular kind of treatment; it is simply not that sort of thing. But between master and animate tool there *is* some relationship of justice, for (presumably by virtue of his limited reason) a slave is capable of 'participating in law and contract' (*EN* 1161ᵇ7); he can keep, or fail to keep, to his natural role; and in the former case he deserves just treatment. The natural concomitant of a just association, *koinōnia*, is friendship (*EN* 1159ᵇ25 ff.); indeed justice and friendship are coextensive in range of situations and persons in which they subsist (1160ᵃ7–8). Hence the crucial distinction is this: with a slave *qua* slave (i.e. *qua* tool) there cannot be friendship, with a slave *qua* man there can be (1161ᵇ4–6). Of the three categories of friendship, (i) for mutual advantage, (ii) for mutual pleasure, (iii) 'because of virtue' (of the friend) (*EN* VIII iii), friendship with a slave is presumably an instance of (i) (see 1252ᵃ24–34, 1255ᵇ9).

This paragraph concludes Aristotle's discussion of slavery in book I. The scattered nature of my own discussion simply reflects that of his; and clarity of exposition is not helped by the bewildering variety of models he employs to pinpoint the natural slave's character, status, and function: owner/possession, tool-user/tool, man/beast, reason/emotion, soul/body, part/whole, animate/inanimate. Each captures part of his overall view, but in several respects they demand reconciliation. The internal consistency and moral acceptability of his shifting viewpoints are a complex and controversial field, and I cannot here attempt a systematic overview. The most thorough and challenging of the recent analyses I have read are Fortenbaugh (1977), Schofield (1990), Smith (1991), Brunt (1993) 343–88, and Williams (1993) 109–17; on slavery in general in the ancient world see Finley (1968, 1980, 1981).

7 (1260ᵇ8–20) rounds off book I, with some reference to the 'parts' of the household in I ii ff.; on the implications for personal freedom of education 'with an eye to the constitution', see on I ii 8, and cf. 1310ᵃ12 ff., VIII i. The reference of 'in connection with the constitutions' at the end of the first sentence is perplexing: there are many relevant remarks and passages (e.g. VII xvi), but no full-scale treatment along the lines indicated; and if Aristotle means those in bk. II, or VII–VIII, he ought to have said something like 'highly regarded constitutions and allegedly best constitutions', or 'best constitution', respectively. Vander Waerdt (1991) argues for a lost or intended but unwritten account of virtue, education, and household-management, in relation to the various constitutions and the ends they promote.

8 (1260ᵇ20–4)   The outline of what is now to follow in bk. II is so extremely compendious that these few lines have been thought by some to be the work of an editor. The matter is impenetrable; see Introduction, on the order of the two books.

PROGRAMME: 'IDEAL' STATES, REAL AND PROPOSED;
THE LIMITS OF SHARING

Introduction If it was indeed Aristotle who made the promise at the end of book I (see comment on 1260^b20–4) to examine the opinions of theoreticians on the best constitution, he now immediately enlarges his programme of inquiry to include actual states with a reputation for good government. This coupling makes sense; for all the constitutions Aristotle will consider have some claim to a principled superiority independent of the rival merits of the four traditional constitutions (kingship, aristocracy, oligarchy, and democracy), which were the staple of normal partisan political controversy, and indeed of Aristotle's own discussion in III–VI. 'Currently existing' (or 'available') (1260^b35) ought naturally to apply to both categories of constitution, but may refer to only the actual ones: cf. 1288^b41, 1289^a2, ^a6. 'Association that is the state': see on 1252^a1–7.

Of the theoreticians, Aristotle discusses Plato at great length (ii–vi), while Phaleas and Hippodamus receive only one chapter each (vii and viii). The pattern of discussion of actual states is similar: Sparta is analysed exhaustively (ix), Crete and Carthage more briefly (x and xi). Chapter xii is a pendant, on certain eminent lawgivers.

It is legitimate to say, loosely enough, that book II concerns 'utopias'; but the term calls for careful definition. In IV i (1288^b21 ff.) Aristotle distinguishes the following subject-matter of political knowledge:

1. '. . . the best constitution, what it is and what sort of thing it would be in absolutely ideal circumstances, with no external impediment';
2. 'the best constitution in given circumstances';
3. 'a "given" constitution, "on an assumption" ', *hupothesis*;
4. an omnipurpose constitution which will 'fit' practically all states; it is 'easier' and 'more common or accessible' (*koinotera*) 'for all of them'.

The purpose of the somewhat different list that appears in the next chapter, IV ii 1289^b11 ff., is to set out the agenda for IV–VI in particular. In that list (3) is hard to find except by implication; on the significance of this for those books and the methodology of the *Politics* as whole, see Rowe (1989).

There is thus, at least in (1)–(3), a series of graded approximations to the ideal. What then is the precise relationship between (1) and (2)? A long series of references, especially in VII and VIII, to 'ideal' conditions (*kat' euchēn*), literally 'according to prayer, wish, aspiration' (e.g. excellent geography and economic resources, 1326^b39–1327^a10, personnel with the right natural qualities, 1325^b35 ff.), implies that the best state is one in which *all* such conditions are present; and if they are, there will be no impediment to that state's 'gelling' (by natural teleology and 'political knowledge', see I i–ii) into a state than which no state could be better. It is therefore initially in terms of facilitating conditions that Aristotle conceives the best state: it needs 'a lot of resources', 1288^b39–40. What the facilitating conditions facilitate is not so clear. Perhaps Aristotle would point to his own 'best' state of VII and VIII, imagined under wholly ideal conditions. At any rate, if all requirements are satisfied, is there any reason why one 'best' state should differ substantially in structure and operation from another? The 'best' state looks like a single thing, a construction whose features are individually not impossible in practice, but only in the ensemble, in that it is wholly unlikely that they will all be present in one place simultaneously. But depending on the number and distribution of conditions satisfied, (2) may take more than one form, each 'fitting' (1288^{b}24) different kinds of person.

Presumably neither (1) nor (2) is a 'utopia' in the sense of a society of wonderful bliss without stress, toil, or strife: there would still be work to be done, interests to be reconciled, decisions to be made. If not, what would the constitution be for? Though Aristotle had no doubt heard of the Golden Age (e.g. Hesiod *WD* 109 ff.), he takes no interest in it as a model for the best state; nor has he any conception of a 'jellyfish', i.e. virtually structureless, run-on-goodwill society (such as in William Morris' *News from Nowhere*). Nor does he show any awareness, at least in the *Politics*, of the elements of fantasy, satire, and irony common in literary utopias, or of the long-term effect of such productions in the eroding of conventional social and political belief. Yet presumably he had read e.g. Aristophanes' *Women in the Assembly* (*Ecclēsiazousai*) 657 ff. He discusses only texts which have face-value as serious proposals for practical conduct (cf. 1265^{a}10 ff.). On ancient utopias in general, see Dawson (1992).

1 (1260^{b}27–36) On the face of it, the whole paragraph is devoted to states at level (2), since their common characteristic (as the first sentence implies) is that they may indeed approach, but do not attain, level (1). Hence the 'near-best' constitution of the first sentence would presumably be Aristotle's own, of VII and VIII (see 1323^{a}18), and the 'other' near-best ones would be all those examined in II. But the 'others', it will turn out (e.g. 1261^{a}16), are to be judged not only by the standard of the 'best', but in the light of the degree to which they attain an assumption (level (3); for the 'given circumstances' of level (2) can modify the achieving not only of 'the best' but also of assumptions). What then is an 'assumption'? According to *EN* 1151^{a}16–17 (cf. *EE* 1227^{b}28 ff.), 'in actions, the goal is the starting point, just as in mathematics the assumptions are'. In politics, the assumption that a constitution (e.g. oligarchy, 1289^{b}20–2) or an institution is best forms the starting-point for activity designed to achieve that best. The assumptions are *false*, since they do not embody the standards and goals of (1) and (2) (1293^{b}1–9, 1325^{b}33–8, 1332^{a}7 ff.), which Aristotle presumably believes are demonstrable from a consideration of human nature. Nevertheless, the assumptions in category (3) are not necessarily wholly wrong, either individually or in sum: they can lead to constitutions which, though inferior, are not without merit, and worth a legislator's attention, with a view to their preservation and improvement (1288^{b}28 ff.). In book II, Aristotle oscillates freely between 'best' and 'assumptions' as criteria of judgement, faulty though the latter often are; but they can sometimes coincide, the execution alone being defective (1269ᵃ34–ᵇ12). Neither when he attacks assumptions nor when he attacks the methods of achieving them does he lose the 'best' from view. See, however, on a wider canvas than book II, Rowe (1989) on Irwin (1985). On assumptions, cf. also 1261ᵃ16, 1263ᵇ29–31, 1269ᵃ32, 1271ᵃ41, 1273ᵃ4, 1296ᵇ9–12, 1314ᵃ38, 1317ᵃ40, 1328ᵇ34–1329ᵃ2, and *Laws* 742d.

'Governed by good laws', *eunomeisthai*, often a slogan, like 'law and order' today, and equally hard to define. In his various accounts of it Aristotle identifies three salient characteristics: (i) sticking to one's own role (*MA* 703ᵃ29 ff.); (ii) careful cultivation of civic virtue (1280ᵇ5 ff.), leading to (iii) observance of good laws (1294ᵃ3 ff.). He chooses the word with an eye on chs. ix–xi; for Sparta (especially), Crete, and Carthage had a reputation for good government (cf. introduction to II ix). He probably had a controlled admiration for such more or less tightly run societies, in that they did at least exhibit some degree of hierarchichal order resembling the order he himself desiderated (cf. 1272ᵇ30–3); but that did not inhibit him from criticism (see e.g. on Spartan education, 1333ᵇ5 ff.). (Abundant further refs. for good government in Schütrumpf, ii. 152–3.)

2 (1260ᵇ36–1261ᵃ9)   At the start of I i the description of the state as a *koinōnia*, association, led to a discussion of various types of *rule*; now, 'association', the 'natural starting point', leads to a discussion of *sharing*. The two topics come together in the next chapter, in which the sharing of political power is a major topic. Meanwhile Aristotle instances two extremes of sharing: merely in territory, which is necessary but not sufficient to make a state (1263ᵇ35–6, 1276ᵃ19 ff., 1280ᵇ12 ff.), and in 'everything'— which immediately suggests the sharing even of wives, children, and possessions in Plato's *Republic*, an arrangement sharply at variance with 'present practice', i.e. private possession of them. Property is in fact the central topic of Aristotle's highly selective discussion of the *Republic* in ii–v. The lynch-pin of the entire scheme of Callipolis ('Beautiful City'), the theory of Forms, is not even mentioned, and the elaborate education of the Philosopher-Guardians, designed to lead to a knowledge of the Forms, is neither described nor assessed. Perhaps he feels these topics may be ignored on the strength of his demolition of the Forms in his *Metaphysics* and elsewhere (see on 1252ᵃ7–16). In v, however, he has something to say about Callipolis' administration; and later, in V xii 1315ᵇ40 ff., he discusses constitutional changes in *Rep.* VIII and IX.

II ii

CRITICISM OF SOCIAL AND POLITICAL 'ONENESS' IN PLATO'S *REPUBLIC*

Introduction   The chief target of this rather difficult chapter is *Republic* V down to 466d, in which Socrates prescribes the life-style of the Guardians, as follows. (*a*) Since the sexes do not differ essentially in capacity for philosophy and political rule, there must be female as well as male Guardians. (*b*) The Guardians must have no private property whatever, neither spouses, nor children, nor material goods; all these are to be held in common. (*c*) The strong sense of community thus engendered should be the basis, in each Guardian, of a total identification of his own interests and those of the group, his fellow-Guardians (cf. 412d). They should act and think like a single living body: just as when my finger is hurt 'I' am hurt, so a Guardian must regard an injury to a fellow as an injury to himself; he must as it were lose his sense of the distinction between *meum* and *tuum*. The state will thus become, as nearly as possible, 'one'; cf. *Laws* 739b ff.

In this frame of mind, and in the light of their vision of the Forms, the Guardians will rule the state with total devotion to its interests. However, their education is prolonged: not until the age of 50 is it complete (540ab). Till then, they are 'trainee' Guardians, auxiliary to the Guardians proper (414b), and more or less open to human weaknesses. When therefore Plato takes precautions against backsliding, and Aristotle talks (esp. in ch. iv) about their doing certain things which we might think inconsistent with the very hypothesis of the moral perfection of Guardians, neither is being unrealistic.

What of the Third Class (i.e. all who are not Guardians or Auxiliary Guardians)? As Aristotle realizes (1262ª40–ᵇ1), Plato describes community of property in connection with the Guardians alone; for he thinks it too hard a prescription for ordinary mortals. But he speaks loosely of the oneness of 'the state' (462ab; cf. 423d); the Third Class is indeed to have some feeling of solidarity with their rulers (e.g. 463ab), but inculcated in other ways. Later (1264ª13 ff.), Aristotle grumbles about Plato's failure to say whether community of wives, etc. applies to the 'other citizens' (and they *are* 'citizens': 463a4). Nevertheless, in our present chapter he seems to assume that it does (see 'all' *ad init.*), and so too the intense feeling of community. Strictly, he *must* so assume; for otherwise he would not be comparing like with like: he would have to play off his own conception of the state not against Plato's state but only against a special cadre of persons within it.

1 **(1261ª10–22)**   In objection (*a*) it is hard to see what is what. Aristotle may mean only that Socrates' arguments for oneness fail in the point of theory, so that it cannot be adopted as an aim, and hence cannot require community of wives in order to achieve it. Or he may have in mind 464ab, where the cause, *aitia* ('reason' in 1261ª11) of community of feeling is claimed to be communal possession of women and children. In that case, his point would be that the necessity for the communal possession does not 'emerge' from the arguments for the community of feeling: either we could achieve the latter without resorting to the former, or the former does not in fact produce the latter.

Or perhaps he is thinking of 457c, where the 'law' of communal possession is said to 'follow on from' the policy of assigning the same occupations to men and to women. He would then be simply denying the inference: the doctrine of common wives and children does not follow on from the arguments for common occupations of men and women; for a woman can do a job equally well whether she is a private wife or a common one (or indeed not married at all). That would be a shrewd blow on Aristotle's part; for to license the inference from common occupations to communal possession we need to import the necessity of a totally unselfish community of feeling, if the male and female Guardians are to be successful in their common occupation of ruling *well*; and that community of feeling, *alias* 'oneness', Aristotle now tells us in (*b*), is 'impossible'. So community of wives can be justified neither by the arguments for common occupations nor by its being needed to achieve 'oneness'; for oneness is in practice unattainable anyway.

In (*b*), 'as it is there described' implies that *some* unity is possible and indeed essential: a functional one, as described in the rest of the chapter; cf. also 1263^{b}29 ff. (*c*) remarks that [although Platonic oneness is impossible] Plato gave no alternative or modified version of it. The 'assumption' refers to 464b; on the term, see comment on 1260^{b}27–36.

The remainder of **1** has earned Aristotle a good deal of obloquy. On the face of it, he captiously deploys a merely mathematical sense of 'oneness', and absurdly suggests that Plato wished to see a state consisting of a single person (even though he used the single person only as an analogy, 464b1–3). But 'a state is by nature a plurality' reminds us of I ii, where the natural historical development of society into the state resulted in part from increases in numbers of personnel: 'pairs', households, villages, state. Aristotle's point is that reciprocal services (see **2**) between large numbers of persons make the state the means of living the good life; but they are not inspired by feelings of unselfishly benevolent 'oneness'. You could indeed attain an approximation to oneness by reducing numbers to those of a household, where personal relations are closer and warmer (cf. Stalley (1991) 188–9); but total oneness is attainable only in the individual. In brief, to require the characteristics of an individual in a state is a 'category mistake', which presumably demands that citizens, though rational and endowed with a moral sense, should bear the same functional relationship to the state as do irrational and non-moral limbs to a body. Aristotle's own man : state :: limb : body analogy at 1253^{a}18 ff. carries no such implication.

Two ripostes may be made on Plato's behalf. (1) Oneness of sentiment is not *incompatible* with reciprocity of service; indeed some forms of reciprocity are built into Callipolis itself (within the Third Class, and as between it and the Guardians, who receive 'pay' for their services as rulers, 463b3, 465d6–7, 543c; cf. in general 423d). It is the motivation for rendering mutual service that would need to change. (2) The motivation *can* change: Aristotle need not assume that because he finds human nature to be of a certain kind 'always or mostly' in existing states, it is therefore fixed. On the contrary, it is highly plastic: men and women can be brought to identify closely with the group. Common possession of wives and children is an attempt to do the moulding.

2 (1261^{a}22–37) and **3 (1261^{a}38–^{b}6)**   In insisting on a plurality of different types of people Aristotle may simply be developing the notion of plurality didactically, for its own sake. But if his remarks are intended as criticism of the *Republic*, they hardly go home; for Callipolis is peculiarly a society based on differentiation of role for different persons with different abilities. Presumably he thinks 'oneness', in entailing the suppression of any sense of conflict between one's own interests and those of the group, entails also a loss of a sense of individual personal identity, and therefore of ability to act independently and differently from others. (See for instance Plato's decrying of *idiōsis*, 462b8, 'sense of individuality'.) In short, Aristotle may believe that 'oneness' generates clones. This is hardly true: Plato himself relies on the Guardians' initiative and individual self-assertion (e.g. 460b), and there also exists among them a clear differentiation of function as between young and old. His reply would be: 'oneness means identity of belief, but not identity in all respects whatever, e.g. in ability, character, role, etc. My Callipolitans will indeed be different, and act differently, but always in such a way that in furthering their own interests they further the state's. The two interests mesh: by furthering the state's interests, the individual furthers his own.' Nevertheless Aristotle is right to call attention to the apparent tension between mental uniformity and practical diversity. For his own recognition that the citizens of a state must have *some* unity of outlook, see 1280ᵃ34 ff., 1328ᵃ35–ᵇ2.

The contrast between (1*a*) the mere weight of large numbers of homogeneous persons who form an *alliance*, and (1*b*) the structured unity of different people in a *state*, is apparently paralleled by (2*a*) *nations* that live scattered in villages, and (2*b*) *states* that do not so live, but live in some more unified manner. I take the point to be that villages offer less opportunity for differentiation of functions than states; the latter are therefore more self-sufficient in point of facilitating the 'good life' (cf. comment on 1252ᵇ15–1253ᵃ1). But what the Arcadians are supposed to be doing is unclear; perhaps (2*a*) and (2*b*) are evidenced in two stages of their history. There is an exhaustive discussion of this awkward sentence in Schütrumpf ii. 163–6. The reference to the '*Ethics*' is to *EN* V v; for discussion of 'reciprocal equality' in economics, see comment on I ix.

The remainder of **2** and the whole of **3** form a short essay on one of Aristotle's favourite topics, ruling and being ruled by turns (cf. e.g. 1277ᵇ7 ff., 1287ᵃ10 ff.). The connection of thought seems to be as follows. A state consists of persons different in type, who exchange goods, services, etc. on the basis of equality (one cow = five pigs, *vel sim.*). These persons are equal (presumably in point of nature, education, virtue, etc., not merely free status, cf. 1301ᵃ28–31), and so have an equal claim to rule; but it is impossible for them all to do so all of the time. So 'even' among them reciprocal equality is essential: they take turns to have the privilege, or do the work, of ruling; the principle that all rule is thereby preserved, and there is reciprocity of service.

Alternation of rule is, then, ostensibly introduced merely as a way of showing the extreme importance of reciprocal equality, which has to apply even among equals, when ideally (on the principle of specialization of function) the same people should rule permanently (just as the same people are permanently shoemakers and carpenters). But is there some more direct relevance to the *Republic*? For there the same people do rule all the time. Nevertheless, Aristotle disapproves: it is likely to lead to civil strife (1264ᵇ6–10, cf. 1281ᵃ28 ff.) obviously because it is unjust (1261ᵇ1, 1287ᵃ10–18; on permanent monarchy, cf. esp. III xvii). If that is Aristotle's thought here, it is simply irrelevant: he has in mind what would happen in actual states, whereas the fundamental hypothesis of the *Republic* is that the Guardians rule permanently in virtue of their special knowledge, and the members of the Third Class are permanently ruled in virtue of their lack of it—and acquiesce in the arrangement, so that permanent rule by the same persons *is* 'possible'. See further on 1273ᵇ8–17.

4 (1261ᵇ6–15) sums up, and adds that a state cannot be self-sufficient if it is too much of a unity. These remarks are reminiscent of the latter part of **1**, and again may constitute a merely mathematical argument (see comment there). One could charitably recast them in some more respectable form, as follows: 'Platonic oneness generates only one kind of person, which militates against diversity of function, which militates against self-sufficiency.' But that is not what he actually says.

II iii

LANGUAGE AND PSYCHOLOGY OF POSSESSION IN A SYSTEM OF 'ONENESS'

Introduction Plato believes that 'the best-run state is that in which the greatest number of people apply "mine" and "not mine" to the same thing in the same respects' (*Rep.* 462c). He therefore proposes elaborate arrangements for mating and breeding. The Guardians are to be kept in systematic ignorance of who their relatives actually are; they have to regard (e.g.) all boys born at a time consistent with their having been sired by themselves as their 'sons' (461cd). The result, Plato hopes, will be that no Guardian will ever be able to regard himself as unrelated to any other Guardian. Whomsoever he meets, he will think he is encountering 'either a brother, or a sister, or father, or mother, or son, or daughter, or their offspring or forbears' (463c). Every Guardian will say of every other Guardian that he or she is 'my' son or sister etc., and that his/her suffering or prosperity is 'my' suffering or prosperity; thus pleasures and pains will be 'shared'; and these results are caused in part by the Guardians' 'sharing' of wives and children (463e–464a).

Now clearly the crucial move is from 'the suffering of my relative' to '*my* suffering'. Plato is often thought to wish to suppress the sense of the private, of what is 'mine', as opposed to the communal. And so he does, in so far as what is private is *exclusive* to the individual 'owner': for instance, in monogamy, 'my' wife, as distinct from 'your' wife. It is truer to say that he wishes enormously to strengthen the sense of the private, by extending it to a very much larger range of people and things (debatably to the Third Class, but certainly not to foreigners). There is to be no distinction between 'my' interests and 'your' interests, because yours are mine, because you are [regarded by me as] my relative by blood or marriage. By these means Plato hopes to make the state 'one', in the sense of having unanimity of outlook and sentiment.

These proposals contain a great many obscurities and difficulties (conveniently summarized and discussed by Halliwell (1993) 16–21, 155–82). Aristotle, however, is extremely selective; indeed, he goes for the jugular. He distinguishes two uses of 'all'. (*a*) is *distributive*: 'this is my book'; there is one owner, and one book; the sense of 'my' is *exclusive*, and strong; and if many individuals say this, each of his own book, then 'all' say it, *but of different books*. (*b*) is *collective*: 'this is my village'; there are several 'owners', but only one village; the sense of 'my' is *inclusive*, and weak; and if many individuals say this, they 'all' say it, *but of the same village*. Aristotle's fundamental point, developed in this chapter, is twofold: the intensity of the feeling in (*a*) cannot be achieved in (*b*), if, as is the case in Callipolis, the speaker of the words (e.g.) 'my son', (1) is not sure that the boy concerned *is* his son, (2) is aware that many other persons are saying the same thing of the same boy, and are or should be acting on that belief.

(1) provokes essentially the same reflection as at the end of the comment on 1261^{a}10–22. Where 'my' is used in a collective sense, it is a very large assumption that one's attachment to a person whom one knows to be a relation must in any circumstances be more intense than to a person whom one knows not to be, or who may not be. For Plato, in virtue of the Guardians' education and life-style, provides highly special circumstances, designed precisely to redirect and extend what he assumes to be normal patterns of attachment and motivation. As for (2), Aristotle simply assumes that the normal inverse correlation between numbers and affection is unchangeable; Plato assumes it is not.

1 (1261^{b}16–32) The train of thought is rather confusing, and it is easy to miss Aristotle's paradox; for the description of the exclusive mode of speaking at 1261^{b}22–4 looks like something *Socrates* 'wants to bring about'. But what Socrates wants is oneness ('this' in 1261^{b}17), which Aristotle claims will be *more nearly achieved* by the apparently selfish and divisive practices implied by the distributive use of 'my'. Hence the argument that 'all say "mine" and "not mine" simultaneously' is *not* a 'sign' of the presence of oneness; the mere use of the terms tells us nothing, for even when they are employed in a collective manner, which Socrates advocates, they do not, according to Aristotle, lead to the *functional* oneness he explained in II ii. It is rather cheeky of Aristotle to suggest that the distributive use more nearly approaches *Socratic* oneness.

That elementary logical fallacies can affect practical decisions is indicated several times in the *Politics* (e.g. 1307^{b}30–1308^{a}3); in particular, they may be used for purposes of constitutional deception (see Saunders (1993) 51–4). 'Contentious', literally 'eristic', is something of a technical term: 'designed to win an argument at all costs'. 'Even in discussion' (1261^{b}30) presumably means 'even when one has time to think clearly, not under pressure of events'.

'Concord' is *homonoia*, literally 'like-mindedness'; it is analysed in *EN* IX vi (cf. 1155ᵃ24–6, *EE* 1241ᵃ15–33) as that friendship which is agreement in relation to the same person on matters of practical political action, e.g. when A and B agree that in their common interest A should rule, not B. If Aristotle has that analysis in mind here, what is his point? Presumably that concord presupposes a sharp sense of the difference between my interests and yours, which have to be rationally reconciled, according to some calculation of balance of advantage. *Republic*-style affection abolishes the sense of difference, and therefore the basis on which the calculation can be made; and that is a 'harm' (see **2** *init.*). No doubt Plato would reply that the lack of a sense of difference makes reconciliation unnecessary, since my interests and yours are, in my eyes and yours, identical; so there is no conflict to start with. On this account, concord is for Aristotle a friendship which is the result of highly specific practical deliberation, and the *Republic*'s friendships are too generalized and uncalculated to qualify. On possible friendship between the Guardians and the Third Class, see on 1264ᵃ22–40.

2 (1261ᵇ32–40)   explores 'other harm' in communal ownership: the neglect that arises both when one object or person has many owners, and when one owner has many possessions (things or persons). Much of this leaves Plato's position untouched; for his hypothesis is that everyone has strong affection for everyone, because private interests are projected on to the communal. But it may be a point against him, if indeed Aristotle means to make it here, that however strong my affection for everyone, I cannot *do* something for everyone: it is physically not possible (see *EN* 1158ᵃ10 ff., IX x, cf. *EE* 1245ᵇ19–25). I have to concentrate my efforts on only a few—though of course that can be construed as having communal relevance. Aristotle would no doubt conclude that such concentration is effectively the system that was supposed to be superseded.

3 (1262ᵃ1–14)   seems to contain a double comparison between the collective and the distributive systems.

In the distributive: (*a*) The 'ownership' is not fractional, or only mildly so (several brothers may say 'my' of a brother); it is 'personal' (*idion*, 'private', or 'peculiar', 1262ᵃ13), and full-strength, not weak; and the care and fellow-feeling is correspondingly more intense. (*b*) The relationship is real, and is known to be so.

In the collective: (*a*) Each individual among 1,000 (Aristotle derives this number from 423a) is, as a relative (say father) to another citizen, only a tiny fraction of that relative. He is not a full or sole father, and his concern for that citizen's welfare or distress (cf. *Rep.* 463e) is weak, since he cannot fully identify it with his own. (*b*) When the relationship is (e.g.) paternal, the 'father' cannot know, of that connection, whether it is *real*; for no more than one of the 1,000 can be the father; and which one, is not known.

(*b*) raises—one wishes Aristotle had pursued it—the very interesting question of a Guardian's state of mind when he says, of each of (say) 100

boys, 'my son'. Obviously he cannot mean the literal sense; yet an analogical sense (as a priest might say to a parishioner, 'my son') hardly does
justice to Plato's clear intention to extend the literal use, and its associated
feelings, into a wider context. 'My son' seems to have, in the mouth of a
Guardian, some special, unique sense; for he must presumably not be
aware of, or at least not think about, (a) the difference between relating to
many sons and relating to one or a few, (b) the distinction between real
sons and analogical sons. Indeed, is he even capable of *formulating* (b)?
Presumably the mildly incantatory effect of constant repetition of the term
has to be allowed for (464a1–2, cf. *Laws* 854c). See further Price (1989)
182 ff.

However that may be, the extensive network of real, personal, and
highly specific relationships, both familial and other, outlined towards the
end of the paragraph is Aristotle's realistic answer to Plato's collectivist
model.

4 (1262ª14–24) Cf. Herodotus IV 180: a neat deployment of anthropology against Plato, in the spirit of *Rhet.* 1360ª33–5 ('travel books are useful
for legislation'), and with the implication that the inevitable discovery of
real relationships will vitiate (as Plato would see it) the Guardians' attitudes. Presumably Plato fears favouritism, and perhaps especially the effects on the power-structure of Callipolis if a Guardian resists the
demotion of an untalented son to the 'silver' or 'iron' class. Aristotle, while
alive to the dangers of the hereditary principle and in favour of
meritocratic rule (cf. e.g. 1271ª18–26, 1272ᵇ33–1273ª2, 31 ff.), would simply
welcome the discovery of relationships as the assertion of 'natural' patterns of conduct; for the state is natural, and embraces the household,
whose internal relationships also are natural, man being a 'pairing' and a
'household' animal (see I ii in general, *EN* 1155ª17–19, 1158ᵇ11 ff., VIII xii;
EE 1242ª22 ff.). It is for these reasons that he approves of such patterns,
not directly because they are focuses of non-state loyalties or 'subsidiarity'
or independence or freedom as against totalitarianism or tyranny; he does
not mention this issue here, though in broad terms he is aware of it
(1313ª34 ff., cf. 1262ª40 ff.).

The mare was 'just' because she produced, in offspring like the stallion,
a 'corresponding' return—good value, so to speak. See *HA* 586ª13.

II iv

DRAWBACKS OF COMMUNITY OF WIVES AND CHILDREN IN
PLATO'S *REPUBLIC*

Introduction In this more than usually vivacious chapter Aristotle turns
from the disadvantages of the Guardians' recognizing blood-relationships
among themselves, to the disadvantages of their not recognizing them.
Which he expects to happen more commonly, is not clear. On the misdeeds
of Guardians, see introduction to II ii.

1 (1262ᵃ25–32) Plato's methods of preventing and containing offences of the kind mentioned are set out at 464d–465b: 'sharing' will reduce personal self-assertion, contemporaries may keep in physical trim by scrapping without intervention from the law, only from older Guardians, and 'fear and respect' will inhibit attacks on elders/parents. Aristotle ignores all this. He fastens on two related points: (i) that since in Callipolis one cannot know who one's real close relatives are, the inhibitory effect of knowledge is absent, and one may commit certain serious offences against them in ignorance of their identity; and then (ii) the customary expiations will be impossible, for the same reason. How far Aristotle himself took such procedures seriously (they were matters of religious scruple rather than law) is unclear (cf. 1335ᵇ25–6 on 'the holy'), but at any rate here is his usual concern for *real* relationships: it seems not to impinge on him that in Callipolis, if putative relationships are to be taken as real ones, the latter are no more important than the former; and that expiations would be performed for every such offence, not just some—since everyone is now a (putative) real relation (463c). He may have in mind the point that if everyone is a near relative, and therefore special, no one is special: the sense of extra outrage at offences against near relatives is lost. (In the second sentence, the material in the parenthesis, which in the Greek is very short and technically ambiguous, has often been translated and interpreted so as to imply that offences against non-near relatives, or complete non-relatives, *are* holy; but that would be an outrageous claim.) For the legal and religious background, see Schütrumpf ii. 182–4, Saunders (1991) 229–30, 241–2, 263–5, 268–79.

2 (1262ᵃ32–40) Although Plato made it clear that only boys born at certain times were to be regarded as a man's 'sons', and sexual relations between them will be avoided (461de), a more sweeping statement comes later (463c), in which he apparently suggests that *all* boys are sons in common to all men. All boy-love is therefore officially incest. (In a few cases it will be actual incest; but unlike in **1** Aristotle does not here seem concerned with the distinction between real and putative.) Nevertheless, Plato permitted, perhaps in a slightly jokey manner ('deplorable facetiousness', Shorey, Loeb edn., p. 489), very limited homosexual relations—kissing and touching—in a very limited range of circumstances (403ac; 468bc). Aristotle regards that as paradoxical: if incest is to be suppressed, then not only must all full man–boy sexual relations be suppressed, but the limited ('other', 'most unseemly') practices also, and the love itself that leads to them. How the inclination itself is to be eliminated, he does not say. But his point may be that it is hard to limit sexual encounters once they have started, and that, as a matter of practical psychology, the inclination is harder to eliminate if it is indulged partially than if it is not indulged at all. On the treatment of incest in Greece, see Parker (1983) 97–8.

3 (1262ᵃ40–ᵇ24) turns from sexual affection (*erōs*) to the personal and social, by reverting to and developing the theme of II iii, the thinness of the 'family' relationships in Callipolis; for they fail to foster *philia*, 'friendship', 'affection', which is 'the greatest of goods for states' (cf. comment on

1261ᵇ32, 'concord'). *Philia* is however a far richer term than our 'friendship'. Aristotle distinguishes very many kinds, and devotes two of the ten books (VIII and IX) of the *EN* to them. Here he speaks quite compendiously of the total network of 'friendships' between various persons in household and state (Price (1989) chs. 6 and 7, esp. 195 ff.), all presumably (see 'private and delectable', 1262ᵇ23) friendships based on pleasure or advantage rather than virtue (*EN* VIII iii), and on the 'reciprocal equality' of 1261ᵃ30–4.

The splendidly waspish opening sentences about the management of the Third Class (cf. comment on 'totalitarianism', 1262ᵃ14–24) embraces both familial and state relationships, between which the rest of the paragraph oscillates rather confusingly. What is Aristotle assuming, and what is at issue? He thought of the various 'friendships' within the household as *preparatory* to the various 'friendships' at the level of the state, between citizens and statesmen, which especially promote happiness (cf. comment on 1252ᵇ9–15, with references). Socrates wished the former friendships, in their collectivist form, to *be* the friendships at the level of the state, between the Guardians. That would generate the 'oneness' he praises (462c). But these friendships, claims Aristotle, are 'watery', because they are not based on 'the private and the delectable'; they therefore cannot prevent faction. But why not? In historical states, precisely because friendships were private and particularized (X is my friend, Y is not), the most sanguinary conflicts arose between competing groups whose respective members were, precisely, friends. It is at least possible that Plato's collectivist system, in which 'my private interest' is always identified with the interests of everyone else, and the category of non-friends does not exist, would be a pretty efficient preventative of faction; for however 'watery' the friendships, they are at any rate universally diffused. And *if* Aristotle's objection is in part that there is no gradation of maturity and quality of friendship first for one's family and then for one's state (cf. *EN* 1242ᵃ40–ᵇ1), the two having been fused, he fails to notice (had he read the text?) the implications of the Guardians' long process of emotional, social, and philosophical maturation. Would not their 'affection' for their fellows and the state at large be better founded at the age of 50 than at 25? The question of their motivation to care for the state is raised indirectly at 1264ᵇ15–25.

The brief excursus (ᵇ11–14) about Aristophanes is by way of comic contrast with the watery friendship, and therefore presumably watery oneness, produced by Socrates' proposals. The reference is to the myth accounting for sexual differentiation in the *Symposium* (192b–e), where lovers wish to come together so tightly as to become 'one'. Aristotle, tongue in cheek, points out the literal consequences. Then with 'however' in ᵇ15 we come back to the real world; and with 'constitution' at the end, in the wide sense of 'socio-political structures', he links the two levels, familial and political.

4 (1262ᵇ24–36). On murders etc., cf. 1. The main texts relating to 'promotions' and 'demotions' (which are not confined to children) are 415b–d, 423cd, 468a. Aristotle is right to complain of their cursoriness; but Plato clearly expected that for genetic reasons children would normally stay in that class into which they were born. Yet in Aristotle's own comments there are two minor mysteries. (1) Why should it matter that the transferrers, who are presumably Guardians, know the identity of the children transferred? Perhaps because while every other Guardian is aware that, in a given age-group, there is no child that might not be his own, the transferrers know that there are some children (the promoted) that *cannot* be the children of any Guardian at all; and this knowledge, to a mild degree, undermines the system. But then, are Guardians supposed even to think about these things? See further on 1262ᵃ1–14. (2) Why are the offences *more* likely to occur? After all, how much social (as distinct from administrative) contact between the Guardians and the Third Class is there to be? But Aristotle is technically correct to point out that the transferred children will (be taught to) regard their real parents as *not* their real parents.

II v

DRAWBACKS OF COMMUNITY OF PROPERTY IN PLATO'S *REPUBLIC*; THE CONSTITUTION

Introduction II i announced, as the 'natural starting-point' of the inquiry into proposals for the best state on a practical level, the basis on which property should be held. Chs. ii–iv were in a sense an immediate digression: they were devoted to a highly unusual form of property-sharing, the community of wives and children in Callipolis. Aristotle now turns to property in the more usual sense of land, chattels, and food-supply; and these topics occupy a large part of the rest of the book. He considers Callipolis first; but even now there is some delay. It is not until **6** that there is any reference to Callipolis; **1–5** are entirely general, and in their urbane shrewdness could practically stand alone as an independent essay in the manner of Addison or Lamb. Nevertheless, the urbanity has an edge: Aristotle has a thesis to argue that would in many states outrage common sentiment. Though he defends private *ownership* of property, he advocates its common *use*—but in precisely what sense, is a question.

The salient facts about property in the *Republic* are these (416c–417b, 419a, 420a, 458c, 463b, 464cd, 543bc, 547bc): (i) In order that the Guardians may suffer no temptation to pursue their own interests, rather than study and rule in the interests of the state as a whole, they are to possess no private property whatsoever, apart from their own bodies. (ii) They will receive their maintenance from the Third Class, as 'pay' for their services as rulers; they will have common meals (*sussitia*), and housing etc. will be provided on a communal basis. They will have such things 'in common', but presumably as common users, not as common owners (not that in practice there would be much difference; at any rate, they are not encouraged to use of property the language they are to use of wives and children:

'mine'). (iii) The members of the Third Class, it seems to be assumed, have private property in the usual way; certainly they pay a levy for the Guardians' upkeep.

Plato wished the Guardians to have strong attachments to 'property' in the shape of wives and children, etc., built on a strong feeling of their being in some sense 'private', i.e. 'mine'. Aristotle argued that these attachments would prove 'watery' (1262^b15). By contrast, Plato wished the Guardians to have the weakest possible attachment to property in the sense of things; Aristotle argues that it needs to be strong (though not obsessive). They agree on the need for strong attachments to people; but whereas Plato believed they would be hindered by attachments to things, Aristotle believes they would be assisted (**5** and **6**).

F. D. Miller (1991) and Mayhew (1993*a*) are excellent analyses of Aristotle's views on property in general.

1 (1262^b37–1263^a8) Aristotle identifies four possibilities: (*a*) common ownership, (*b*) common use, (*c*) private ownership, (*d*) private use; and he mentions every combination of two except (*c*) + (*d*), the practice that prevailed in Greece in his day. It is clear (1329^b36 ff.) that his own preference is for (*b*) + (*c*), subject to certain conditions. (i) Some land should be owned communally, to support religion, and common meals. (ii) Poorer citizens should enjoy a safety net (cf. 1320^b9–11). (iii) There should be generous forms of 'workfare' (1320^a29–$^b9$). (iv) Those who actually work the (private) land should ideally be slaves (1330^a25 ff., conformably with the principles of I iii–vii). It is not easy to fit Callipolis into this analysis: perhaps (*c*), in that the Third Class have private land (but cf. 1264^a14–16), and (*b*), in that the Guardians take part of the produce for common use; but in Aristotle's own intention the private ownership and the common use are apparently to be within the *same* class of people.

2 (1263^a8–21) 'A different system': private ownership, with slaves ('others') doing the work, is 'easier' than communal. To judge from the contrast with the last sentence of **1**, and from the rest of **2**, 'themselves work hard for their own benefit', in spite of an apparent contrast with the use of slaves on private land, does not describe free men doing their own work on their own land, but free men working communally for the communal benefit. The difficulties in such a system arise from a sense of outraged justice (cf. *EN* 1131^a20 ff.), and Aristotle dwells on them at length.

3 (1263^a21–30) 'Habits': Aristotle agrees with Plato that habituation is effective in the formation of a virtuous character (*Rep.* 444c, *Ph.* 82ab, *EN* 1103^a14 ff.). Nevertheless, on the face of it he takes a somewhat roseate view of the zeal of private owners who know that some of the produce of their own labour will be consumed communally; but cf. comments on **4–6**, especially on 'liberality'. Keen though he is to insist that the difficulties of private property are not intrinsic to it, but are due merely to depravity and are curable by habits and correct laws, he omits to make the point in relation to communal property (cf. 1261^b32–40 and Irwin (1991) 218–21).

4 (1263^a30–40) It is rather difficult to see the practical limits of the common use of property that Aristotle recommends. 'Outline form' may suggest he has in mind something stronger than the Spartan practice he describes. He specifies 'common use' for friends (cf. 1329ᵇ41–1330ª2), not generalized charity; reciprocity is presumably required, or difficulties similar to those of **2** would arise; and spongers would rapidly cease to be friends. On the other hand, he seems to regard the practice as a means of relieving poverty (1320ᵇ9–11, 1330ª2); in particular, he commends the Cretan system, which does not exclude from the common meals and citizen-rights those unable to pay their contributions (1271ª26–37, 1272ª12 ff.). But these are public measures; Aristotle is probably thinking primarily of private, face-to-face generosity between relations (*EN* VIII ix), and 'friends, and strangers and companions' (**5** *fin.*); and that is different again from the 'liturgies' (public services, e.g. paying the expenses of a dramatic festival, demanded of wealthy individuals in Athens.

5 (**1263ª40–ᵇ7**) and **6** (**1263ᵇ7–14**) are important: they bring us to the pith of Aristotle's psycho-social objections to the 'oneness' of Callipolis, namely that by suppressing private property it vitiates the generation of other-love from self-love. However, taken strictly at face value the two paragraphs make a far more limited claim; it is only when they are interpreted in the light of evidently cognate but long and difficult passages elsewhere (*EN* IV i, VIII iii, IX iv, viii, ix, *EE* III iv) that their wider implications become clear.

5 and **6** seem to state 5 propositions; I add a few comments and references.

1. Self-love is natural (as natural as, say, the sex urge, see 1252ª28–30); it has a purpose.
2. The active expression of that natural love is the pursuit and attainment of one's own welfare; this is a natural activity, which causes pleasure (this is true of natural processes and states in general: *Rhet.* 1369ᵇ33 ff., *HA* 589ª8–9).
3. Private property causes a very great 'difference' to this natural pleasure of furthering one's interests; common property generates *less* pleasure, or so it seems to be implied by **5** *init.*; we are not told why.
4. Private property is similarly more effective than common property in the 'helping and gratifying' of friends, which is *very* pleasurable (**5**); again there is no explanation; and the implied distinction between self-love and love for others is left in the air.
5. That property should be private is necessary for the exercise of liberality, *eleutheriotēs*; but yet again we are not told why, nor the nature of that virtue.

We seem to be facing a set of swift observations, which Aristotle presumably thought likely to command ready assent (note the heavy emphasis on pleasure). But as a defence of *private* property, they are decidedly questionable; for could not the same activities and benefits be equally possible if property were common? The argument will work, however, if one supplements it somewhat as follows.

A. My reason is what makes me distinctively human; action in accordance with it is not merely pleasant but a crucial part of my overall welfare, my total happiness as a human being; and my rational conduct is necessarily in part concerned with the use of resources.

B. Now if at least some of those resources are not *mine*, and so subject to my unfettered discretion, then my self-sufficiency is diminished (*cf. EN* 1099ᵃ31 ff. 1125ᵃ11–12, 1177ᵃ27 ff.), and my rational conduct, and therefore happiness, is impeded. Further, self-love (distinguished from selfishness and by implication from other-love in 5) is (i) precisely the love of one's reason, since one's reason 'is' oneself, and (ii) arises in particular from the *judgement* of oneself as 'good', i.e. as a rational agent achieving happiness (*EN* 1166ᵇ2 ff., cf. 1170ᵇ8–10, and the sense of individual success in getting, not inheriting, property implied at 1120ᵇ11–14). *To the extent that* private property is essential to that achievement, it is essential to that judgement and so to self-love.

C. Finally, self-love is essential to the development of other-love, i.e. friendship, which is in turn essential to the unity of the state as Aristotle conceives it (1280ᵇ38 ff., and comment on 'concord' 1261ᵇ32). At any rate, 'from' or 'out of' self-love comes other-love, with the implication that without the former the latter does not come into being (1166ᵃ1–2, 1168ᵇ5–6). (But in that case, is the rational and thus laudable activity of other-love an essential part of the basis on which I build up my self-love, from which my love for others springs? If so, other-love requires for its generation its own prior existence.)

The extension of love from oneself to others is apparently on the basis of some kind of likeness or sympathetic affinity in point of family relationship, character, interests, etc. (On the very difficult psychology of other-love, see Annas (1977), Kahn (1981), Engbert-Pederson (1983) 37 ff., Irwin (1988) ch. 18, esp. 395–7, Annas with Kraut (1988), Price (1989) 110 ff., Benson (1990).) One now seeks the welfare of others also, for their own sakes, as 'parts' of oneself, or as 'second-selves', as one would one's own welfare for one's own sake (*EN* 1156ᵇ7 ff., 1161ᵇ27–9, IX iv, viii, 1170ᵇ5–8). In *EN* VIII iii Aristotle lists three kinds of friendship: two common-or-garden types, based on what one friend finds useful or agreeable in the other, and a further 'perfect' (but rare) type, between good men, who love each other for their moral excellence. The 'helping and doing favours to friends and strangers and companions' in 5 are presumably cases of common-or-garden friendships, and the exercise of the virtue of liberality in 6 *may* be intended as characteristic of 'perfect' friendships; for liberality is the giving away of property, especially money, where there is no obligation to do so, and without expectation of reciprocal benefit (*EN* IV i). It is perhaps a reasonable guess that this is how 'perfect' friends would treat each other in the matter of property.

What is the relevance of the virtue of restraint in 6? I take it that whereas liberality *enhances* the welfare of others, restraint is simply another expression of other-love, which ensures that that welfare is not *diminished*. On the Guardians' restraint in the matter of women, see *Rep.* 443a; but no Guardian woman *could* 'belong to another'.

If we take a simple instrumental view of the virtues—that they are exercised not only 'for their own sake', as constitutive of or conducive to happiness (*EN* 1097ª34–ᵇ5, 1174ª4–8), but also in order to achieve some goal or cope with the difficulties of some situation or institution (cf. 1332ª7 ff.)—then **6** can read rather oddly; for Aristotle could be construed to claim that private property with all its problems ought to be preserved simply in order to permit liberality to go on coping with them. This seems topsy-turvy. What we need to find is some special value in liberality such as to justify the retention of private property, its prerequisite (cf. Irwin (1991) 214–17). The special value is surely its selectivity. 'The liberal man will give for the sake of the noble, and rightly, for (he will give) to whom he ought, in the amounts (he ought), when (he ought), and in the other ways entailed by right giving' (*EN* 1120ª24–6); see also the discrimination in giving at *EN* 1120ᵇ3–4 and 20–4. The recipients will presumably be qualified by virtue of social or familial status or moral merit (cf. the careful priorities of persons specified in connection with moral dilemmas in *EN* IX ii). Aristotle's point is that without private property this network of direct, face-to-face discrimination is lost; common property reduces entitlements to a homogeneous level, in a system (in Callipolis at any rate) of 'watery' friendships of everyone with everyone. To Plato, of course, it is this private economic patronage that is objectionable, because it can all too easily degenerate into cronyism (cf. *Gorg.* 492bc), and because it constitutes a focus of loyalties all too likely to be corrupted by criteria alien to his own moral orthodoxy. Liberality is something the Form of which the Guardians must recognize (402c); it plays no other part in the *Republic*, at least among the Guardians. On liberality in the *Laws*, see 1265ª28–38 and comment.

Plato and Aristotle addressed the same problem, of harnessing private interest to the common good. 'All persons' (within the Guardian class) 'are my son or wife etc.', and 'self-love is extended to other-love', are as policies not wholly dissimilar. This harnessing is the context for Aristotle's insistence on the value of private property: as Irwin (1991) 222–4 notices, he takes no interest in liberality on the basis of *communal* property. Nor does he defend private property as a right, nor on grounds of economic efficiency or productivity, nor as a way of preventing or relieving poverty, nor as a means of ensuring individual autonomy, over and against the power of the state, in the making of practical, moral, and political decisions.

What then *is* the role of private property? (i) It creates, as common property cannot, the pleasant feeling that it is exclusively mine and my own achievement, and so furthers self-love, without which other-love cannot exist, for its psychological basis will have been lost; (ii) it is the tool by which other-love can be expressed in practice, for the ultimate benefit of the solidarity of the state as a whole. **5** and **6** thus contain, in spite of their allusiveness, the essence of Aristotle's case against communal ownership. See further Irwin (1991), a full and especially stimulating discussion.

7 (1263ᵇ15–29) 'Such legislation': presumably Plato's in the *Republic*, but Aristotle may have in mind other thinkers too, now unknown. 'Bene-volence', *philanthrōpia*, is general goodwill, apparently more or less inde-pendent of ability to act on the feeling, and of desert in its object (see Irwin (1991) 209–13); it is only a shadow of liberality, which is selective and therefore more effective.

On lawsuits etc., Aristotle seems to be thinking chiefly of *Rep.* 464d–465c. He hardly meets Plato's fundamental point, that if men will persist in fighting, the obvious way to stop them is to take away their battle-field, i.e. private property (though that negative step merely opens the way to virtue; it does not force men to become virtuous; cf. 556a). He stresses that education can mitigate the evils of private ownership, but seems unwilling to admit that it could mitigate those of common ownership, perhaps be-cause, as he claims here, the quarrel-rate is empirically higher in the latter circumstances than in the former; but this point, in spite of the confident 'we see' and 'we observe', is little more than anecdotal and rhetorical, since he can hardly have collected pertinent comparative data. Cf. comment on 1263ᵃ21–30.

8 (1263ᵇ29–1264ᵃ1) The 'blunder' is common property, the 'assumption' (see on 1260ᵇ27–36) is the oneness of the state. The paragraph first restates ii–iv in summary form ('before' refers to 1261ᵃ22 ff.), and then develops the paradox that although Plato 'introduced' education (i.e. the advanced education of the Guardians), he never thought to use 'habits, laws, and philosophy' (this last in a loose sense, 'intellectual training') for securing the advantages of private property, while eliminating its drawbacks; the proper scope for common property is that of the common meals of Crete and Sparta. This is a trifle odd, as Plato *did* prescribe common meals for the Guardians—though of course as part of a system of replacements for private property, not in tandem with it or as a supplement to it, as it was in Sparta and Crete: see 1271ᵃ26–37, ᵇ40–1272ᵃ27.

The 'legislator' (in Sparta presumably Lycurgus, see on 1269ᵇ39–1270ᵃ11) will have lived a long time ago; this prompts the reflections on history which now follow.

9 (1264ᵃ1–11) 'Collected', i.e. the data has not been assembled and ana-lysed; Aristotle has in mind the kind of factual survey carried out in the Lyceum of 158 constitutions, of which the *Constitution of the Athenians* alone survives. The paragraph is a kind of blocking manœuvre. Aristotle's history is teleological (see especially I ii, 1268ᵇ22–1269ᵃ28, 1271ᵇ23–4; good review in Schütrumpf ii. 204–8). Mankind has discovered, more or less fully, not only how to 'live' but how to 'live well'—in states, which are pluralities, i.e. they contain many different organizations (households, brotherhoods, etc.) that mesh to make the whole. Now it is typical of 'ends' that they are complete and 'best' (see 1252ᵇ27–1253ᵃ1): the process of development and improvement stops and can go no further. In constitu-tion-making, therefore, the room for new suggestion is now limited: if radical change does come about it will be *disimprovement*, and recognized as such by mankind. So Plato simply will not be able to create a state which is radically 'one': men will insist on brotherhoods, etc. That will leave him, as Aristotle notes, only with the proposal that the Guardians shall not farm, which (*mutatis mutandis*: the parallel with Sparta is very broad) is nothing new (on the problems of the Lacedaemonians, cf. 1269ᵃ34–ᵇ12). Plato, however, though not bound by teleological assumptions, was well aware that he would meet strong opposition; hence his demand for a clean sheet (*Rep.* 540e–541a: the first persons to be trained as Guardians must be not above 10 years old, and so be mentally malleable, unlike their seniors). This requirement occurs at the end of book VII, and Aristotle mentions neither it nor (except obliquely in **8**?) the higher education of the Guardians in V 473b–VII; perhaps he had not read this material, or only cursorily; cf. 1264ᵇ37–9.

The last sentence puts Aristotle in mind of Callipolis' farmers; and the rest of the chapter sprays Plato with a rapid series of complaints about obscurities and difficulties in the relationship between the Guardians and the Third Class; the most far-reaching of the issues he raises is in **14**. In general terms, he is right to complain of obscurity: Plato is overwhelmingly interested in the Guardians, and the information he gives about the Third Class is decidedly sketchy.

10 (1264ᵃ11–22) Aristotle is perfectly aware (see 1262ᵃ40–ᵇ3) that community of wives, children, and property is not required of the Third Class; but now he assumes that it might be, and explores the consequences. Presumably he is not suggesting that the Guardians and the Third Class have the same wives etc. in common, but each class its own; in that case, since such community is the cause of the state's 'greatest good' (464ab), namely 'oneness' (462a–c), we shall have either two states identical in that excellence, or one undifferentiated state, but with no means of distinguishing who should rule and who should be ruled—since all its members will be 'alike' in so sharing. But this is mare's-nesting. (i) Even if there were no such distinction, one could be introduced artificially (see 1261ᵃ22–ᵇ6, on alternation). (ii) The Third Class could have community of wives, etc., but in some imperfect form (Mayhew 1993*b*), without the Guardians' special frame of mind. (iii) Even if such 'communism' applied in exactly the same way in both groups, Plato obviously did not think of it as in itself a sufficient condition for ruling, but only when combined with the advanced metaphysical education of the Guardians. That is how the two groups will 'differ'; and Plato is quite clear that the members of the Third Class will be content to be ruled because they recognize the Guardians' superior wisdom in ruling them and efficiency in protecting them (432a, 465d). Once again Aristotle is curiously indifferent to important themes in the *Republic*.

The *Realpolitik* of the final sentence is far from Plato's intentions. It is true that, on the principle of specialization of function, only the Auxiliary Guardians bear arms; but this is only for protection against foreign aggression (375b ff.), and in spite of 1268ᵃ17 ff. it does not make 'slaves' of the Third Class. The Third Class is to regard the Guardians as friends and protectors (416b, 417ab, 463ab; cf. 547c); hostilities against it by the Auxiliaries would be a sign that civic harmony had broken down (but cf. 415de).

11 (1264ᵃ22–40)   explores some difficulties which will arise if the Third Class is to have private families and private possessions (= 'such things'; or does this mean 'weapons'?). In view of Plato's strong desire for civic harmony (432a), and his reluctance to tolerate 'two states in one' (422e ff.), there is some tendentiousness in the description of the Guardians as 'like a garrison', with the implication of forcible control over 'citizens' (as the Third Class is called at e.g. 416b2). So too *apophora* 'rent', which half-suggests that the Guardians own the land worked by the Third Class, or, if translated 'payment' (to masters, by slaves hired out, a common meaning of *apophora*), that that class comprises slaves—perhaps on the Aristotelian model, providing necessities in return for protection (cf. 1252ᵃ30–4). Yet in ordinary practical terms Aristotle has a point: it is dangerous to concentrate all political and military power in one group, and all economic activity in another.

'But no decision . . . these things' (i.e. communal families and property) repeats the complaint of **10**, about the obscurity of Plato's intentions. But the 'related questions' are important; and they are related because the familial and economic arrangements affect moral character, and moral character will determine the kind of constitution, education, and laws that are required. Conversely, since the members of the Third Class are citizens, *politai*, Aristotle may assume that there will be some *politeia*, constitution, conferring specified citizen-rights, notably to deliberative and judicial office (see III i *fin.*); and that this will in turn call for a certain type of education and laws (1282ᵇ10–11, 1289ᵃ10–25, 1337ᵃ11–18). That is the highly specific way Aristotle's mind would naturally work; but it is not Plato's way in the *Republic*, who is operating on the assumption (scorned by Aristotle: see comment on 1252ᵃ1–16) that the Forms can dictate correct moral and political decisions. Such hints as can be gleaned from the text suggest that therefore the Guardians themselves exercise a total control over all administrative, deliberative, and judicial decisions, and that is the only 'constitution' Plato intends (421a, 425c–e); for if the Guardians rule as they should in the light of the Forms, what need of conventional constitutional machinery? As for education, it would certainly exist for vocational purposes (456d), but beyond that there would apparently be little or none (as Aristotle complains), except presumably moral education based on simple injunctions ('do not steal', etc.), and an insistence on acquiescence in the Guardians' rule. Some laws there would have to be (425e, 427a), but surely not laws framed by anyone but Guardians. All this has implications for the 'quality' of the members of the Third Class; for that quality affects 'the association of the Guardians', i.e. among them, as a distinct group, because if the Third Class were rebellious (cf. 'full of their own ideas'), that association could hardly be maintained, at least in the form Plato intends; cf. 465b. (Or does Aristotle mean '*their* association *with* the Guardians', as their rulers? Cf. 1254ᵃ24–6.)

12 (1264ᵃ40–ᵇ6)   As Aristotle must know, the Guardians are not to live in households; so his objections hardly go home—except on his own assumption that human beings simply do live in households. In the third sentence, he faults Plato's observation (451d); for animals do not manage households, human beings do; so Plato is not comparing like with like, and cannot argue that female human beings are free to follow the same occupations as men, on the grounds that bitches can do the same work as male dogs, and just as efficiently.

At 1256ᵇ7–20 Aristotle draws attention to extensive parallels between the naturalness of certain patterns of animal behaviour and the naturalness of certain patterns of human behaviour. How far does our present paragraph imply that normative inferences from animal behaviour to human behaviour are legitimate, and under what conditions? He might have argued (not implausibly) that just as female animals tend their 'households' (nests etc.), so (contrary to Plato) ought human females.

13 (1264ᵇ6–15) In practice, 'the same people rule permanently' normally entails that the same *set* of people rule permanently, and that within the set different individuals rule at different times and for different periods determined in some principled manner (1261ª37–ᵇ6, 1277ᵇ7–16, 1287ª8–23, 1329ª2–17, 1332ᵇ12–32, but cf. 1273ᵇ8–17). The Guardians proper are no exception: each alternates periods of rule and periods of study (520de, 540b), and even during the former might not be on duty every day. But in ordinary life rulers temporarily not ruling are ruled. Can one say that of those Philosopher-Guardians who are (so to speak) on study-leave? Presumably disobedience is ruled out; or could two Guardians disagree on a practical issue, in spite of their equal supreme wisdom? The Guardians who are genuinely ruled are the Auxiliary Guardians, i.e. the soldiers and administrators of Callipolis (414b, d), who in that respect are in exactly the same position as the Third Class: both are ruled by the same permanent rulers.

That is the point that Aristotle acutely fastens on. Both those without standing (presumably the Third Class) and the spirited and warlike (presumably the Auxiliaries) will resent their subjection (1281ª28–32, ᵇ28–30, 1330ª25–8) and cause faction (*stasis*), either one or the other alone or jointly (for an exhaustive analysis of the causes of faction, see V and VI *passim*). If jointly, we should have in the state what in the soul is the alliance of the middle part (spirit) with the lowest (appetite), contrary to the natural alliance of spirit with the highest part (reason: 441a). The possibility of revolt *within* the Guardian class is particularly damaging. However, Aristotle assumes, as Plato does not, that the inhabitants of Callipolis will have ordinary motivations, which have not been, because they cannot be, eliminated by education designed to produce civic harmony: i.e. agreement about who should rule and be ruled, in a Platonic state; for that education has to work against the grain of human nature. He appraises Callipolis as if it were a real state with ordinary people; and that is both the strength and the weakness of his approach.

The rest of the paragraph, on the myth of the metals (415a–c), is nicely ironic; for the myth is designed to legitimize the changeless power-structure of Callipolis, which has obviously been designed antecedently and independently, not as an 'unavoidable' entailment of it.

14 (1264^{b}15–25) The happiness of the Guardians is partly psychic and partly practical: (*a*) the harmonious integration ('justice') of the three 'parts' of the soul (reason, spirit, appetite), under the control of the highest, reason, and culminating in knowledge of the Forms; (*b*) the instantiation of that knowledge in the state as a whole. The happiness of the state resides in the corresponding harmonious integration of its three parts—Guardians, Auxiliaries, Third Class—under the control of the highest virtue, the wisdom of the Guardians, to which the courage of the Auxiliaries and the restraint of the Third Class are subordinate. (See books IV–VII in general, but esp. 419a–421c, 443c–444e, 465d–466d, 519e–521b, 580bc.)

This highly compendious summary conceals a host of problems both theoretical and practical, notably:

(i) Does 'happiness of the state as a whole' imply that the state is a sort of super-individual with interests conducing to a happiness distinct from that of the individuals who comprise it? And if so, are the individuals to sacrifice their interests/happiness to the state's? Or in subserving the state's, do they thereby also subserve their own?

(ii) Do the practical duties of the Guardians, who find supreme pleasure in intellectual activity, constitute a diminution of their happiness? For they are under a compulsion to undertake those duties (421bc, 520a–e, 540b).

If Aristotle has any inkling of all this, it is hard to discern in this paragraph. What then is its focus? Normally, when Aristotle makes a criticism, he gives a reason (commonly heralded by *gar*, 'for'). Here he gives none: that no part of Callipolis is happy is simply asserted, as though it were obvious. He is presumably relying in part on **5** and **6**: the Guardians' lack of private property not only robs them of substantial pleasures but prevents their practising two important virtues. Now happiness is activity in accordance with the virtues (see *EN* I vii; cf. 1323^{b}21–3, 1328^{a}37–8, 1329^{a}22–3); so the Guardians cannot be happy, or not completely so.

But Aristotle is probably thinking in particular of *Rep.* 419a–421c, where Socrates faces the objection that the Guardians are not happy, because they lack private material goods to give them pleasure. He hints (420b) that on the contrary they may prove 'most happy' (this presumably refers to (*a*) and (*b*) above); but his immediate answer is that it would be wrong to concentrate on the happiness of only one part of the state, and that the Guardians need to do without private property in order to carry out efficiently, without distraction, the task that belongs to them peculiarly, that of ruling; for that is decisive for the happiness of the whole state (421a–c). It would be easy to construe this a demand for some non-happiness (i.e. lack of pleasure) in one part of the state for the sake of happiness in other parts. Aristotle may be thinking only of that; more probably, whereas Plato presents the lack of private property only as a necessary (but not sufficient) condition of good guardianship, Aristotle presents it as a vitiating of the practice of (some) moral virtue, and hence as a preventative of happiness. In that case, he may have felt no need to tackle head on Plato's more sophisticated account, (*a*) and (*b*), of the happiness of the Guardians. On the difficulties in that account, see Annas (1981) 260–71, Mahoney (1992).

As for manual workers, Aristotle is not arguing that a lack of happiness among the Guardians would prevent the workers also from being happy; he simply casts around for other candidates for happiness, and eliminates them. But why? Workers have little or no share in virtue, and therefore in happiness (1260ᵃ36–ᵇ7, 1328ᵃ38–40, ᵇ33–1329ᵃ2, 1329ᵃ17–26, 1331ᵇ40–1), and Aristotle seems to think (**10, 11**) that the Third Class is a sort of slave class, and slaves are if anything in an even worse case (I xiii, esp. comment on 1260ᵃ36–ᵇ7; cf. 1280ᵃ31–4).

The mathematical illustration is another fallacy that may mislead practical calculation (cf. 1261ᵇ16–32). 3 + 5, both odd numbers, add up to 8, which is even; but unhappy parts of a state do not add up to a happy whole.

II vi

CRITICISM OF PLATO'S SECOND-BEST 'IDEAL' STATE IN THE LAWS

Introduction   A brief description of Magnesia, the state of the *Laws*, will set the scene for this chapter; a longer summary is in Saunders (1970) 26–33; id. (1992) provides a short critical survey, Stalley (1983) a full one; Morrow (1960*a*), a comprehensive historical and philosophical analysis, is fundamental. The classic discussion of this chapter is by Morrow (1960*b*).

Without actually mentioning the *Republic*, Plato makes clear that Magnesia is an ideal second-best to Callipolis (739a ff.), in that each citizen (there are 5040) has private property (land, movables, money, slaves) and a private family. The economic basis of the state is agricultural, not commercial. Manual work, handicrafts, and trade are in the hands of non-citizens, i.e. slaves and resident aliens (e.g. 842d–850d, 919c–920c). The hypothesis of incorruptible supreme rulers, the Guardians of the *Republic*, is abandoned, or at any rate not employed (874e–875d); for the basis of the governing of Magnesia is not metaphysical insight but a code of good laws, administered under a political constitution midway between monarchy and democracy (756e ff.). However, certain of the citizens qualified by age, intellect, and experience constitute the Nocturnal Council, the 'anchor' of the state, and are required to undertake advanced study (951d ff., 961a ff.). Much attention is given to an elaborately prescriptive system of education (book VII), and to religious belief (X). In sum, the fundamental differences from Callipolis centre on property and philosophy, and therefore governance.

1 (1264ᵇ26–1265ᵃ1)   'Later': in the last years of Plato's life (d. 347). 'Constitution', twice: in the broad sense of 'socio-political structure' not specifically 'system of offices'; contrast 2 *init*. 'Office' and 'arms': on a strict application of the principle of specialization of function, the Third Class would have neither; 1264ᵃ18–22 perhaps implies no arms, cf. 374cd; yet how plausible is it to see the *Guardians*—even the Auxiliaries—as jurymen and petty officials (see 425cd and 433e)? Some lower-echelon administrative structure within the Third Class is not to be ruled out. 'Extraneous matter', 'education of the Guardians': staggering indifference (cf. comment on 1260ᵇ3b–1261ᵃ9) to huge areas of the *Republic*: the definitional, psychological, historical, and social preliminaries of the early books, the analysis of imperfect societies in VIII and IX, and the literary criticism and eschatological myth in X. 'Extraneous' is harsh; but Aristotle is concerned only with what Plato wants to *do* in (a–c), which Aristotle thinks impossible; he is not interested in its theoretical underpinning.

2 (1265ᵃI–10) starts with an exaggeration which permits a glum joke: the actual proportion is 1/3 or less (England (1921) i. 1). Aristotle distinguishes laws and constitution confusingly: for there are (i) laws *prescribing* a constitution, (ii) the kind of laws apparently meant here, those *administered under* a constitution, which is a 'system of offices' (1289ᵃ15–16 cf. *Laws* 735a, 751a, 768e4; comment on 1273ᵇ27–34; Mulgan (1970) 521 n. 7). To charge that Plato said 'little' about the constitution in that sense is brusque: about half of book VI, with important supplements elsewhere. By 'more acceptable' (*koinotera*, 'more common or accessible') he means in effect 'middling', 'practicable', or 'easier for ordinary men to live under' (cf. 1288ᵇ38, 1295ᵃ25–31); and he implies that Magnesia turned out to be in effect an oligarchy, like Callipolis; see discussion of **9–12**. He then reverts to the wider sense of 'constitution', by listing certain social and economic practices which he alleges are the 'same' in the two states. These parallels are extremely broad-brush, and conceal vital and obvious differences, of which he could hardly have been unaware (notably as regards education). Nevertheless, his judgement is sound. He realizes that Magnesia is essentially the same Platonic state as Callipolis, incorporating the same principle of rule by philosophers with unquestioning obedience by others, but expressed in practical terms that entail all sorts of modifications and compromises, in moral, social, and economic matters; and that the various individual institutions of the *Laws* point in the same direction as those of the *Republic* (cf. Saunders (1992)). That is why the Nocturnal Council has to embark on what sound like the preliminaries to the theory of Forms (963a ff.). By 'same' Aristotle means 'identical in ultimate tendency, however different in practice'.

In respect of the common meals, the difference is almost certainly not as Aristotle states it: in Callipolis women Guardians seem to dine communally with men (458c); in Magnesia citizen women dine communally apart from them (780a ff., 806e); probably Plato thought this a slight but prudent modification.

On arms-bearers, see **9**(a) and *Rep.* 423a.

3 (1265ᵃ10–18) The chief speaker in most of Plato's dialogues is Socrates; in the *Laws* it is an 'Athenian Stranger'. Aristotle may only be committing a minor blunder (so too in 2); or he may think that the Stranger is Socrates in disguise, rather than Plato; or, just conceivably, Socrates was indeed the leading interlocutor in early drafts (cf. Morrow (1960*b*) 161–2). One is even more startled to read 'extravagance, brilliance, originality, and a spirit of enquiry', not the first words one would reach for to describe the *Laws*, at any rate in the form in which we have it. I suspect ironic jesting, a comic contrast between the liveliness of the Socratic dialogues of Plato's early and middle period, and the staidness of his last and most lengthy work. But the *Laws* does have many bold ideas and proposals (e.g. about women), and that may be enough to prompt Aristotle to assimilate it to Plato's other work, with respect to content rather than form.

Demographic calculations for the ancient world are notoriously tricky; for Magnesia, the best estimates are by Morrow (1960*a*) 129 n. 105 and (1960*b*) 156–7: a maximum population of 80,000 (1960*a*) or 60,000 (1960*b*), that is about 1/4 or 1/5 of the estimated population of Attica in the fourth century, 300,000, of whom roughly 30,000 were adult male citizens (Hansen (1991) 90–4). At 1270ᵃ29–30 Aristotle claims the Spartan territory can support 1500 cavalry and 30,000 hoplites, all apparently non-productive; Plato proposes only 5,040 heads of household (or 10,080 if each estate is to support two families: see **8**). Even so, Magnesia will obviously be a big place (most Greek states had less than 1000 adult male citizens, Hansen (1991) 55), and Aristotle obviously thinks it grandiose; his specific objection is the sheer size of the territory required for the food-supply; but why, provided the territory is available and manageable, is that an objection sufficient to arouse an 'emotion' which has 'upset [his] judgement' (Morrow 1960*b* 157)? The unstated reasons are surely in 1326ᵇ2–25. A state can become so big that it is no longer a state: *inter alia*, people cannot know each other well enough to make good appointments to office (cf. *EN* 1171ᵃ8–20, on the difficulty of forming genuine friendships with numerous people); the territory cannot easily be surveyed, and communication and therefore the running of a constitution become difficult. Aristotle's objections are thus probably as much social and political as strictly economic. Such difficulties seem not to have struck Plato; at any rate he expected the Magnesians to know each other well, e.g. 751de, 771de; cf. *Rep.* 423bc.

Aristotle speaks of 'idleness', a strong word. What he has in mind is the householder without routine tasks, at leisure to pursue affairs of state, etc. (cf. 1278ᵃ6–13, 1328ᵇ33–1329ᵃ2). It is however by no means clear that the poorer Magnesians would be thus privileged: see Morrow (1960*b*) 152–3 on the somewhat inconsistent implications of 806d ff. and 842e ff. On ideals and possibilities, see introduction to II i and comment on 1260ᵇ27–36.

4 (1265ᵃ18–26) 'It is stated' presumably refers to some or all of *Laws* 704a–708d, 735a–741e (esp. 737c), 745b–e, 747de, 847e–849a; cf. 763ab.

The burden of the paragraph is that whether a state has active relations with other states ('life of a state', *bios politikos*, i.e. life as between states, cf. 1327ᵇ5), or keeps itself to itself, it will need an army. But in the former case, it will have to consider neighbouring territories too, from a military angle; in the latter, apparently not, presumably because defence is sufficient. Whether or not that is sound military strategy, Aristotle (in 'reject') may well have divined Plato's policy accurately, who concentrates on defensive war (760e–761a, 806a–c, 828e–831b); only at 737d, and 813e–814c (men only?), does he seem to envisage limited fighting abroad. Magnesia certainly will not have an active political foreign policy, or at any rate not an aggrandizing one; but she will have certain carefully controlled foreign contacts (952d ff.), and is not quite a 'closed' society, in that she is open to such new ideas from abroad as the Nocturnal Council judges salutary.

The paragraph indicates that both individual and state have a choice of two lives: solitary, and other-related. There is more in this than meets the eye. Aristotle holds that happiness lies in *activity* in accordance with virtue; and obviously both other-related lives involve activity: the members of a state interact, and states interact with other states. But if the state is self-sufficient for happiness, what is the status of its foreign relations? Certainly aggrandizing warfare must be ruled out (1324ᵇ22 ff.); but even other relations ought ideally not to exist; for the state's business is the good life and happiness of its own members (1324ᵇ41–1325ᵃ15). Foreign relations are only a means to the furtherance of those ends, a means adopted for purely prudential reasons if circumstances dictate (cf. 1333ᵃ30–ᵇ4, *Rhet.* 1359ᵇ33–1360ᵃ5). In that case, the ideal is the solitary life; but that is not an inactive one, since the internal parts of the state interact (1325ᵇ23–7).

The choice for the individual is set up in quite different terms: the active life of the statesman, and the life of private contemplation (1324ᵃ23 ff.; the main discussions are *EN* 1095ᵇ22–1096ᵃ5, X vii, viii). The latter is preferred; and here again Aristotle has to insist that the solitary life is not inactive. For contemplation and thought which are 'their own end and for the sake of themselves' are *more* active than thought directed to external results (1325ᵇ14–23). (Apparently if thought is 'for the sake of itself', it functions both as agent and as aim: it acts for the sake of an *end*.)

Presumably the other-related life apparently rejected for the individual in this paragraph is involvement in his state's foreign relations, and is rejected merely as an entailment of the state's having forsworn them, rather than because he has adopted the life contemplative. The latter seems intrusive here, unless the point is that the absence of foreign relations makes the contemplative life more possible. At all events, Aristotle prefers the solitary life both for state and for individual: for they are both active lives with higher ends than their alternatives. So when he claims that the 'same' life is best both for individuals and state, and means 'active' in the non-contemplative sense (1325ᵇ15–16, 30–2), it is awkward that the preferred life for the state, i.e. of interacting parts, is the dispreferred life for the contemplative individual.

5 (1265ᵃ28–38) At *Laws* 737cd Plato prescribed that Magnesia's land should be sufficient to support the population 'as being moderate people', i.e. in a moderate life-style—and no more land than that is needed on top.

Aristotle's objection seems to be that Plato employs 'moderation', *sōphrosunē*, a particular virtue, as though the exercise of that one virtue constituted the 'good life', which is a far wider term, embracing the exercise of several other virtues besides, notably liberality (cf. 1263ᵇ7–14: private property facilitates this and *sōphrosunē*, there translated 'restraint'). Both are needed for a suitable life-style, for each prevents the other from running to an excess (cf. 1326ᵇ30–9). Since liberality requires more property than moderation does, the amount of property allowed in Magnesia ought to be revised upwards; cf. 1326ᵇ30–2. To broaden the perspectives somewhat: Aristotle would claim that Plato's repentance in the matter of property does not go far enough; for although he now allows private property in the *Laws*, and indeed speaks of the 'good life' (828d–829a), he sets it at a level which suppresses part of that life, namely liberality. This is no accident. Plato devotes much space to the virtues in general; but liberality is nowhere mentioned as part of Magnesia's life, doubtless for much the same reasons as account for its apparent absence from Callipolis (see comment on 1263ᵇ7–14). Cf. Morrow (1960b) 154–5.

6 (1265ᵃ38–ᵇ17)   All the 5,040 allotments of land in Magnesia are roughly equivalent in value, and each is inalienable from the holder's family; no increase or diminution in number or size/value is allowed. Hence only one son may inherit; others must either be adopted by other families in which there are no sons, or leave the country for a colony; in case of a shortage, recruits must be sought from abroad (740a–741e, 745cd; cf. 784ab, 855a ff., 930cd).

In criticizing Plato for failing to bring the supply of potential inheritors into balance with the number of estates to be inherited, by regulating births rather than by rationing properties, Aristotle seems (i) to be unaware that Plato discusses the point at length, and mentions measures to increase and decrease births (740a–3); (ii) not to realize, or to ignore, the provision about colonies (740e): he assumes *all* non-inheritors will remain in Magnesia permanently, as an impoverished underclass, and so a source of faction and crime (but cf. 1273ᵇ18–21). Was the passage not available to him, or did he simply miss it, or has he carelessly forgotten it—or is he just being perverse?

I believe he has read the passage carefully, and has noticed (i) that Plato writes it in such a way as to imply that measures of control would be resorted to only *after* an imbalance has occurred (as Schütrumpf has pointed out in a good discussion, ii. 227–9), and (ii) that, in the time before the balance is restored, surplus non-adopted males *will* have to live 'in want' (loosely attached to their brother's estate?), since dispatch to a colony (cf. 1273ᵇ18–21) is a very last resort. Aristotle, presumably on the assumption that a state should be self-sufficient for the good life, which includes material provision, attacks on both fronts; for it is a diminution of the good life if most male children bar one have to go without land or, in the end, emigrate. Measures of birth-control are necessary, but they should be taken in advance of the problems (cf. 1266ᵇ8–14, 1270ᵃ39–ᵇ6): prevention is better than cure (cf. 1302ᵇ19–21). It is revealing that whereas Plato mentions the childlessness of some couples merely as one cause of the problem (740cd), Aristotle apparently wishes to incorporate calculations on this point (and on the survival rate of children) in 'fixing' the number of births to be allowed. On Pheidon, cf. comment on 1274ᵇ2–5.

Both Plato and Aristotle are aware that measures to increase or limit births are likely to be inexactly successful. Plato prefers to wait and see (contrast *Rep.* 460a), and then take ruthless measures to ensure precisely 5,040 holders for 5,040 estates. Aristotle, who shows no sign of insisting on an unvarying number of lots, can tolerate the inexactness more easily. Both, too, are hazy about the measures to be adopted. Plato, typically, relies heavily on social pressure. Aristotle apparently requires abortion under certain conditions, but forbids exposure, except of deformed children (1335ᵇ19–26). 'Later': presumably *inter alia* VII v, x, xvi. For Spartan practice, see 1270ª34–ᵇ6. On population policy in the two philosophers, see *Arethusa* (1975).

7 (1265ᵇ18–21) A curiously inconclusive fragment on an important topic (see 1332ᵇ12 ff.). The reference is to book V of the *Laws*, 734e–735a (cf. *Pol.* 308d ff.); but Aristotle must have been aware of at least some of the many passages whose upshot is that rulers should differ from the ruled in point of superior ability, education, and virtue (e.g. 689e–690e, 694ab, 701a–c, 751cd, 756e–758a, 818a, 951d ff., 961a ff.). I suggest that in **7**, embedded as it is in a discussion of property, Aristotle meant to ask what relation there is in Magnesia between property and political power; he had asked the same question about Callipolis (1264ª11–27). Book V of the *Laws*, apart from one glancing remark at 744c, contains no answer to that question; and as **6** and **8** too concern material in that book, he has probably not read beyond it when writing **7**. In **9**, however, he turns to book VI, and in **10** and **11** he discusses the answer he finds there. Cf. Morrow (1960*b*) 157–8.

8 (1265ᵇ21–6) 'Five times', says Aristotle (so also at 1266ᵇ5–8); 'four times', says Plato (744e). They are both right. There are 4 property-classes in the *Laws*: the *4th* class possesses a lot of land of value x, plus at least 1x in movable property and up to 2x; *3rd*: up to 1x on top of that; *2nd*: up to 2x on top; *1st*: up to 3x on top. Plato omits the 1x in his calculation of the multiple, as a basic invariable; Aristotle includes it. These rankings will be assumed in **10**, on filling offices; but the property-classes have several other uses besides that. Cf. Morrow (1960*a*) 131–8.

The answer to Aristotle's query about land (cf. 1267ᵇ9–13) is that Plato thinks of private property as a concession to human frailty (739e–740a). To allow differentials in land-holding would be to allow different opportunities for wealth-creation, and an unacceptably wide gulf between rich and poor. Some differences in movable wealth are acceptable, but only on the basis of the same opportunities for acquiring it. The system neatly and judiciously blends the principles of equality and inequality: see 744b ff., 745cd, and comment on **10** for the constitutional implications. Aristotle himself limits neither land nor other property: he relies on common use, 1329ᵇ36 ff.; but as the state's territory must not be too extensive (see comment on **3**), there is some implicit limit on the number and size of large estates.

Each Magnesian lot has two homes, one near the centre of the state and the other near the boundary (745e); presumably the latter is intended for the son who is in time to inherit the estate as a whole (775e–776b); and the implication seems to be that he will work and manage it independently of his father (who would of course remain the owner). If that is right, Aristotle's objection falls; this is perhaps another indication that he has not yet read book VI, where the second passage above occurs. Cf. 1330ᵃ14 ff., for Aristotle's own division of estates.

9 (1265ᵇ26–1266ᵃ5) A rich but confusing paragraph. The central issues are these:

(*a*) *Plato's unnoticed aristocracy.* Aristotle's description of Magnesia's constitution as midway between oligarchy and democracy is not Plato's own, who says 'monarchy' instead of 'oligarchy' (756e); but it is in substance correct as far as it goes (see esp. 756e–758a, and cf. **10** and **11**). However, his attempt to pigeonhole it in terms of the approximations to the ideal which are outlined in IV i (see the *schema* in the comment on II i) goes sadly but revealingly astray. Hesitantly, he first locates it at level (4): 'the most acceptable' (or 'accessible') constitution for states (cf. **2**). But he knows that *Plato* thinks he is aiming at level (2), the second-best to the ideal (739a ff.). That too is wrong, says Aristotle, in effect because the second-best is an aristocracy (the best itself being monarchy: 1279ᵃ32–7, III xiv–xviii, IV ii). He then, very oddly, alleges that Magnesia is a mixture of democracy and *tyranny* (see (*c*) below). Finally, at the start of **10**, he settles for analysing it as a 'polity', i.e. a mixture of oligarchy and democracy; that is, he in effect places it at level (3), a constitution constructed 'on an assumption'.

Plato's first-best is direct rule by Guardians, underpinned by communism of property. His second-best is a constitution and laws, underpinned by private property held within a narrow range, and with a strict maximum (739a ff., cf. 807b; 744e–745a; 875d). Some limited political preponderance is accorded on oligarchic principles, i.e. on the basis of greater wealth (see **10** and **11**, with App.); for industry and thrift are virtues (or so 744c seems to imply). More importantly, the basis on which offices should be filled is precisely *not* wealth, but personal merit, education, and virtue (715b–d, 726a–734e, 757c; cf. e. g. 766ab, 746a, 751d ff., 961a ff.). The (democratic) use of sortition is to be only minimal (757e–758a), since it can take no account of such criteria. The sense in which Magnesia's constitution is midway between *oligarchy* and democracy is much less important than the sense in which it is midway between *monarchy* and democracy—which is exactly how Plato himself defines it at 756e (cf. **10** *init.* and **12**). By this he means something midway between (i) the power, exercised moderately, of a single meritorious and benevolent ruler, (ii) a populace enjoying modest freedom in a spirit of obedience and moderation: see the lengthy historical description of the two at 689e–702a. He does not mean something midway between a good principle (monarchy) and a bad (democracy), but between two good ones, moderate authoritarianism and moderate freedom. Magnesia is in intention 'midway' in being a kind of aristocracy, with controlled infusions of the freedom of democracy. Cf. Morrow (1960b) 158–9.

Why therefore does Aristotle see in Magnesia only a 'polity', i.e. a mixture of oligarchy and democracy operating in the common interest? (Cf. 1297ᵃ37–ᵇ4, and IV ix, which however admits that some polities are aristocratic: 1294ᵇ10–13, cf. 1290ᵃ16–17, 1295ᵃ31–4.) We may grant him that Magnesia is not an aristocracy of the pure kind, in which a small (or even a large) number of excellent persons rule permanently (1279ᵃ34–5, 1288ᵃ9–12, 32–ᵇ2). But he himself allows for a modified form of aristocracy, in which a certain number of good but not excellent persons combine aristocratic rule in what is effectively a mixed constitution, which pays attention to oligarchic and/or democratic considerations also (1293ᵇ7–21, 34–42, 1308ᵇ31–1309ᵃ9). On the face of it, Magnesia satisfies that description rather neatly. But it does not. Aristotle assumes that even in modified aristocracy the aristocrats will be a more or less constant body of people with wealth, breeding, and education, set off against the rest, who will be *less* good. Plato is more ambitious. In Magnesia, everyone receives the same education, which does not depend on wealth; everyone, even the less wealthy, aims at the highest moral virtues, in effect aristocratic values; and that is why Plato avoids using the term 'aristocracy' of Magnesia: for it implies that lesser moral achievements by some are acceptable. They will of course occur in practice, but they are not part of the aspiration. Aristotle sees that Magnesia does not fit his own model for aristocracy, and reaches for the nearest and easiest description: a mixture of oligarchy and democracy, in which each side acts in its own interests. That is not Plato's purpose at all. Cf. Morrow (1960a), 230–1, 528–30. On 'polity', see Johnson (1988).

Heavy-armed troops, hoplites, characteristically the citizens in a 'polity': cf. 1279ᵃ37–ᵇ4, 1297ᵇ1–2, 12–14, 22–5, and **2** *fin*. Aristotle himself thinks of this as an oligarchic property-qualification for citizenship (1321ᵃ12–14); but if the start of this paragraph means to imply that that requirement applies in Magnesia, he is simply wrong. For in Magnesia even the poorest lot-holder, who would be light-armed, is a citizen; see most aptly 753b.

(b) *The mixed constitution.* Having chosen Sparta as an example of a state with an aristocratic bent (cf. 1293ᵇ16–21), Aristotle now develops the notion of mixture; for Sparta (described in II ix) was a celebrated hybrid (1294ᵇ13–36, *Laws* 712de). 'Some say': we know not who.

The theory and practice of the mixed constitution from antiquity to the present day is an extensive and complex subject; as a political ideal, it is one of the two most potent that the Greeks developed (the other being democracy). The term is a comprehensive one: it denotes the very many different ways in which different economic and social groups could share political power; for it was early learnt that unmixed or pure constitutions are socially destructive. It was not a means whereby legislature, executive, and judiciary could operate in creative tension (the so-called separation of powers); nor did it serve to facilitate a 'mixed society', in which competing religious, racial, philosophical, or national ideologies could exist peacefully. On the whole topic see von Fritz (1954). Aristotle's chief discussions: IV viii, ix, xi.

(c) *The consent of the governed*. This important theme emerges by implication. Aristotle assails Plato for wishing to mix what are two non-constitutions (cf. *Laws* 712e and 715b) or the worst of all, namely democracy and tyranny (presumably because two bad ingredients cannot yield a good whole, just as a happy state cannot be produced out of unhappy parts, 1264ᵇ19–22). He then concludes that it is 'therefore' better to mix a 'larger number' of constitutions (than two). But that seems hardly to follow: the natural conclusion is, 'therefore mix two *good* constitutions'. Why do the merits of a mixed constitution increase with the number of constitutions that enter into the mixture? The point is presumably that the more numerous the political and economic interest-groups satisfied by a constitution, by seeing features of their own favoured constitution built into it, and the more the varying criteria employed to fill offices and distribute other goods, the more people will support that constitution, and the more stable it will be (see e.g. 1270ᵇ17–28, 1272ᵃ27–ᵇ1, 1294ᵇ36–40, 1296ᵇ15–16, VI v; cf. also 1273ᵇ35–41, *Laws* 691e ff.). This is in effect to acknowledge the importance of the consent of the governed; it does however fall far short of a theory of how different interests, once in the power-structure, may be reconciled or put in an order of priority.

The argument contains one misrepresentation and one exaggeration. (i) Plato never proposed (see on **9**(*a*)) to mix *tyranny* and democracy (in spite of 709e ff., on the use of a tyrant as a rapid *ad hoc* means of *founding* a state, cf. 735d); (ii) some forms both of democracy and of tyranny have some limited merit (VI iv, 1296ᵇ17 ff., IV x).

10 (1266ᵃ5–14) and **11 (1266ᵃ14–22)**   Aristotle now summarizes his evidence for ascribing oligarchic bias, i.e. in favour of wealth (1294ᵇ10), to Magnesia's constitution. The texts on which he is presumably relying are numerous and complex, and are therefore relegated to the Appendix, with some comment on detail.

Just how strong is his case? (i) In general, all Magnesian citizens are eligible for all offices, and that is democratic; such oligarchic bias as there is, is a modification of that fundamental position. (ii) In particular, there is no restriction on the right to sit as a juryman in the regular tribal courts; on the other hand, the verdicts of these courts are subject to appeal, as they were not in Athens; and the composition of the appeal court is partly oligarchic at one remove, in that every board of officials elects one judge from among their own number, and some of these officials have been appointed to their substantive posts under procedures with an oligarchic bias (on the details of Magnesian courts, see esp. 766d–768c, 956b–d; cf. 855c–856a, on the special court for capital cases). (iii) For some offices, including the most important, are indeed filled under rules according some limited preference to the wealthier citizens, either as voters or as candidates; and the Assembly (see (2) in App.) has similar bias built into its rules of attendance. (iv) Certain cases (e.g. (6) in App.) seem justified by commonsensical utilitarian reasons. (v) Plato has a distinct preference for election over the lot (757e); but that is to ensure that the best people are appointed, not because of an admiration of wealth.

Given Plato's professed hostility to wealth as a criterion for office (see refs. in comments on **9** (*a*)), the high number of cases of oligarchic preference is surprising, and not justified even by the apparent claim at 744c that wealth is an indication of some moral virtue. The matter is hard to judge, but my own impression is that the 'edge' given the wealthy is a modestly pervasive influence, not an overwhelming force. However, the question must remain whether Plato is entirely consistent (or indeed frank). Aristotle does not even consider the inconsistency: he treats the *Laws*' oligarchic preference at face value, as straight class-interest; he is insensitive to Plato's general scepticism about wealth as a qualification for political power.

12 (1266ᵃ22–30) At last, Aristotle brings himself to cite Plato's own description of Magnesia's constitution (756e). He does not say why democracy and monarchy ought not to be compounded. Nor is the reference to a later discussion clear: IV vii–ix, xi–xii have relevant material, but do not address the matter directly. If his point is merely that in practical terms the rule of one excellent man is hard to combine with the rule of the many, that is a fairly mechanical objection, and misses Plato's meaning (see on **9**(*a*)).

He adds the further thought that Plato (for two important offices, the Guardians of the Laws and the Scrutineers) abandons the (democratic) lot as the final stage of election, and substitutes a further round of selection (753b ff., 945e ff.; for details of this and cognate procedures see Morrow (1960*a*) 233–8).

II vii

THE CONSTITUTION OF PHALEAS: THE PROBLEMS OF EGALITARIANISM

Introduction Of Phaleas we know nothing but what Aristotle tells us here. **3** indicates a date considerably later than Solon (archon 594), say mid- or late 5th century. His relationship to the politics of his own state, Chalcedon, is conjectural: see Lana (1950), and Schütrumpf's discussion, ii. 238–40. The sweeping and somewhat naïve simplicity of his proposals, and apparent indifference to matters military and commercial, and to constitutional structures, perhaps suggest he was not a practising 'statesman' (cf. xii *init.*); the apparent lack of theoretical underpinning for his ideas suggests he was not a 'philosopher' (see **1**); but these may be distortions introduced by Aristotle's mode of reporting, and the conclusion that he was a 'private person' is far from certain. Presumably he wrote some treatise, which Aristotle has read.

It is equally difficult to pin an ideological label on Phaleas. Aristotle gives only three pieces of hard information, namely that Phaleas advocated: (i) equality of (landed) property, to be achieved by certain specified means; (ii) equality of education; (iii) that all skilled workers should be public slaves, and hence not part of the citizen-body. The first two sound, to a modern ear, democratic; yet Greek democratic sentiment, though egalitarian in political affairs (witness the use of the lot), was not so in *these* matters (cf. VI ii, the finest ancient account we have of Greek democratic tenets). Revolutionary demands for redistribution of land were certainly not unknown (Rhodes (1981) 479); in an existing state, Phaleas would be a gradualist advocate of that policy (**1**; cf. Pheidon of Corinth, 1265^{b}12). (iii) is decidedly oligarchical, for it excludes many of the poor from office (cf. 1277^{b}1–3); yet few oligarchs—or indeed anyone, Greek society being competitively acquisitive (cf. **4**)—would have been willing to accept (i). Nor do modern terms help: 'socialist' is misleading because it implies communal, centrally directed economic (and other) activity and certain provisions for welfare, without a class of politically disadvantaged artisans (see on **9**); and 'communist', because Phaleas did not envisage *common* ownership of property; cf. Schütrumpf ii. 240–1. Nor did he have any large notions such as 'all men are created equal': his egalitarianism has the strictly limited purpose of preventing civil strife.

1 (1266^{a}31–^{b}8) 'Both of these': the constitutions of Callipolis and Magnesia. 'No other person': apart from Plato. Nevertheless, so far from coming 'closer to established constitutions', Phaleas is in some ways more extreme even than Plato; for even Plato did not require all artisans to be slaves, either in the *Republic* or in the *Laws*. Aristotle apparently thinks Phaleas' proposals, though radical, are at any rate within the bounds of practical politics, and less extreme than Plato's common possession of wives, etc.

The distinction between the ease of innovation at the foundation of a state (i.e. colony) and the difficulty of it later is discussed at length by Plato also, at *Laws* 708a–e and 736c–737c. Evidently at the foundation of a colony equal estates of land were indeed commonly allocated, as in Magnesia (Graham (1964) 59); but nothing was done to equalize movable possessions (cf. *Laws* 744b), which according to Aristotle (**8**) Phaleas' proposal also did not touch. In that case, its novelty lies not in the estates' initial equality but in their *enduring* equality and therefore their exclusion from dowries—unlike in existing states, where, under Phaleas' policy, by being included in dowries they are to be the instrument of their own equalization. Plato's policy on marriage and dowries was calculated merely to prevent existing differences in wealth from becoming wider: see *Laws* 742c, 772e–773e, 774c. On the limits to movable property in the *Laws*, see 1265^{b}21–3. But why does Aristotle mention this at all, if movable property is not affected by Phaleas' proposals (**8**)?

2 (1266^{b}8–14) The argument about children is similar to that of 1265^{a}38–^{b}17: see comment. It depends on the assumptions (i) that the state is of a fixed extent that cannot be increased so as to allow the creation of more lots of land of the same size as the existing ones; (ii) that it is impermissible to reduce all lots to some smaller size, while preserving their equality; (iii) surplus children cannot be removed to a colony. Granted all these, if the number of children greatly exceeded the available lots, the law providing for equality of landed property would probably have to be abrogated—but Aristotle is chary of changing laws: see 1268^b22–1269^a28 and comment there. The final sentence is a blow at the practicality of introducing equality in an existing society; cf. *Laws* 736c ff.

3 (1266^b14–24) Aristotle concedes that experience does something to support Phaleas' case; for the extensive legal detail see Asheri (1963). However, it seems that none of the laws mentioned would have kept or rendered landed property equal, only less sharply unequal ('levelness'). 'Association which is the state': see on 1252^a1–7; extreme disparities in the benefits to the association's members cause trouble: Schütrumpf well refers to 1295^b13–28. As to Leucas, the point is presumably that the splitting up of landed estates among a larger number of holders meant that some holders who were formerly able to meet the property-qualification for office could no longer do so; the qualification had therefore to be lowered, which had the effect of enabling to qualify for office not only this larger number but many others too, whose possessions had been small to start with.

4 (1266^b24–1267^a2) It is not until **8** that Aristotle informs us that Phaleas' proposals apply to landed property only; meanwhile he speaks in general terms, as if to include movable property too. His remark that evening out desires is preferable to evening out possessions does not imply that he thinks the latter desirable at all, at least if that means their strict equality: he merely wishes to see possessions kept within a certain moderate range, because the possessors have only moderate desires (IV xi; cf. 1323^a38 ff., *Laws* 736e, 742e). He does not make the point, but he may also think that strict equality of property would militate against liberality, just as Plato's communism did, at least in so far as that virtue depends on some *inequality* of property (see comment on 1263^b7–14).

Aristotle complains (we can only take his word for it) that Phaleas (i) did not specify that the amount of the equal property should be neither too little nor excessive, so as to yield a reasonable standard of living (cf. **5**); (ii) did not specify the content and purpose of the 'one and the same' education to be given (Aristotle's own account is in book VIII); and (iii) wrongly regarded inequality of property as the only cause of civil strife (cf. **1, 5, 7**).

(i) is similar to 1265^a28–38, on Magnesia: see comment there. (ii) Since the acquisitive persons Aristotle describes are hardly compatible with equality of property, Phaleas presumably did not intend the kind of moral education that would produce *them*. Indeed, he may not have meant moral education at all. He may have meant an education designed merely to produce the same practical skills in the use of the same amount of property: reading, writing, household-management, horsemanship, hunting, etc. He may have thought that acquisitiveness would in time simply disappear, once equality of property had robbed it of its point. (iii) Aristotle seems to think that a system of distinctions, and a class of 'sophisticated' people, would exist in Phaleas' state and be potential sources of discord.

Phaleas could plausibly deny it. As Aristotle himself implies here (cf. refs. in Schütrumpf ii. 249), a major means to distinction is wealth; so if everyone's wealth is the same, how can anyone be distinguished? If that is right, Phaleas' egalitarianism would have considerable social consequences. For Aristotle's own discussion of equality, see V i ff.; on honour, *EN* 1095ᵇ22 ff. 'The sophisticated': persons of wealth *and culture*; perhaps equality of education would eliminate refinement in artistic taste and achievement. The quotation is Hom. *Il.* IX 319.

5 (1267ᵃ2–17)   By an easy linkage (cf. 1265ᵇ12), and apparently following Phaleas, Aristotle turns from civil disturbance to crime; both arise from wanting more. His central claim rests on the tacit assumption that Phaleas' equality of property will guarantee a minimally adequate standard of living. That will indeed make less likely petty crime arising from poverty in necessities; but it cannot achieve more than this, since most serious crimes are committed by people who desire property in excess of their needs (cf. the greedy traders and others in I ix). Phaleas could reasonably reply that the continuous enforcement of equality of property, and the education he envisages (see **4**), will have trained the inhabitants of his state not to *want* more. But Aristotle, as always, talks of men as they are, not of men as they might become under the schemes of those whom he criticizes. At any rate, we may perhaps infer from his discussion that the standard of living in Phaleas' state would be modest.

None too clearly, Aristotle distinguishes two types of person who desire more than necessities: (i) those whose purpose is pleasure, by which they allay the pain they feel in desiring it (i.e. in *lacking* it); (ii) those who seek pleasure *without* that pain: excess resources allow them indulgence such as (they think) permits them not even to feel an antecedent desire/pain. For (i) Aristotle prescribes, merely and bleakly, restraint. For (ii) his remedy is more interesting, but very allusive: he tells them to do philosophy. For it is the pleasures of knowledge that have no antecedent pain (*EN* 1173ᵇ13 ff., *EE* 1225ᵇ30–1). (Is this plausible? Why are the pleasures of knowledge not preceded by the pain of ignorance, of wanting to know but not knowing?) At any rate, contemplation needs few material resources (*EN* 1177ᵃ28–ᵇ1, 1178ᵇ33–1179ᵃ9), whereas 'the other desires stand in need of people' (i.e. their company, co-operation, and the goods they produce). The advice is comically high-falutin', given the kind of person those in category (ii) presumably are.

6 (1267ᵃ17–37)   The counterpart of 1265ᵃ18, on the foreign and military relations of Magnesia. 'Chiefly' perhaps implies some minimal attention to non-military foreign affairs; and Phaleas may have expected that social and political cohesion achieved by equality of property would render his state militarily formidable (cf. 1272ᵇ7–16 ff.; further refs. in Schütrumpf ii. 252). Yet Aristotle alleges that he did not consider military strength at all, and that he did not specify a level of wealth high enough for that purpose but low enough to make the enemy think conquest not worth the candle. Clearly the calculation of the right level would be nice; for the first purpose would have to take priority, and require a level of property that might militate against the second. The anecdote about Atarneus apparently dates from the mid-4th century.

We may also wonder how in an egalitarian society it is possible to achieve differentiation in military roles. For in ancient Greece they were determined by individual wealth: heavy-armed troops needed longer pockets than light-armed. So the differentiations in movable property we can probably infer from **8** must be at least large enough to accommodate this requirement—unless indeed everyone is to be wealthy enough to be heavy-armed, at need.

7 (1267ᵃ37–ᵇ9) Broadly similar to **4**, and notably in the attention paid to the feeling of 'the sophisticated', that they do not deserve 'equality' (i.e. that they deserve *more* than equality, cf. 1301ᵃ32–3). Again Aristotle pins his faith on education as a cure for excessive desires, rather than on economic measures; but he has a decidedly patrician attitude to the lower reaches of society. In **5**, the cure in the case of those who have more than necessities was a *virtue*, restraint, the effects of which are described in **7** as being 'such as not to wish to get a larger share'. In **5** the poor were prescribed merely 'employment and modest resources'; in **7**, merely a weak position and freedom from ill-treatment (cf. 1305ᵃ37–ᵇ1).

'Two obols': a reference to the *diōbelia*, probably a small grant made to relieve poverty towards the end of the Peloponnesian war; see Rhodes (1981) 355–6.

8 (1267ᵇ9–13) Belated but crucial information. Phaleas may have expected, *if* land was to be the sole source of wealth in his state, that equal allotments of land would automatically act as a control on opportunities for getting movable property; or that movable property might indeed be made equal, but a system of enforcement would have to be unduly rigorous and intrusive into private affairs. It is hard not to sympathize with Aristotle's suggestion of a moderate degree of regulation across the board; yet the alternatives he poses are unnecessarily exclusive and extreme. To control non-movable property but not movable could itself have seemed to Phaleas to *be* moderate regulation—a middle or mixed system, acceptable precisely because it neither allowed total licence nor imposed total restriction. In that case, so far as economics go, Phaleas may be an advocate of a 'middle' or 'mixed' constitution of a kind, blending equality with differentials. If so, Aristotle ought perhaps to have recognized his purpose.

9 (1267ᵇ13–21) 'Small scale': not necessarily physically, but in the number of citizens; perhaps Aristotle thinks it *too* small: it could not function as a state (cf. VII iv). The requirement that skilled workmen (and *a fortiori* unskilled labourers) be not only not citizens but not free either, but slaves, and state-slaves at that, looks like an extreme expression of the 'banausic prejudice', the view that their very occupations unfit them for the life of reason and virtue demanded of a citizen (cf. 1260ᵃ36–ᵇ2 and comments, 1277ᵇ33–1278ᵃ26, 1321ᵃ26–9, 1328ᵇ33–1329ᵃ2, 1337ᵃ4–21). That is an extreme policy: the sole property-qualification for citizenship and office is possession of land; there is no class of free but non-enfranchised persons intermediate between citizens and slaves (except perhaps traders, who are not mentioned) who could compete with landed interests in point of wealth and influence. (Even in Magnesia, by contrast, skilled workmen were metics, i.e. free resident aliens—though under strict control: 846d–847b, 850a–d, 920–921d, 949b.) But slaves, unlike free men, do not have to be paid; Phaleas' proposal looks decidedly exploitative.

But there are obscurities. (i) Such extensive use of state slaves is a big innovation: how did Phaleas intend to introduce it? (ii) If the slaves are to belong to the state, under what terms are the private landowners supposed to use them (cf. 1330ᵃ25–33)? (iii) Does 'common' mean simply tasks which the citizens at large need to get done for themselves individually, i.e. common to all of them (cf. 1278ᵃ12), or 'communal or public' (cf. 1330ᵃ30–1)? (iv) We know nothing of Diophantus' proposal.

II viii

THE CONSTITUTION OF HIPPODAMUS: PROBLEMS OF PROPERTY, LAW, AND INNOVATION

Introduction   This long chapter, on a notably versatile thinker, is for my money the best in book II. Its structure is simple and clear. **1** concerns Hippodamus the man; **2–4** describe his proposals, in some detail but mainly without comment; **5–11** criticize them; **12–15** are a splendid extended essay on the management of change.

Hippodamus' penchant for trinities is curious. Three was a popular significant number, which he uses to give an appearance of unity and coherence to his proposals—spuriously enough, since apart from the linking of two of the three citizen groups to two of the three divisions of the territory (**2**), the trinities seem to have no functional or conceptual connections. But three was important also in Pythagorean number-theory, and Hippodamus may have supposed that a state permeated by threes had a certain *rightness*, as somehow reflecting the structure of the cosmos and therefore something significant in human life (*Cael.* 268ᵃ6 ff.); or, perhaps cynically, that such a state would at any rate give that impression.

1 (1267ᵇ22–30)   Hippodamus' career and life-style are described at surprising length. Obviously we are dealing with someone of far greater range and ingenuity than Phaleas, and far more in the public eye. Yet there may be a note of faint disdain: mere mechanical expertise, eccentric dress, ambition, the presumption to advise on 'political' matters without practical experience, and an (unsuccessful?) attempt to gain a reputation for knowledge of 'nature', *phusis*, the structure and operation of the physical world. If so, Aristotle is perhaps sailing (whimsically?) close to the wind: he himself dressed stylishly (D.L. V 1), took no part in running at any rate Athens' constitution (he was a resident alien), yet had a lot to say about the best state, and indeed about nature. On the whole, his report seems to show a sort of detached fascination; that he takes Hippodamus' proposals seriously is evident from the scale and elaboration of the chapter as a whole.

'Division of states': presumably by planned areas devoted to particular purposes (cf. 2, on the division of land). 'Streets of the Piraeus': on an orthogonal grid pattern (cf. 1330ᵇ17–31), at an uncertain date after the end of the Persian Wars; but the pattern itself seems not to have been Hippodamus' invention. The main objective may have been no more than ease of communication and maintenance (with perhaps some Pythagorean regard for the figures of the rectangle/square?). Whether he related town planning to some deeper social theory of communal living is not known (nor how, if at all, he connected 'nature' with social and political life: was he in some sense a precusor of Aristotle himself?). See in general Lana (1949), Burns (1976).

2 (1267ᵇ30–7) The number of 10,000, presumably male heads of household, is nearly the same as the number in Magnesia (745c), which Aristotle thought unrealistically large (1265ᵃ10–18). He does not so complain here, no doubt because Hippodamus' farmers are not 'idle', i.e. unproductive. Yet the soldiers may be, if the common land that sustains them is to be worked by others. Perhaps they are to be only a small group, but highly trained, cf. Plato *Tim.* (24b); at any rate the ratio of soldiers to farmers (and indeed to the craftsmen) is not specified. On the working of the land see further **7**.

3 (1267ᵇ37–1268ᵃ6) If 'he held the view that' reports simply an opinion about contemporary facts, then Hippodamus is presumably indulging his liking for threesomes—unilluminatingly, since the categories are very broad and (certain religious laws apart) could embrace in one way or another practically the whole of at any rate Athenian law (we know little of the law of other states); and nothing seems to hinge on them. ('Outrage' = *hubris*, despiteful ill-treatment of a weaker or defenceless person, or calculated to impair the victim's standing; the term may be meant to cover assault and wounding also; 'damage', *blabē*, presumably relates to property.) But the same problems arise if we translate 'he intended there to be'; for what is 'only' meant to exclude, and what are the implications? Hippodamus may merely be impatient with the sheer number and complexity of laws applying to all areas of life, and wish, in a simplifying spirit, that his own laws should remedy only substantive damage to person or property, as centrally important.

But his view may be the more precise and radical one that the sole purpose of law ought to be to prevent and remedy harm, not to achieve positive moral or social or physical good. That would be very interesting, and would connect broadly with Lycophron (1280ᵇ10–12 ff., cf. on 1252ᵃ1–7) and J. S. Mill (see Guthrie (1962–81) iii. 139–40). However, (i) Hippodamus' own state seems to require laws to achieve positive good (e.g. in regulating the food supply, and in rewarding innovation); (ii) the contrast do good/prevent harm, though easy to express in Greek, is nowhere in the text: Aristotle offers no elucidation, but simply hurries on to the next point; nor (iii) does he anywhere in the chapter reproach

Hippodamus for ignoring law as a means of securing not just life but the good life. I am therefore inclined to think that he is only reporting a piece of schematization by Hippodamus.

Appeals. Presumably Hippodamus has in mind the popular jury courts, *dikastēria*, of Athens, from whose verdicts no appeals were permitted. These courts were the bastion of Athenian democracy: they handled a wide range not only of private and criminal but of public and political cases, in front of very large juries which were felt effectively to *be* the Athenian people, *dēmos*, the final sovereign power in the state. The notion of appeal from that which is sovereign would have seemed paradoxical. Nevertheless, it was widely recognized that verdicts were subject to prejudice, emotion, and caprice. Hippodamus' suggestion is therefore in principle sound; and it was adapted in an elaborate form by Plato in the *Laws* (e.g. 956b–d). We are not told how the system would work: perhaps the dissatisfied would apply for review, which the 'single sovereign court' would grant if it thought the verdict indeed unsafe; but other procedures can be imagined, e.g. the single court might itself take the initiative. The political implications can hardly have escaped Aristotle: the very existence of such a court would be in itself a derogation of the powers of the popular courts, and its composition (election, of the aged only) has an oligarchic flavour (1294ᵇ8–9). The Greeks never believed that their courts were independent of politics.

The obligation of the Athenian juror to vote to condemn or to acquit, no third option being allowed, presumably has its origins in the informal self-help from which the legal system developed (when two men conflict, often one wins outright, the other loses outright). Yet the choice was not as crude as it sounds: forensic speeches presented jurors with a whole battery of competing arguments, excuses, aggravations, mitigations, the accused's good or bad record, considerations of equity etc., which could persuade them to adopt a flexible attitude to the bare facts. Even in those cases in which, after a verdict of guilty, prosecutor and defendant, in the light of arguments advanced and the temper of the court, delivered supplementary speeches on the penalty to be awarded, the court had to choose between the high estimate of the one litigant and the lower estimate of the other: intermediate, nuanced decisions were not allowed (see Saunders (1991) 93 ff., esp. 95 n. 26, 101). Hippodamus therefore has a sharp point in alleging enforced perjury (cf. **10**); and one wonders whether he thinks the crudeness he complains of in reaching verdicts could be in some cases grounds for an appeal. (Does he envisage the three kinds of vote as another 'trinity'?)

The significance of Hippodamus' proposal may be that it is a first step towards a more inquisitorial and less agonistic mode of trial. Again, Plato probably follows him, for his own special purposes: in Magnesia, the verdicts are to be determined by finely graded calculations of guilt, i.e. 'injustice' in the soul, in order that it may be effectively 'cured' by equally finely calculated penalties (Saunders (1991) 184 ff., esp. n. 188).

4 (1268ᵃ6–14) On discoveries, see **12–15** (did Hippodamus himself feel unhonoured?). The proposal about the children may be part of or an addition to the regulations for the militia's maintenance; the Athenian law is of uncertain date: see Rhodes (1981) 308–9. On the recruitment and role of the officials, see 5; nothing is said of an assembly, but that does not necessarily imply a policy of weakening or abolishing it in favour of power-ful officials. Unlike Phaleas, Hippodamus does not disdain handicrafts: his inclusion of artisans in the citizen-body is extremely democratic (1277ᵇ1–3, 1317ᵇ41). But no mention is made of traders, nor of slaves. Communal/aliens/orphans: yet another threesome.

5 (1268ᵃ14–29) presents a single, clear-cut issue. The three parts of the state seem intended to have no political relationships simply as parts or blocks; but Aristotle explicitly states that all three 'take part in the consti-tution'; in 4 their individual members are to elect 'all' the officials; and the implication of 'sharing all offices' in 5 is that it was Hippodamus' intention that they should also *be* officials (the right to appoint officials and the right to hold office did not necessarily go together, 1274ᵃ15 ff., 1281ᵇ21–38, 1318ᵇ6–27). In the terms of 1300ᵃ32–3 ('all appoint from all by election or by lot or by both'), the state is then a democracy (the elderly appeal judges apart, 1268ᵇ41). But Aristotle believes that it cannot succeed. In actual Greek states, the militia was normally the citizen-body itself; each citizen bore arms, light or heavy, at his own expense; he was (e.g.) a farmer first and a soldier second, at need (cf. 1291ᵃ28–31). In Hippodamus' state, however, the militia is a distinct and dedicated part of the citizen-body, one necessarily more powerful physically than the other two. Aristotle assumes that that power will be used for political ends: not only generalships ([Xen] *AP* I 3, 1309ᵇ4–5) but other high offices will inevitably be filled not by all citizens but by the militia, who will become dominant, like masters of slaves (cf. 1264ᵃ11–40, on the Auxiliaries of the *Republic*). That will de-stroy the 'affection' of the other two parts for the constitution, because their participation in it becomes pointless. The regime will have lost the consent of the governed (cf. comment on 1265ᵇ26–1266ᵃ5).

Aristotle has his eye on Greek practice (arms-bearers always had politi-cal clout; see e.g. 1297ᵇ12 ff.), and on men as they are, ignoring Hippodamus' assumption that they would not abuse their power (though we are not told what preventive measures he would have taken). It is however fairly clear that Hippodamus did not expect arms-bearers to hold a *large* number of high offices—or what then would become of their specialization in matters military? Nor are they necessarily numerous, convenient though the assumption is for Aristotle's argument. The issue is, then, civilian control of the military—not that Aristotle puts it in those terms: he speaks only of the lack of 'affection', and in effect points out that Hippodamus' state will fail to achieve its 'assumption' (see comment on 1260ᵇ27–36), that all should share in all offices.

Plato is firmly on the side of the civilians and statesmen, e.g. *Laws* 921d–922a; for, like Aristotle, he believed that military activity must subserve the specifications of the good human life, as worked out by statesmen and philosophers, not dominate them. This insistence on the primacy of 'poli-tics' foreshadows the modern orthodoxy that the military should be sub-ordinate to government.

6 (1268ᵃ29–35) and 7 (1268ᵃ35–ᵇ4)   Aristotle is not necessarily correct to assume that there will be as many fighters as farmers (see **2**); but the status of the 'public' land is indeed obscure. Hippodamus may have meant only that each farmer cultivates, in addition to his own private land, a small area of land that is public in that its produce is reserved for a select band of fighters, as their 'pay' (cf. *Rep.* 464c). A similar arrangement might apply to the 'sacred' land. On fighters and farmers as functional 'parts' of a state, see 1290ᵇ38 ff.

8 (1268ᵇ4–11)   This section and the next two raise important issues of law and legal procedure. On Athenian forensic practice, see on **3**, and MacDowell (1978) 251–4; on arbitration, Harrison (1968–71) ii. 66–8, MacDowell (1978) 203–11.

Arbitrators, *diaitētai*, operated either singly or in small groups; their business was to bring about a solution agreed between the disputants; failing that, they delivered a verdict on their own authority (cf. *AP* LIII 2). As Aristotle implies (cf. *Rhet.* 1374ᵇ19–22), they were free, unlike jurors in the courts, to side neither with the one disputant nor the other: after due discussion among themselves, they could compromise, in the light of all the circumstances (*epieikeia*, 'equity'). Aristotle calls this 'making distinctions', i.e. saying 'guilty in one respect, not in another'. He argues that such nuanced verdicts are impossible in courts, presumably because discussion between (say) 501 jurors is impossible, and/or because it would destroy the secrecy of the ballot (Dem. XIX 239). Plato by contrast envisages the possibility of (smaller?) juries whose members could debate the issue among themselves: *Laws* 875ᵉ–876ᵇ. Yet discussion is not a *prerequisite* of verdicts based on equity: there is no reason why an individual juror cannot arrive by solitary reflection at his own private nuanced verdict; but if he did so in an Athenian court, he was nevertheless forced to vote unqualifiedly either for condemnation or acquittal. No doubt some rather more elaborate voting system would be required to pemmicanize 501 verdicts, all perhaps different, into a single verdict; but Hippodamus' proposal deserves more sympathy than Aristotle gives it.

9 (1268ᵇ11–17)   The obvious answer to Aristotle's question is, 'add up the figures, and divide by the number of jurors'. Why does he make such heavy weather of the matter?

10 (1268ᵇ1–22)   Evidently Aristotle maintains (i) that if 20 minae are claimed in the charge, and the juror thinks 19 are due, it is not perjury to vote for acquittal, for the charge is of 20, which in the juror's opinion has not been demonstrated to be justified; (ii) that if he votes for condemnation, on the grounds that 19 is a nearer approximation to 20 than 0 is, that *is* perjury. Yet jurors in Athenian courts must frequently have experienced the dilemma of choosing acquittal or condemnation as more nearly expressing some intermediate view. Aristotle seems prepared to tolerate the grave injustice to the injured party in (i), of not receiving *any* compensation, but not the slight excess of punishment of the offender in (ii). Is it then his position that excess punishment is a greater evil than lack of compensation? (At *Rhet.* 1374ᵇ2 ff., arguments of equity are used only to *abate* penalties, apparently without regard to the effect on compensation to the victim.) Probably not; but rather curiously, a juror observing Aristotle's rules about perjury would in some cases be acting as though he were following some such penological policy. (But what if he decided *more* than 20 minae are owed?)

The Athenian juror's oath required jurors to vote according to the laws, but on matters on which no laws existed to decide by 'the most just judgement' (Dem. XX 118, XXXIX 40); these matters evidently included questions of equity, which are obviously impossible to express with precision in formal law (1282ᵇ1 ff., 1287ᵃ23 ff., *EN* V x, VI xi *init.*, *Rhet.* 1374ᵃ26 ff.). Orators could easily stress law and exclude just judgement, or vice versa, as suited their case (Aesch. III 6, Dem. XXIII, 96, cf. *Rhet.* 1375ᵃ27 ff.). Rather similarly, whereas Aristotle takes an objective, legalistic view of perjury, Hippodamus' view is by contrast subjective and internalized. But we must not conclude that Aristotle is hostile to equity. The crucial difference between him and Hippodamus is that he believes equity should be *taken into account in reaching* an either/or verdict: note 'returns in a "just" manner a simple verdict of condemnation or acquittal' (equity = justice, *Rhet.* 1374ᵃ26–8, 1375ᵃ27–9); whereas Hippodamus believes equity should as it were *constitute* the verdict—which could then take any one of very many more forms than the two bald alternatives of Athenian practice. But Aristotle believes that impracticable (see on **8**); so he makes the best case he can for the existing system, at the cost of a brusque dismissal of an intelligent and surely justified suggestion.

11 (1268ᵇ22–31)   Greek literature on rewards and honours, on social and technical progress, and on the merits and demerits of making changes to laws and customs, is full of echoes of the points made here and in **12–15** (e.g. Thuc. I 71 iii, Xen. *Hiero* IX 9: cf. also introduction to I ii, and, on Hippodamus in particular, Edelstein (1967) 30–1; of **11–15** as a whole there is a perceptive analysis by Brunschwig (1980)). Aristotle himself here mentions current controversy on changes to laws. His own discussion is distinctive in at least one way: he attempts to explore some *limits* to the analogy between technical innovation and innovation in law; and he *perhaps* attempts to indicate the relationship between *ad hoc* adjustments to law in particular cases, and permanent changes to them.

Hippodamus may have intended to embrace practical and technical innovation in his proposal (his interest in town planning would support this hypothesis); but Aristotle takes him to be concerned only with social, legal and constitutional questions. Nor is it clear whether Hippodamus assumed that innovation would stop when some state of perfection had been reached, or that society was or ought to be changing perpetually; and what is the relationship between his proposal and his own 'best' (= unimprovable?) state, if indeed 'best' is what he called it? At any rate Aristotle's initial scepticism is purely practical: such matters all too easily become politicized. Vexatious prosecutions (the technical term in the text is 'sycophancies', cf. 1304ᵇ19 ff.) can be brought by demagogues or by enemies of the innovations or of their proposers, with a view to winning the rewards the law provided for successful prosecutors, or to blackmail the proposers into giving money in return for the abandonment of the prosecution; and pleas of 'common good' can attractively disguise proposals which would lead to undesirable constitutional upheaval (1307ª40 ff. contains a telling instance). Such political manœuvrings of course happen anyway; but honour for innovation would serve only to increase their number. By 'a different enquiry' he means that Hippodamus' proposal needs to be related to an antecedent inquiry into the conditions under which constitutional and legal change becomes justified; for (as will appear) the fact that a given change is advantageous is not invariably a compelling reason for adopting it.

12 (1268ᵇ31–1269ª8)   Aristotle now embarks on a sketch of the antecedent inquiry. Initially, the argument is swift and inconsequential. (i) Statesmanship must be regarded as a skill (see III xii *init.* and IV i: the assumption goes back to Socrates and Plato). (ii) Therefore, in virtue of its status as a skill, it *necessarily* benefits from change. Now the historical anthropology that follows certainly provides evidence for such benefit; but it would have been sufficient on its own to demonstrate that. It is the suppressed reasoning in (i) that is important, namely that there are some objective truths about the human condition that statesmanship must discover and implement. The mark of any skill is to have an aim, human *eudaimonia*, or some intermediate aim conducive to it, and means (methods and resources) to attain it (see I viii–xi in general, and *EN* I i–ii; cf. 1282ᵇ14 ff.). Neither the aims nor the means are immediately present to man, either to the individual at birth or to the race at its beginning; they need to be learnt; and that demands time, reflection and effort (cf. *EN* 1098ª20–6, *Soph. Ref.* 183ᵇ17–184ᵇ8). Early men, as Aristotle conjectures, were imperceptive or undiscerning: their mental framework was unsophisticated, and their power to generalize and conceptualize their experience was as yet undeveloped. Their institutions, like their technical products, were therefore rudimentary, and only rudimentarily conducive to human happiness (the regulation at Cyme, providing for mere compurgation, could obviously lead to injustice, and injustice militates against happiness). By treating statesmanship as a skill, Aristotle can, if need arises, head off a relativistic view of historical changes in it.

The translation of *anoētoi*, 'undiscerning', needs justification. The Greek word is often translated 'silly', 'senseless'; 'unintelligent'. But Aristotle can hardly mean that, since *some* early men must have been clever enough to make some progress somewhere; and in any case it is possible to be intelligent and yet fail to make much technical and social progress, for which certain cultural attitudes are needed, and a certain view of the social environment and the physical world. He probably means literally 'lacking *nous*', reason, in the sense of an ability to formulate general concepts, to which particular situations may be related in some principled manner. That is, some idea of (human) 'good', 'function', 'virtue', 'happiness', etc. is necessary for the conceiving and proper development of particular practices. If that is not to over-interpret the text, Aristotle is writing a very brief history of the human intellect. Cf. *Laws* 676a ff., esp. 679c on the uncritical mentality of early man, after the flood.

If the parallel between technical skills, which can presumably be refined to a point where no further improvement is possible, and 'political' skill is followed through, Aristotle ought to be thinking of improvements in the latter that would eventually hone it into some state of perfection; and that would potentially produce 'best' socio-political structures, not merely imperfect states and constitutions 'according to a hypothesis': see on 1260ᵇ27–36. At any rate, it is very clear that fundamentally he is in favour of change, provided of course it is for the better, i.e. more greatly contributing to human happiness; a law's ancestral status is secondary or irrelevant; cf. introd. to I ii, on his developmental view of history. For while it is true that 'pretty well everything [i.e. possible constitutional practices] has been discovered' (1264ᵃ3–4, cf. 1329ᵇ25–35), the good ones are very far from having been adopted universally. They are as it were lying around waiting to be picked up by statesmen, hopefully when they read the *Politics*, or from each other; cf. IV i, *EN* 1103ᵇ26–9, and comment on 1274ᵃ31–65. Aristotle does not believe that 'nothing should ever be done for the first time' (F. M. Cornford, *Microcosmographia Academica* (5th edn., Cambridge 1953), 15).

13 (1269ᵃ8–12) Something of an afterthought. (i) It may be supposed that once laws have been formulated in writing, at a latish stage in the historical development of statesmanship, they would need no further change. But they still need the flexibility of 'customary' laws, in that their strict letter will need to be modified when they are applied in particular circumstances, presumably in the light of equity, which Aristotle has just discussed in **8–10**. In a sense, that amounts to 'not leaving written laws unchanged', that is in their application; however, in themselves they *are* left unchanged, throughout the whole series of day-to-day departures from them (cf. *Rhet.* 1375ᵇ13–15). (ii) Aristotle may therefore (Brunschwig (1980) 526: 'sans doute') be hinting at something crucial to the *development* of law. When a law has over and over again to be modified *ad hoc* by reference to the same generally acceptable principle, then instead of forcing litigants to argue for that principle on each occasion, one may as well incorporate it into the law and have done; and this will ensure uniformity of practice for the future. Aristotle may well have accepted this suggestion; but on the face of it he makes only point (i).

14 (1269ᵃ12–24) Although throughout **12–14** Aristotle is thinking chiefly of legislators who formulate and change laws, he now considers also the effect of change on the individual person who is expected to obey them. For laws are both a means by which statesmen produce virtue in their citizens, through habituation, and a code of conduct by which the virtuous citizen is guided in his pursuit of happiness. Cf. *EN* 1129ᵇ14–25 ff., 1179ᵇ31 ff.

To judge from the restrictive tone of the opening sentence, Aristotle has some sympathy with the 'caution' enjoined by the conservative views he now summarizes. In general terms, it is not hard (cf. on **11**) to parallel these views in Greek literature, (e.g. Eur. *Bac.* 890–2, Thuc. III 37 iii). Plato's ferocity about the undesirability of change, stemming ultimately from a desire to produce a perfect, metaphysically based society (see on I ii), which would never even need it, stands somewhat apart from the main stream: 424a–c, 797a–798d (*acceptable* change is discussed at 769a ff., *Pol.* 295b ff.). But there is no reason to believe that Aristotle is here thinking of Plato in particular.

Aristotle's own contribution to the debate is to impose some practical restriction on the parallel between moral and political action and the skills on which he had himself relied in **12** (cf. *EN* 1105ᵃ26 ff.; also 1261ᵃ34 ff., but contrast 1287ᵃ32 ff.). He claims, startlingly, that the laws have *no* power to secure obedience except habit (repeated acts of obedience to the law engender the disposition, i.e. virtue, of so acting; cf. *EN* II i). But does not the sheer utility of good laws have that power? Or the prospect of punishment they hold out for infraction? Do not such considerations themselves engender habit? Apparently not; or rather, not invariably; and this is the crucial difference from the skills. The skills have rules, which must be followed (by habit: *EN* 1103ᵇ7–12) if a good technical product is to be obtained; and a good product is unmistakable, at least to experts (cf. *EN* 1181ᵃ19–21). Social life also has 'rules', i.e. laws, which have to be followed if a good 'product', i.e. good actions amounting to happiness, is to be obtained; but happiness is not unmistakable. If therefore a man conceives some mistaken notion of happiness, and is tempted to disobey the laws, and thinks he can get away with it, the only thing to restrain him will be habit (in which case he is not genuinely virtuous, *EN* 1144ᵃ13–20); for the constraint of good product will have been lost. Therefore, habit being something that takes time to grow, and is weakened by frequent change, the laws ought not to be changed 'casually', even when they are to some extent deficient. For the habit of disobeying slightly imperfect laws, or the rulers who frame and administer them (ᵃ16–18), encourages a general disregard even for good law; and that will damage one's *eudaimonia*, happiness, to a greater degree than it will be benefited by changes in slightly imperfect laws for the better. In the skills, presumably a new rule does not diminish respect for rules in general, because there is demonstrable improvement in the product. In brief, technical rules and communal laws are importantly different in their modes of operation.

Aristotle does not explore the obvious practical dangers in demanding obedience to mildly substandard laws (cf. 1294ᵃ6–7), e.g. a feeling of injustice and resentment in litigants (such feelings can be passionate, even about minor matters), leading to further suits. He can hardly be unaware of them, but he evidently believes them to be less than those of weakening habit. No doubt if the defects in the laws were substantial, the calculation of advantage would change.

15 (1269ᵃ24–8) Already apparently reluctant to embark on the subject (**11**, **12** *init.*), Aristotle now declines to pass from general principles to particular detail. If the last sentence constitutes a promise to do so, it is not fulfilled. For the mode of making and changing laws at Athens, see MacDowell (1975), (1978) ch. III.

II ix

CRITICISM OF THE CONSTITUTION AND SOCIAL SYSTEM OF SPARTA

Introduction In ix–xi Aristotle leaves theoretical utopias and examines actual constitutions with a good reputation. These three chapters speak to historians rather than to philosophers; for political and social theory to which the particular judgements may be related is conspicuous by its absence, though in general terms it may be inferred easily enough (see Introduction). Nor do we know how much factual evidence Aristotle had collected, or had arranged to be collected, in the *Constitutions* credited to him, by the time he wrote these chapters. His treatment of the three constitutions is often lacunose or compendious—but is the cause ignorance or compression? At any rate, his methodology makes him mostly censorious (see comment on **1**), and his accuracy and fairness are matters of intense debate. In particular, his apparently contradictory judgements about Sparta, usually critical but sometimes admiring, have generated several complex hypotheses (well appraised by Schütrumpf (1994) 328 ff.), e.g. that they reflect different stages in Aristotle's intellectual development, or different periods of Sparta's history. However, common sense suggests that different judgements on different topics from different perspectives in different contexts are only natural; and 'legislation which has been enacted' in **1** (cf. 'constitutions in use', 1260ᵇ30) makes clear that Aristotle proceeds on the basis of institutions and practices contemporary with the time of writing (Schütrumpf (1994) 339), but with historical excursuses designed to reveal how they came about. A full assessment of the controversies about his analysis of Spartan laws and institutions, and a summary of the voluminous scholarly literature, with a critical bibliography, is in Schütrumpf ii. 283–98 and (1994); cf. Cartledge (1987) 116–20. For the extreme admiration of Sparta as a paradigm of authoritarian 'law and order' and robust moral virtue, especially military valour, see Tigerstedt (1965–78) i. 155 ff.; both Aristotle and Plato have strong reservations: 1333ᵇ5 ff., *Laws* I *init.*, 666d–667a.

1 (1269ᵃ29–34) is a brief second procedural preface to the second book: see introduction to II i and comment on 1260ᵇ27–36. The existing constitutions examined in ix–xi are to be judged by reference both to 'the best system' and to their 'assumptions', i.e. the aims which they themselves set for themselves. The latter part of this exercise is in effect the identification of inconsistencies with those aims, factors which militate against them; and the same analysis may be applied to utopias also (see 1262ᵇ3–7). Hence the somewhat negative flavour of these three chapters.

By 'contrary' Aristotle does not mean that a 'mixed' constitution, say one composed of oligarchy and democracy, is necessarily internally vitiated, since democracy is contrary to oligarchy; for a *well*-mixed constitution modifies and blends both its elements and is in itself a praiseworthy aim (e.g. IV ix, with particular reference to Sparta). In this case he would look for elements hostile to the combination.

2 (1269ᵃ34–ᵇ67) and **3 (1269ᵇ7–12)** discuss the helots (*heilōtes*, probably 'captives'), indigenous Greeks treated as a conquered enemy by Sparta; they were not privately-owned slaves but belonged to the state, and enjoyed certain familial and property rights. The Cretan 'peripheral populations' (*perioikoi*) are not to be confused with certain free but subordinate communities around Sparta, for it is implied here and at 1272ᵃ1, 18, that in Crete peripheral populations were the economic counterparts of the helots; but their precise status is unclear. For further detail, see Willetts (1955) 37–9. Aristotle's discussion is entirely clinical and pragmatic: he shows no indignation about the subjection of helot and Cretan peripheral peoples, just as he shows none about the status of slavery in I iii–vii; for no doubt the criteria for the naturalness and justice of slavery can be applied *mutatis mutandis* to helotry also (see esp. introd. to I v). He sticks closely to his brief as stated in **1**: in so far as Sparta aims at the 'assumption' of freedom from essential tasks, she is correct; but partly for accidental reasons (foreign relations), and partly because of bad management, she has a 'way' of achieving it that is 'contrary' to it; for the Spartans purchase that freedom at the paradoxical cost of constant worry about insurrection. He presumably thinks that some mode of dealing with helots that is neither oppressive nor too permissive would be preferable, but he does not enlarge on the issue; indeed, he does not even mention the cynical brutality with which the Spartans were at any rate commonly alleged to have treated the helots, who outnumbered them, though in 1269ᵇ10 he may have something like that in mind ('wretchedly'). His own preferred way of ensuring that adult male citizens have the leisure from 'essential' (i.e. routine, cf. 1253ᵇ16, 24) tasks to pursue moral activity and affairs of state emerges sketchily from 1330ᵃ25 ff.: workers on the land should ideally be slaves, presumably non-Greek, who should not be akin to each other nor men of spirit; for that will ensure good work, with the danger of revolt diminished by the lack of intimacy among them; and they should be offered freedom 'as a reward'. A second-best to chattel slavery is 'non-Greek peripheral people'. Both there and in **3** he has an eye to the (limited) moral virtue of workers (cf. I xiii); but he does not say how he proposes to inculcate it (cf. however 1260ᵇ3–5). For a related treatment of the problem, see *Laws* 776ᵇ ff.

On the importance of leisure to the life-style of 'statesmen', see 1255ᵇ35–7, 1292ᵇ25–9, 1333ᵃ30–ᵇ5 1334ᵃ11–40, VIII iii, *EN* 1177ᵇ4 ff., *Laws* 803d, and Solmsen (1964).

4–8 (1269ᵇ12–1270ᵇ6) I xii and xiii are essential background reading to this difficult and confusing stretch of text. There, Aristotle argues that a women's deliberative capacity is 'without authority' (1260ᵃ13) and inferior to a man's; her natural role is in the household, as wife and mother, under the rule of her husband. In **4–8** he gives us a kind of QED: he shows us in detail the disastrous consequences of allowing women to step outside that role. But it is important not to exaggerate the connection with I xii and xiii. Aristotle in **4–8** refers neither to the psychology of females nor to the social theory of book I; he nowhere claims that women are inferior by nature;

and the entire passage relies merely on ordinary unspoken assumptions of male superiority: apart from a couple of technicalities ('chosen aim', 'happiness') at the start of 4, one would hardly have needed to be Aristotle in order to write it. And in any case it is probable that book I was written *after* book II (see Introduction). Nor is he 'gunning' at women in particular: there is hardly anything (5 *fin.*?) of the abusive misogyny of e.g. *Laws* 781a, and certainly no claim that women are the root of all evil; contrast Hes. *WD* 94 ff., cf. 373–5. Presumably, in view of e.g. I ix, he could hardly deny that men can perfectly well be greedy independently of any female influence.

On the complex (and greatly controverted) historical detail concerning property and women in Sparta, see Cartledge (1981*a*) and Hodkinson (1986). As the latter points out (387), Aristotle's account of Sparta's troubles 'relies not on a single cause but provides a sophisticated analysis which lays stress on a *variety* [my italics] of contributory factors'.

4 (1269ᵇ12–23)   Again we have the distinction of 1, between the 'assumption' of the state (here called its 'chosen aim', *prohairēsis*, i.e. toughness for military success, cf. 'target' 1333ᵇ13), and the 'happiness' of the best state, which Sparta fails to achieve (cf. 1333ᵇ5–25). 'Licence' (*anesis*, echoing *Laws* 637c) means not freedom to *treat* women just as one wishes; it is nicely ambiguous as between (*a*) 'permission granted' to women, if only by default, here on the part of the 'lawgiver' (probably Lycurgus, cf. 6), and (*b*) their exploiting of the permission, in order to engage in the licentious conduct described sweepingly and with a play on words (see Plato *Gorg.* 505b11–12, *EN* 1119ᵃ38 ff.) in the final sentence of this somewhat heated paragraph. (Cf. 'not legislated for', the same term as at *Laws* 781a1, which totally ignores laws of education, marriage, property, etc., which certainly applied at all times, and the rhetorical question of 5 1269ᵇ32–4.) Aristotle is well within the strong tradition of indignation about the conduct of Spartan women; cf. *Laws* 637c; it is his attempt to analyse its historical *causes* and wider social and economic effects that makes his account distinctive.

On the real issue, however, Aristotle lacks Plato's radical drive. How far ought a legislator to seek to control private life? Plato, who entertained dire suspicions about what women got up to in the secrecy of their homes, believed, like Aristotle, that private and public life had an intimate effect on each other, but he reluctantly acknowledged, as Aristotle here evidently does not (see 'mistake', 6 *fin.*), that there are practical limits to interference in domestic matters. His solution was to flush women *out* of their homes, and compel them to take, so far as possible, a full part in public life, on an equality with men (see Saunders (1995)), so that they should be subject to the same public educational and moral influences (*Laws* 781a–e, 804e–806c, passages of which Aristotle has here several echoes). To Aristotle, such an assimilation of role is, on the showing of I xii and xiii, unnatural (cf. *EN* 1161ᵃ22–5); indeed, it is a major part of his complaint against Sparta that women used to manage 'a great deal' (1269ᵇ31–2). Cf. on 1252ᵃ34–ᵇ9.

5 (1269ᵇ23–39) An attempt to trace the growth of avarice in Sparta. Its psychological origins were explored in I 1257ᵇ40 ff.: zeal for pleasure, for 'life' rather than the 'good life'; since the pleasure lies in excess, people seek to acquire wealth over and above their real needs. Now in this paragraph Aristotle leaves the psychology to be inferred; indeed, he is somewhat vague even about the social mechanisms. Presumably self-indulgent women bring pressure to bear on their husbands to get wealth (cf. *Rep.* 549cd), and the resultant esteem given it is all the greater, (i) because Spartan men, being warlike, have exceptionally strong sexual drives, and greatly desire to please their wives, (ii) because the wealth accorded to women gives them a hold over men, and they win some control even over public affairs, as powers behind the ostensible rulers.

'Over-boldness', shown by the women by thrusting themselves forward in this way, is a quality related to but distinct from courage (*EN* 1108ᵇ31–2, 1109ᵃ8–9), and inappropriate (as indeed courage itself would be) for 'routine' tasks (perhaps for superintending them, as the wife of the head of the household, not just for doing them: 1255ᵇ25, 1277ᵇ24–5; but cf. 1260ᵃ23–4: the courage of women is, unlike a man's, 'of a servant' or 'servant-like'). The jibe that follows (cf. *Laws* 806a ff., 813e ff.) probably refers to the year 370/369 (Xen. *Hell.* VI v 28), and 'the days of supremacy' to the period till then from the end of the Peloponnesian War in 404. 'As in other states': formally ambiguous, but probably meaning that women in other states *were* useful, not that they were not.

Ares, god of war; Aphrodite, of love; the two are frequently associated, cf. the rationalizing interpretation of myth at 1341ᵇ2 ff., and the discussion of *Met.* 1074ᵇ1 ff. At 1327ᵇ40 ff. Aristotle makes a brief psychological connection between *thumos* ('spirit', 'aggressive drive') and love or friendship. At Sparta, deities were often represented armed, even Aphrodite (Paus. III 15, 10). On male homosexuality in Sparta, see Cartledge (1981*b*).

6 (1269ᵇ39–1270ᵃ11) This paragraph would have been better placed before **4**; for the men's absence abroad, in pursuit of a false 'aim' for the state, was the start of the troubles. Lycurgus' date and achievements, if indeed he existed, are uncertain; on his alleged retreat, cf. *Laws* 781a, 806c.

7 (1270ᵃ11–34) Aristotle passes from the informal means by which women gained a social and political ascendancy in Sparta, to certain features of property law which both accentuated that problem and generated several others. A few brief and inevitably dogmatic notes on historical matters are needed. (i) 'He' (1270ᵃ20–1): surely Lycurgus (see ᵃ7). (ii) 'Land already possessed' (ᵃ20) may or may not be meant compendiously, to include, in addition to other land acquired at whatever time, the 'ancient portion' given to each man at the foundation, which according to Aristotle fr. 611.12 Rose (1886) and Plut. *Agis* 5 it was illegal to sell. At any rate, from the start it was possible, albeit strongly discouraged, to sell part of one's total holding, with risk of impoverishment. Alienation by gift or by (presumably partible) bequest had the same effect; but that was not even discouraged. See Hodkinson (1986) 386–94. (iii) 'Heiresses': Aristotle misleadingly uses the Athenian term, *epikleros* (in Sparta it was *patrouchos*), for the daughter who could in the absence of a male heir of her father, notably in cases of intestacy, 'inherit' an estate; she was then married to the nearest male relative (complex rules existed), so that the estate would stay within her kin. In Sparta, by contrast, where frequent wars presumably gave rise to frequent intestacy, marriage to that relative (the 'heir') was not compulsory, and she was evidently able to retain the estate in her own right, whomsoever she married: and if she married outside her kin, her new *oikos* would gain a considerable accession of wealth. The antiquity of this practice is not known; for further detail see MacDowell (1986) 96–7, 107 ff., Hodkinson (1986) 394 ff. (iv) The figures at the end relate to the early 4th century, before the battle of Leuctra, 371 ('a single blow'). (v) 'Men' (final word), i.e. the Spartiates, adult male Spartan citizens, not merely 'population'.

The passage is not overtly critical of women: there is no claim, except possibly in the first sentence, that women through greed brought pressure to bear for the *creation* of the laws about the alienability of land and the rights of 'heiresses'. As in **6**, they may simply have taken opportunities presented to them; and as Newman (ii. 330) notes, the trouble is less that the land is possessed by females (though cf. *EN* 1161ᵃ1–4, on heiresses) than that it is possessed by few persons (who then presumably intermarry and become even richer); for the poor lack resources to rear children, and this weakens the state's 'assumption', military prowess. Both Plato and Aristotle favoured confining inheritances to kin, restrictions on or absence of dowries, and a broad diffusion of moderate but not equal amounts of private property, without undue concentration or fragmentation: see e.g. **8**, **15**, **19**, 1263ᵃ40–ᵇ7, 1265ᵃ28–ᵇ17, 1266ᵃ31–1267ᵃ17, 1309ᵃ23–6 (in oligarchies), *Laws* 736c–745b, 772e–773e, 774c, 922a–925d.

8 (1270ᵃ34–ᵇ6) 'It is better': presumably because the admission of foreigners is socially and culturally disruptive; cf. 1278ᵃ26 ff., *Laws* 741a. Aristotle's central point is that the policy of maximizing the Spartiate population generates poverty, because of the numerous progeny of some households. Presumably sons, having eventually divided their indigent fathers' property equally (the normal practice in Greece), would be even poorer—a predicament the more likely to arise in that Sparta was untypical in allowing daughters too to share in the inheritances (Hodkinson (1986) 98 ff.), so that the sons would receive that much less. (The constitutional implications of the poverty are set out in **15**.) 'Levelling' should come first, as a *basis* for a large population. Hence Plato's care to balance resources and numbers: the estates of Magnesia are not only inalienable but indivisible, and surplus offspring have in the end to emigrate (*Laws* 740b ff., 1265ᵃ38–ᵇ17 and comment; cf. 1266ᵇ8–14).

9 (1270ᵇ6–17), **10 (1270ᵇ17–28)**, and **11 (1270ᵇ28–34)** concern the Ephors, a board of five officials elected annually by and from the whole body of Spartiatae. Their powers were executive, disciplinary, and legal, and extraordinarily wide and strong (1265ᵇ40, *Laws* 712d, Xen. *Const. Lac.* VIII 4; further material in Andrewes (1966) 8–14 and Forrest (1980)). Whether their discretion extended to overriding what laws Sparta had, is not clear; **11** may imply only that there *ought* to have been more written laws for them to observe than there were. The two hereditary Kings, taken from two separate royal houses, had certain important executive, judicial, religious, and military functions; their actions were subject to scrutiny and control by the Ephors (cf. *Laws* 692a). The Andrian affair (1270ᵇ11–12) is not securely identifiable. The 'lawgiver' (1270ᵇ19): probably Theopompus (1313ᵃ26–7), but possibly Lycurgus. 'Childish' (1270ᵇ28): possibly acclamation; cf. 1271ᵃ9–10 and *Laws* 692a. 'Intention' (1270ᵇ32) is an alternative for 'assumption', 'aim'; see on **1**. 'Court popularity' (1270ᵇ14), i.e. as demagogues, popular leaders, do with the common people, at least in the eyes of anti-democrats.

Sparta enjoyed a considerable reputation for operating a 'mixed' constitution (see *Laws* 712de, 1265ᵇ33–1266ᵃ1, 1294ᵇ14 ff.). Schütrumpf ii. 319 distinguishes two possible senses of the term, which I would call (*a*) the static and (*b*) the dynamic. (*a*) all the powerful interest-groups in the state share in its government (cf. III i), by means of a clearly identifiable organ in each case (**10**; cf. 1268ᵃ23–5, 1272ᵃ31–3, 1320ᵃ14–16); (*b*) the various organs interact dynamically and functionally (e.g. 1313ᵃ18 ff., *Laws* 691e–692a, Plut. *Lyc.* V 6–7), so that one balances another. Schütrumpf rightly says that Aristotle's emphasis in **10** is on (*a*). However, the focus of **9–11** as a whole is not on the merits of the Spartan constitution, but on the demerits of the Ephors, and **10** is something of a digression. Aristotle's central point is that, although the constitution attracts the loyalty of the various groups (cf. 1294ᵇ34–41, 1296ᵇ15–16, 1309ᵇ16–18), in the matter of Ephors it is to be *censured*, for bribery (cf. *Laws* 955c), tyrannical power, undue discretion, silly election procedures, and a tendency to generate a democracy (cf. 1307ᵃ23–5); and the system allows the Ephors undue self-indulgence to boot. In other words, the Spartan and other admirers of the constitution are attracted to it for reasons that sound edifying, but which they might have to modify if they knew, or chose not to ignore, the truth about Ephors. They suppose the constitution works in one way, in reality it works in another; but on a pragmatic level their misapprehension does serve to cement its stability (cf. IV xiii). Aristotle implicitly comes close to Bagehot's distinction in *The English Constitution* (1867) between 'dignified' and 'efficient', between the show, the way a constitution is thought to operate, and the way it operates in practice; cf. Saunders (1993).

So Aristotle's observations, in so far as they focus on a 'mixed' constitution, simply undermine, for reasons that are as much moral and sociological as political, Sparta's reputation for operating a successful one. But it is by no means clear that Aristotle thinks that the faults of the Spartan constitution arise *because* it is a mixture, a clumsily executed one; on the contrary, he reckons it a good mixture (1294ᵇ14 ff.) and that its faults arise despite that. For the faults of a mixture can arise in isolation in each of the parts, from features intrinsic to them individually, regardless of their status as parts of the mixture. A powerful official can be equally open to bribery in *any* kind of constitution, mixed or not. Criticism of a mixed constitution can more easily be brought under heading (*b*) above; but apart from the tension between the Ephors and the Kings (1270ᵇ13–15), Aristotle here

COMMENTARY 1270^b6–28

undertakes, explicitly at least, little by way of such 'dynamic analysis'. (But perhaps 1271^a6–8 qualifies also.) He may, of course, simply assume it; for even a simple static analysis implies some principled relationship between the parts: e.g. the people 'stay quiet because they share in the highest office' (1270^b18–19); presumably the lower offices would not have satisfied them. The powers and actions of one part are not easily isolated from their effect on those of the others; cf. also comment on **14**. For limitations on the usefulness of 'written rules', see 1286^a7 ff., and cf. comment on viii **8–10**.

The Assembly has no role in Aristotle's analysis, except presumably by implication at 1270^b25–8. Perhaps he believes it was a political cipher, which may indeed be true (Cartledge (1987) 129–31; dissent in Andrewes (1966) 1–8).

12 (1270^b35–1271^a8) and **13 (1271^a9–18)** The *Gerousia*, 'senate', consisted of the two Kings plus twenty-eight Elders over the age of 60. The latter were elected for life on the basis of personal merit by and from the Spartiatae (cf. 1294^b30–1), or perhaps from a restricted aristocratic number of them (1306^a18–19), in an elaborately conducted process of acclamation (Plut. *Lyc.* 26) designed to preclude bias in those who estimated the volume of shouting for each candidate when presented. Presumably it is this attempt to gauge noise produced in part by crowd psychology rather than to count votes cast after due reflection that Aristotle considers 'childish'; it would be better to say 'inexact', or 'not securely accurate' (when two shouts are of similar volume). The Elders had extensive powers, notably to judge capital and other serious cases (MacDowell (1986) 126–8), and possibly to prepare business for the Assembly; further detail in Andrewes (1966) and Forrest (1968) esp. 46–9; cf. *Laws* 691e–692a. It is not clear whether their life tenure was granted on the assumption that judgement improves with age (Aristotle rightly contests this, cf. *Rhet.* II xiii, *Anim.* 408^b18 ff.), or in order to ensure independence of judgement without fear of interference or attack; but not even the members of the Athenian Areopagus enjoyed total freedom of action (Dem. XXVI 5, Aesch. III 20). Nor is it clear what evidence Aristotle had of 'distrust' on the part of the legislator (^a2), nor what effect it had. On the need to give authority to the able and virtuous, willing or not, not to the ambitious, cf. *Rep.* 499bc, 519c ff., 540b, 557e. On Elders in Crete see 1272^a33–^b1.

The scrutiny, *euthuna*, was a democratic device to ensure control over office-holders (cf. 1274^a15–21, 1281^b32–4, 1282^a25–32, 1322^b6–12), but was readily usable by non-democrats also (*Laws* 945b ff.). It was normally undergone at Athens by officials at the *end* of their term; it covered financial and other matters, and was conducted by Scrutineers under certain procedural rules which permitted public participation (*AP* XLVIII iv–v, LIV ii). Aristotle does not say *why* 'we' (who?) say that scrutiny of officials under the Ephors' general powers is undesirable. Probably he means that it lacked written procedures and legal safeguards (cf. 1270^b29–31), allowed no formal public participation, and could be capricious, malicious, politically motivated, and incessant throughout the officals' tenure (see Xen. *Const. Lac.* VIII 4); for officials (he might argue) must be allowed to exercise 'political knowledge' as best they can, and not be held

155

on too tight a rein. If that is right, perhaps he would wish to see Elders, who hold office for life, scrutinized at specified intervals; cf. 1308ᵃ19–20.

14 (1271ᵃ18–26) 'Postpone': in his long and confusing taxonomy of five types of kingship in III xiv–xviii Aristotle defines the Spartan variety as a permanent (= lifelong) hereditary generalship, according to law, not sovereign over everything but with absolute personal power in matters of war in foreign territory, and with religious duties (to summarize 1285ᵃ3–16, b26–8). Given that Sparta's preoccupation was military might (**17**), the office was clearly vital, and it is hardly surprising that the Kings were sometimes at loggerheads with the Ephors (1270ᵇ13–15), especially since the hereditary principle does not necessarily throw up natural generals, as Aristotle notes (though on the question of inherited character he is apt to vacillate: see 1255ᵇ1–4, 1283ᵃ36–7, 1286ᵇ22–7, *Rhet.* 1367ᵇ31, 1390ᵇ21–31). Yet he must be exaggerating when he claims that the lawgiver regarded the Kings as 'not good', apparently without exception. The combative dynamics of Spartan political life are somewhat puzzling. 'Fellow-ambassadors' may refer to normal foreign diplomacy exclusively or to the practice of sending out two Ephors along with a King on campaign (Xen. *Hell.* II 4, 36); in the latter case, the diplomacy would be negotiations with the enemy. The 'faction' may be personal wrangling, or disagreement about policy.

Aristotle has no conception of a 'constitutional' kingship above the political battle, with only ceremonial and advisory functions: all his five types of king are active in the running of the state. He is however in general terms aware that in the course of history some kingships have lost power (1285ᵇ3–19); paradoxically, that is why they survived, as in Sparta (1313ᵃ18–33).

15 (1271ᵃ26–37) The *phiditia* (in Attic, *sussitia*) were the (fairly frugal) common meals which were attended by every Spartiate; for they were an important part of the Spartan attempt to de-emphasize private life and to foster group solidarity and civic loyalty; and citizen-rights depended on membership, presumably because such sentiments, acquired in such conditions, were felt essential in a citizen (cf. Plut. *Lyc.* 10, 24, 25). No doubt the institution worked so long as all Spartiatae could afford the contribution; but with increasing disparities of wealth the poor could not (cf. **7** and **8**, with comment), and so became disfranchised, i.e. not one of the *homoioi*, 'Similars' (as the Spartiatae called themselves) in political rights, and indeed in general life-style too. That is the point of saying (cf. 1265ᵇ40–1) that the common meals were intended to be 'democratic' (anachronistically, since the founder could hardly have known the word); for political equality is the hallmark of democracy (1301ᵃ25 ff.). However, in effect an *unplanned* oligarchy developed (on property-qualifications for citizenship in an oligarchy, see *Rep.* 551ab, 1292ᵃ39–41)—though presumably the tendency to democracy decribed at 1270ᵇ13–7 did something to counteract it. In other words, what started in part as a moral or social qualification for citizenship became an economic one, subverting the state's 'assumption' (see **1**). On common meals in the *Laws*, see 762c, 780a–781e, 806e, 842b,

955, Morrow (1960a) 389–98; in Aristotle's ideal state, 1330ᵃ3–13; on the Cretan common meals, see 1272ᵃ12–27.

16 (1271ᵃ37–41) Aristotle speaks as though the matter were purely one of constitutional rivalry, perhaps arising from a vague demarcation of power, and uncertainty which office took precedence in policy and action. In fact, as an analyst of constitutional tension and change, he knows there are more issues than those (see book V *passim*). No doubt he is thinking of the Naval Commander Lysander (d. 395), who wished to make the Spartan Kingship elective (Diod. Sic. XIV 13, cf. 1271ᵃ20–2), probably because he felt the Naval Command unfairly lacked the prestige of the Kingship (1270ᵇ23); and he was apparently slighted personally by several Kings (1301ᵇ19–20, 1306ᵇ31–3). What lies behind this cryptic paragraph is a distinction between the principles of and tensions between the various parts of the constitution and the relatively trivial occasions that trigger changes to them: see e.g. 1302ᵃ22 ff., V iv.

17 (1271ᵃ41–ᵇ6) A common complaint, e.g. 1324ᵇ5 ff., 1338ᵇ9 ff., *Laws* 631a, 666e–667a, 688a ff.; refs. to other authors in Schütrumpf ii. 326. Aristotle speaks in black and white terms, as though the Spartans had no other 'part' of virtue, i.e. any other particular virtue, in view, and therefore *possessed* no other; but clearly if that had been so Sparta would have fallen apart as a state; and indeed **6** 1270ᵃ5–6 says the military life itself has 'many' parts of virtue. But it is a question how Aristotle's official Socratic-style account of the virtues accommodates the Spartan situation (and indeed the perfectly common cases of a person's possessing different virtues in different degrees). According to *EN* VI xiii, we may have one merely 'naturally' occurring virtue but not another, but not one virtue 'in the sovereign sense' (*kuria*, i.e. a developed or mature virtue) but not another; for any virtue in this latter sense is inseparable from mind (*nous*) or practical wisdom (*phronēsis*). Practical wisdom (presumably because it is a comprehensive or general faculty, not easily compartmentalized, life being complex) is therefore inseparable from each of the whole range of the virtues, so that if you have one sovereign virtue, you necessarily have practical wisdom, and therefore *all* the sovereign virtues. The implication may then be that practical wisdom is of some single intensity, i.e. not possessed by the same individual in varying 'strengths' in different parts of life. At any rate, apparently the Spartans have great practical wisdom, and hence great virtue (courage) in one area (war), but limited practical wisdom and hence only partly-developed virtue in a range of cognate areas (political and family life, economics, etc.). But the practical result is clear: by allowing the growth of ambition and poverty etc. the Spartans have lost the worldly goods they achieved by military prowess (1333ᵇ5–26, cf. 1334ᵃ6–10, Isoc. VIII 95 ff.).

'Assumption': see **1**. On 'leisure', which is not for relaxation but for leading the 'good life', see references at end of comment on 1269ᵇ7–12. On the term 'sovereign', see comment on 1252ᵃ1–7 (*b*).

18 (1271ᵇ6–10) And why should they *not* so suppose, we may ask, on an instrumentalist view of virtue? But to Aristotle the 'good things men fight about' (wealth etc., 1168ᵇ15 ff.) are themselves only tools, of which we need only a few, for the attainment of human good, i.e. happiness, virtuous activities, which ideally *exclude* goods-getting. Cf. I viii–xi, esp. 1323ᵃ38–ᵇ21, *EE* 1248ᵇ26–1249ᵃ16.

19 (1271ᵇ10–19)   Commonplaces about Spartan finance: see references in Schütrumpf ii. 329. The lack of inquiry suggests not just greed and reluctance to pay but systematic corruption.

II x

CRITICISM OF THE CONSTITUTION AND
SOCIAL SYSTEM OF CRETE

Introduction   In this chapter Aristotle pursues roughly the same themes as in ix, but even more selectively and allusively, and with little reference to political theory; and again there has been a great deal of historical controversy. His sources (on which see Perlman (1992) 197–8) are uncertain, but at least in places he seems to have used the historian Ephorus (d. 330); whether he himself, or one of his pupils, compiled a '*Constitution of the Cretans*' is not known, but is more than likely. Certainly the similarities between the Cretan and Spartan constitutions, and the (alleged) derivation of the latter from the former, were widely known and debated (see e.g. Her. I 65; Plato *Rep.* 544c, *Laws* 630d, 780e). For interest in inter-state influence, cf. 1274ᵃ22–ᵇ5.

There were of course many Cretan states, traditionally 100, and Aristotle evidently thinks they all had a constitution of the same basic pattern. This belief is hard to square with the historical facts, which suggest much diversity; it may well be 'an artificial construct of the political philosophers of the late Classical period' (Perlman (1992) 195, in an attempt to trace its origin).

1 (1271ᵇ20–32)   'Finished' (*glaphuros*) seems glossed in ᵇ24 as 'elaborated'; contrast the rude simplicity of early laws at 1268ᵇ31–1269ᵃ8; and in biology too there is a pattern of increasing complexity, in the development and articulation of embryos (e.g. *HA* 489ᵇ9–10; cf. Perlman (1992) 204–5). But elaboration is not in itself a merit: a state's administrative and legal structure can be so complex as to be unworkable. At 1274ᵇ7–8 the lawgiver Charondas, though ancient, is 'more finished' than modern legislators in the *precision* of his laws: presumably the implication is that they were not merely unambiguous but detailed, and so able to cope successfully with a wide variety of situations. So 'finished' seems to mean 'complex, but nicely calculated to suit relevant purposes' (cf. the finely intricate web of the 'wisest and smoothest (*glaphurōtatos*)' spider at *HA* 623ᵃ8 ff.). Perhaps then, the Spartan constitution is more finished in that it has more, and more elaborately interlocking, organs: a double Kingship, Elders, Ephors, etc.; and the ensemble works, more or less. Crete on the other hand has effectively only Elders and Cosmoi (**3**); and certain rules of office (**6**) allow the latter practically to destroy the constitution. If Aristotle does not mean that, what *does* he mean? At any rate, it obviously suits his general teleology to point out development and refinement: see also I ii and introduction, 1264ª1–11, 1329ᵇ25 ff.

The implications of the last sentence are unclear. Were there two parallel and generally similar systems of law? Did at least some of the peripheral people (counterparts of the Spartan helots, see 1269ª36 ff. with comments) *observe* Minos' laws unmodified, while the incoming Spartans *adapted* them? Aristotle may even think it possible to distinguish *three* systems of law, of increasing refinement: (i) Minos'; (ii) the Spartan colonists'; (ii) Sparta's. That would be a remarkable exercise in comparative law. Cf. Strabo X iv 17, and, on Lyctos, Perlman (1992) 200–1.

2 (1271ᵇ32–40) For an awareness of the importance of geography to political affairs, see VII v–vii; it is not for nothing that Plato sited Magnesia in a remote area of S. Crete, a longish distance from the sea and the undesirable people and practices it can bring (*Laws IV init.,* cf. 1272ª41–ᵇ1). Evidently in Aristotle's own day Crete did not have an aggressive foreign policy (1272ᵇ19–20); presumably he thinks that absence of empire conduces to Cretan happiness (cf. 1324ᵇ22–1325ª15).

3 (1271ᵇ40–1272ª12) A systematic list of parallels between the two constitutions, with notes on certain differences. *Andreia*: 'men's meals or quarters'; the Attic term is *sussitia*, 'common meals'. The 'plain indication' is plain only if we know antecedently that the Spartan constitution derived in general from the Cretan.

The final sentence presents difficulties. (i) Are these Elders Spartan or Cretan? Probably the latter, at any rate if the Spartan Assembly had substantial power (see on 1270ᵇ25–8). Considerable obscurity surrounds the word Aristotle uses for the voting in the Assembly (*sunepipsēphizein*): if it means 'vote for', 'ratify' rather than 'vote on', it is an odd 'final' power that cannot say 'no' but only 'yes'. At all events, an Assembly hobbled in some such way is typical of an oligarchy: 1298ᵇ26–1299ª2. Whether debate was allowed the Cretan Assembly is equally unclear (cf. 1273ª9–13).

4 (1272ª12–27) Many details of the Cretan economy are uncertain. Athenaeus 263f may indicate the existence of both private land and public; but 'public produce' may mean either 'from public land' (alone) or 'from a public *stock* of produce', built up by contributions at least in part from private land. If the latter is right, Aristotle seems to imply that the basis of the contribution to the meals was not a set sum per head (contrast 1271ª26–37); presumably it was a proportion of a man's produce (possibly one tenth, Athenaeus 143ab), which ensured that no adult male lost his political rights because of a *failure* of his crops, and no one starved (cf. 1329ᵇ36–1330ª13, esp. ª2). If that in turn is right, we have here the rudiments of a 'welfare' state (cf. Huxley (1971) 511 for further details), though how far its inspiration was philanthropic it would be hazardous to speculate; 1309ª14–32, ᵇ35–1310ª12 for some hard-headed reasons why an oligarchy (as **5** with 1272ᵇ9–10 implies Cretan states were, if they were anything) should look after the interests of the poor. And given those political and economic guarantees, what incentive is there to work one's land energetically? At any rate, in Crete the effective citizen-body does not *fluctuate* for chance economic reasons; it Sparta it did. But no doubt the main reason for Aristotle's approval of the Cretan system is that it chimes with his own principle, 'private property, common use' (1263ᵃ21–30). However, he can hardly mean, though he seems to imply, that women and children actually joined in the 'men's meals'; see comment on 1265ᵃ1–10.

It is hard to know what to make of the remarks about homosexuality (see Dover (1978) 185 on its origins and distribution). Nowhere in the *Politics* does Aristotle fulfil his promise to discuss further its practice in Crete (cf. however 1262ᵃ32–40, 1269ᵇ23–31). Indeed, it is not even clear whether 'acted ill or not' refers to the desirability or otherwise of male homosexuality in principle (*EN* 1148ᵇ24–9 is disapproving; cf. *Laws* 636a ff., 836a ff.), or merely to the way it is *utilized* in Crete. 'Bring about' is odd language to use of it: 'recognize' or 'find a place for' *vel sim.* must be meant. One may doubt if it was effective for the purpose stated (Spyridakis (1979)). On the 'segregation' of women, see Willetts (1955) 18 ff.; it means not merely social seclusion but delayed cohabitation, perhaps facilitated by the male homosexual activity. On the birth-rate see 1265ᵃ38–ᵇ7, 1266ᵇ8–14, 1270ᵃ34–ᵇ6, VII xvi (esp 1335ᵇ19–26).

'Public services', *leitourgiai*, such as paying for a festival; in Athens they fell on rich private persons.

5 (1272ᵃ27–ᵇ1) Cf. the commentary on ix 9–13. Aristotle's central point is that Cretan states are more oligarchical than Sparta: the Cosmoi come from certain families only, without regard to merit (contrast 1272ᵇ34–7), and the Elders from former Cosmoi; what regard is paid to wealth as a qualification, and so leisure, is unclear: cf. 1273ᵃ31–ᵇ7.

In the last sentence, the lack of corruption (bribery) among the Cosmoi, which is in principle laudable (1308ᵇ31 ff.), is said to account for popular apathy: there is no profit in the office, so the people are not disturbed by seeing others gain from it, and are not concerned to hold it themselves. Aristotle presumably prefers the interest shown in the Ephorate by the Spartan people, since it helps to cement the constitution (1270ᵇ17–28), but without the corruption. Indeed, not to be attracted to an office because it offers no prospect of illicit gain is itself a kind of corruption. On written rules, see Perlman (1992) 196–7.

6 (1272ᵇ1–15) The 'fault' is the very great power described in **5**, checked paradoxically and crudely by faction among the powerful, *dunatoi*, who form 'power-groups', *dunasteiai* (an extreme form of oligarchy, employing personal and arbitrary rule rather than law: 1292ᵇ5–10, 1293ᵃ30–4, cf. 1298ᵇ2–5). '*Absence* of Cosmoi': akosmia, pointedly, as the word normally means 'disorder' (*kosmos* = 'order'). 'Sectionalize': by appealing for support to various groupings within the people; cf. 1305ᵇ22 ff.

'Association which is the state', *politikē koinōnia*, cf. comment on 1252ᵃ1–7. The faction prohibits or at least impedes the cooperation and interchange of services essential to a state, in particular that form of co-

operation which is a constitution. (Hence we could here translate *politikē*
as 'to do with a constitution', *politeia*, rather than 'to do with a state',
polis.) That is, a collection of people does not amount to a state unless they
have a constitution, which is defined as a 'system of offices' (1278ᵇ8–10).
But why not? The Cretan states did not simply disintegrate when their
Cosmoi quarrelled and generated a power-vacuum. Aristotle is using
'state' in a strong sense. A community founded merely for 'life' (production, exchange, etc.) is not a state, which has to aim at the 'good life'; and
to further that aim it needs men of education and character to administer
and lead it, *under the law* (1292ᵃ30–8, cf. 1252ᵇ27–1253ᵃ1, 1253ᵃ29–39,
III ix).

7 (1272ᵇ15–23) Cf. **5** *fin.*, and 1305ᵇ16–18. On expulsions of foreigners in
Sparta and elsewhere, see *Laws* 950b, 953e. On peripheral populations, cf.
1269ᵃ40–ᵇ5 and comment. On external dominion, see **2** and comment. The
'foreign war' perhaps refers to the invasion by Phalaecus the Phocian
in 345.

II xi

CRITICISM OF THE CONSTITUTION AND
SOCIAL SYSTEM OF CARTHAGE

Introduction   Aristotle evidently compiled, or supervised the compilation
of, several *Constitutions* of non-Greek states, but Carthage is the only one
whose constitution he treats systematically in the *Politics*, perhaps because
he was impressed by the sight of a non-Greek state adopting aristocracy as
its 'assumption' (1273ᵃ4–5). Brief and scattered references to the social and
political character and practices of Carthage and other non-Greek states
may derive from his *Customs of non-Greeks, Nomima Barbarika* (e.g.
1252ᵇ5–7, 1285ᵃ19–22, and 1324ᵇ5 ff.); the *Constitutions* may well represent
a later phase of his political researches (see Weil (1960) 100, 116–21, 228–
31); and the existence of a *Constitution of the Carthaginians* is probable but
not certain. At any rate, we have plenty of evidence of an impressive
catholicity of interest; and his willingness to take the Carthaginian constitution seriously, and his admiration of certain features of it, are surely
maturer than the advice Plutarch alleges he gave to Alexander, 'to treat
Greeks in the manner of a leader, and non-Greeks in the manner of a
slave-master' (*Fort. Alex.* I 6). In this chapter the common Greek division
of mankind into themselves (superior) and others (inferior) is transcended;
cf. also its handling at 1327ᵇ18–38. On Aristotle and non-Greeks, see
Badian (1958) 440–4.

Some of the points made in this chapter are similar to those made in II
ix and x (see **3** *init.*). But caution is needed: the likenesses between the
Spartan constitution and the Cretan gained in conviction from a known or
at least a widely believed historical connection, but Aristotle can claim no

such support in the case of Carthage, and in **2** one suspects a degree of over-schematization; at any rate there are considerable obscurities. See Weil (1960) 246–54, esp. on the comparative dating of Aristotle's various reports of Carthage, and Newman ii. 401–8. In spite of grouping the three constitutions together in **1**, he compares Carthage in detail with Sparta alone, and is content to indicate only vague resemblances to Crete, presumably on the strength of its likeness to Sparta.

From **3** onwards Aristotle analyses the Carthaginian constitution in terms of 'deviations', a concept characteristic of his typology of constitutions in III–VI (see esp. III vi–vii, cf. *EN* VIII x). This is a departure from the dominant mode of analysis in ix and x, where Spartan and Cretan institutions were assessed in terms of their failure to meet the requirements either of the 'best system' or of the 'assumption' or 'aim' (i.e. military virtue and conquest) embodied in the intended constitution (see 1269^{a}29–34 and comment, 1271^{a}41–^{b}6, 1324^{b}5–9). The fuss that has been made (Weil (1960) 248 ff., on which see Bertelli (1977) 73–4 and Schütrumpf ii. 352–3) about the apparent change of method misses the point. For the Spartan constitution, being 'mixed', was notoriously hard to classify (1294^{b}14 ff., *Laws* 712c ff.), the Cretan was not really a constitution at all (1272^{b}9–11), and military prowess is not in itself a constitution. In ix and x analysis by typology was therefore inappropriate (though it surfaces briefly at 1270^{b}16–17). In Carthage, however, the 'assumption' *is* (Aristotle thinks) a constitution (aristocracy, or 'polity', **3** *init.*; cf. 1293^{b}7–21), so typology becomes relevant. That is the point of the first sentence of **3**: objections to the Carthaginian constitution are cast in terms of deviation, but they are not new: we have already met them in ix and x, though not in the garb of deviations. His method throughout ix–xi is entirely consistent: to assess by reference to the 'assumption' adopted by the people in question, or occasionally and incidently to such wider concepts as 'the best way' (1269^{b}11–12) or 'happiness' (1269^{b}14). For a full review of the Carthaginian constitution, see Huss (1985) 458–66.

1 (1272^{b}24–33)   The paragraph seems to presuppose extensive comparative study of constitutions, but why Aristotle isolates these three is not entirely clear; for obviously not all features found within the group are peculiar to it. Perhaps 'a long-established oligarchy, relying on common meals to maintain its ethos, and with a "managed" people', is about as close as one can get to catching a peculiar *combination* of features. The extraordinariness of Carthage lies presumably in her strong elements of aristocracy, which put her closer to Sparta than to the power-groups of Crete. There may be a related point lurking in 'among them' (= all three, or the Carthaginians alone?); perhaps 'them' ought to be italicized, to catch an implied contrast with other states. For *why* does a given institution work in one constitution but its counterpart in another does not? This practical interest is prominent in ix–xi; for example, in **2**, the Kingship in Carthage, which is meritocratic, is better than the Kingship in Sparta, where it is hereditary. Aristotle is also very much exercised by the comparative political role of the people: cf. **3** (in Carthage, considerable power), 1270^{b}17–28 (in Sparta, willing acquiescence in the constitution from good motives), 1272^{a}39–^{b}1 and 1272^{a}10–12 (from disreputable motives in Crete, and with little power).

2 (1272^{b}33–1273^{a}2) The state of our knowledge permits us to do little but take Aristotle's word for these parallels; cf. esp. 1270^{b}6–1271^{a}37. Were the common meals primarily military in purpose (cf. 1324^{b}12–15)? The 104 are presumably the 100 of **4** *init.*; but how such a large number can be or operate 'like' five Ephors is not clear. It seems likely that the electors of the Kings (two, the 'Suffetes') were the people; cf. **5**. 'Age': Sparta used modified primogeniture, if Her. VII 3 is to be trusted; cf. comment on 1271^{a}18–26.

3 (1273^{a}2–13) The point of 'aristocracy "or" polity' is that, of mixtures of oligarchy and democracy, those inclining to oligarchy are (in virtue of the education and virtue that wealth can bring) called aristocracies, while those inclining to democracy are called polities (1290^{a}13–19, 1293^{b}34 ff., 1307^{a}5 ff.). Carthage's constitution somehow manages to lean in both directions, and the leaning to democracy is here explored first.

A leaning or deviation is something which a constitution has towards or away from some stated standard (e.g. 1319^{a}38 ff.); it is often some element which is discrepant with its fundamental or predominant character; and it can be expressed also by constitutional adjectives and adverbs ('more democratic' etc., e.g. 1317^{a}2, and 1299^{a}41–1300^{b}1, 'characteristic of a polity in an aristocratic way'). In the contrast between 'straight' and 'deviated' constitutions, the notion of deviation implies something undesirable: 1290^{a}24–9, 1293^{b}22 ff.; so too here at the start of this paragraph, the deviation *from* aristocracy and polity *towards* democracy and oligarchy; for deviation-constitutions look to sectional interests, not to the common good (1279^{a}17–^{b}10). The term is used in biology also (e.g. *GA* 767^{b}7–8).

The constitutional procedures are desperately hard to fathom. An obvious ambiguity in the sequence described is the scope of the 'agreement': does it mean 'on the substantive issue or proposal', or 'to refer to the people'? A further ambiguity lurks in 'all', which in the Greek can imply unanimity of Kings and Elders together, or 'both together', with a majority vote of Elders. In either case it looks as if the two Kings in concert could not be overruled. 'These matters too': i.e. as well as matters which are referred to them in the normal way, *with* the agreement of King and Elders. Referrals, which presumably concerned major matters of state policy, were apparently not obligatory; however, there would be this constant pressure on the Kings and Elders, that if they failed to come up with an agreed proposal for referral, the people, if they wished, had the right to adopt and decide the business. Whether or not that is the correct interpretation of these foggy lines, the people's powers of decision are, in Aristotle's view, excessive, which is perhaps why, if indeed the text is correct, he calls Carthage a democracy outright (1316^{b}5–6). But in the 'best' democracy, their powers should be confined to election of officials, their scrutinies, and judging in courts: see in general III xi, VI iv, 1274^{a}11–21.

'This practice': to debate and decide (contrast 1272ᵃ10–12 and comments), not merely the former?

4 (1273ᵃ13–20)   We now explore in detail the leaning to oligarchy, in the shape of the Boards of Five, 'Pentarchies'. (*a*) 'When some [i.e. a restricted number] appoint from some by election, that is oligarchical', 1300ᵇ1–2, cf. 1294ᵇ7–9, 31–3; in Carthage, the electors are the 'some' who already hold the office in question, and the 'some' eligible for election are the rich (see **5**, but also on (*e*) below). (*b*) It is unclear from whom the 100 are elected: from the Boards themselves, or from other rich individuals? If the 100 are the 104 of **2** *init.*, who correspond to the Spartan Ephors, who are chosen by and from the people (1270ᵇ8–9, 25–8), then the election of the 100 is indeed a considerable deviation towards oligarchy, as compared with Spartan practice. Neither in (*a*) nor in (*b*) is the degree of formal voting clear. (*c*) Short tenure is democratic (1308ᵃ15–16, 1317ᵇ24–5, cf. 1299ᵃ3–12 ff.). Ruling 'before' tenure may point to an interval between election and entering office, ruling 'after' may be by virtue of acquired personal authority. At all events, evidently the tenure is unusually long only because of the periods before and after; did the latter extend indefinitely? (*d*) Pay, and (*e*), the lot, are democratic (1317ᵇ35, ᵇ20–1); but why is their mere absence aristocratic rather than oligarchic? Probably Aristotle means both: the office is oligarchic in point of numbers of appointers and appointees, aristocratic in that electing to it permits personal merit to operate as a criterion, whereas the lot does not. Cf. comment on **3** *init.*

On (*f*), the judging of lawsuits, cf. 1275ᵇ5–12. There are three issues, at least potentially. (i) Both Sparta and Carthage try cases oligarchically, before officials, not popular juries; that is clear by implication (cf. 1270ᵇ28–9). But the Ephors, in at least some suits, sat alone (1275ᵇ9–10); the Carthaginian Boards each have five members; so in a purely numerical sense, Sparta's practice is more sharply oligarchic. But surely that is not all Aristotle is thinking of. (ii) For he talks of aristocracy, and is probably thinking of the advantages of collective judgements (see III xi), by *meritorious* persons (cf. 1287ᵇ11–15), not individual judgements by Ephors, who might be nonentities and/or bribable (**2**, 1270ᵇ8–10). (iii) The Boards evidently judged all types of cases indiscriminately, unlike the Ephors (1275ᵇ9–12). Is there some implication here that a wide experience of many types of case promotes *better* judgements than specialization? That would be concordant with the view that aristocracy is concerned with 'the best' for the state (1279ᵃ36–7). It is hard to know which point is uppermost in Aristotle's mind: probably (ii), as the personal merit or otherwise of office-holders is central to his typology of constitutions (cf. 1294ᵃ10–11); but his words read as though (iii) might be at issue. On the other hand, in **7** he espouses the principle of specialization in office-holding. On Spartan judging, see Macdowell (1986) ch. 7.

5 (1273ᵃ21–30) and **6 (1273ᵃ31–ᵇ7)**   Of the two reasons for appointing the rich to office, Aristotle discusses here only one: that they alone have the leisure for it. He claims that the result, evidently unlooked for, is a kind of commercialization of office: giving bribes to obtain it, taking bribes during tenure, or resorting to peculation in order to recoup the expenditure (cf. 1286ᵇ14–16, 1302ᵇ5–10, 1308ᵇ31 ff.); and then the state at large catches from its rulers the habit of honouring wealth rather than moral and political virtue (for the force of example, cf. *Laws* 711a). He does not discuss the other reason for office-holding by the rich, advanced by the rich themselves: that they *deserve* a greater share of political power, in all justice, on grounds of 'superiority', i.e. their very wealth and therefore utility to the state, and the virtue they display in getting it (see 1301ᵃ25 ff. and the concession at *Laws* 744c2; contrast 1288ᵃ15 ff.). Elsewhere Aristotle is careful to distinguish that sort of virtue from political virtue, with which it is easily confused (1283ᵃ16–22, 1293ᵇ34 ff.).

In the final sentence of **6** Aristotle in effect pleads for payment to office-holders, as a substitute for personal wealth; yet in **4** he says it is aristocratic that the Boards of Five are *not* paid. Presumably he wants it both ways, that his office-holders should be both virtuous and rich. Certainly he thinks leisure should be provided by the labour of slaves, helots, etc.; cf. 1269ᵃ34 ff., 1278ᵃ8–21, 1328ᵇ33–1329ᵃ2, 1330ᵃ25–33. On the Carthaginians' criteria for election, cf. 1293ᵇ7–21: their attention to wealth prevents their aristocracy from being the 'best'. On love of money in Sparta, see 1269ᵇ23 ff., 1270ᵃ11–34, 1271ᵇ10–19.

7 (1273ᵇ8–17) On the face of it a simple plea for specialization in office-holding, as conducive to efficiency. But there are issues that do not meet the eye. (i) Pluralism can in some circumstances be oligarchic, and import the danger of tyranny (1310ᵇ22–3), which Carthage has nevertheless escaped (**1** *fin.*, but cf. 1307ᵃ5, 1316ᵃ34); we are not told how. (ii) The allegedly *natural* principle 'one person, one job' was invoked in 1252ᵃ34–ᵇ9 to justify a permanent differentiation of function as between slave and female, and in I xii–xiii as between female and male, for each has different natural capacities; notably, the male's natural role is to rule the others. In the state, ideally the same persons should rule permanently; but this is often impossible, on grounds of justice, since all the potential rulers are 'by nature equal'; alternation in rule is therefore necessary (1261ᵃ22–ᵇ6). But now we learn that 'one man, one office' is desirable apparently on a more or less permanent basis, as in the military example, where obviously the ruled do not alternate duties with the rulers. So unless everyone is to have *some* office, we seem to be left with a permanent cadre of officials, each entrenched in a single post, and alternation is subverted. If that is so, is 'one man, one (particular) office' to be justified on grounds of nature (e.g. a naturally bellicose man should be a permanent general), and/or on one of Aristotle's favourite principles, that practice makes perfect (e.g. *EN* 1103ᵃ32–ᵇ2)? At 1299ᵃ31–ᵇ13, however, it emerges that Aristotle thinks 'necessary' the holding by one person of several offices *successively*; but in each office there will be only one job to do, so that the principle of specialization is up to a point preserved. He does not consider whether transferring from one post to another entails a loss of efficiency. Our paragraph seems therefore to be written with an extreme regard for the analogy between the crafts and 'statesmanship', whereas 1299ᵃ31–ᵇ13 more easily accommodates alternation of ruling and being ruled. (In small states, however, pluralism is acceptable, on grounds of shortage of manpower: 1273ᵇ12, 1299ᵇ1 ff.)

'More statesmanlike', *politikōteron*: deployed vaguely, but I take the point to be that the more persons hold office, the more *politikoi* there are, statesmen acting in the interests of the state, *polis* (or of a 'polity'?) and its citizens, *politai*. 'More democratic': democracies require many to hold office (VI ii). 'More communal', *koinoteron*: more people contribute to the state as an association, *koinōnia*, see 1252ᵃ1–7. 'As . . . persons': the Greek, if the text is t, is rather obscure, being only 'of the same' (plural). Perhaps neuter, 'each task (since it?) is of/concerns the same matters', i.e. a permanent holder of a single office always has the same familiar *matters* to deal with, and so becomes efficient in them. The masculine, adopted in the translation, conveys rather the sameness/permanency of the single *incumbent* of each single office, each with its single task.

8 (1273ᵇ18–26)   On the instability of oligarchies, and their problematical relationship to the common people, see e.g. 1302ᵃ2–15, 1309ᵃ20–32, V vi, 1301ᵃ2–12. The Carthaginian measure described here is mentioned again at 1320ᵃ35–ᵇ9, as one of several which may be designed and paid for by rich persons to prevent poverty and hence civil unrest. Given its admitted practical effectiveness, Aristotle's censure of it as the work of Fortune seems harsh; for it is not accidental but planned (cf. *EN* 1099ᵇ20–5). His point is not merely that Carthage lacks legal means to cure faction, nor even that prevention is better than cure (cf. 1302ᵇ19–21), but that a state that can remain stable only by ejecting parts of itself has not been designed by its lawgiver (cf. 1270ᵇ19–20, 1284ᵇ17–20) as a genuine association, *koinōnia*: its benefits and burdens are not distributed justly (see on 1252ᵃ1–7 (*a*)), so that it cannot be 'free of faction'. Compare commentary on 1265ᵃ38–ᵇ17, on Plato's population policy in Magnesia. The exact nature of the 'sending out', and the identity of 'the states', are not clear; nor indeed is the Greek itself: perhaps '. . . escape faction by being rich, i.e. by sending out some section . . .' (i.e. by being rich enough to send it out with the appropriate resources).

The concluding accolade is a trifle unexpected, given the severity of Aristotle's criticisms; but cf. comment on 1260ᵇ27–36.

II xii

DEFENCE OF THE CONSTITUTION OF SOLON; SIGNIFICANT MEASURES OF CERTAIN OTHER LAWGIVERS

Introduction   This chapter is a standing puzzle. At 1260ᵇ27–36 Aristotle promised (*a*) to examine constitutions of high quality, both those in force in certain states reputed to be well governed (ix–xi), and others merely proposed but thought to have merit (ii–viii); and (*b*) to do so in a critical spirit, in order to discover what was right and useful in them. In II xii he departs from both promises. He (*a*) concentrates on the careers and certain miscellaneous enactments of several lawgivers, without constitutional analysis, and (*b*) adopts a factual and entirely non-committal methodology: there is none of the sharp scrutiny and forthright criticism we encounter in the rest of the book.

The only exception is **2–4**, an intelligent but angled analysis of the original form and subsequent development of the celebrated constitution of Solon, Athens' most famous lawgiver. Even here, however, the conflicting assessments of Solon are presented as those of other people, and the writer's apparent wish in **4** to defend him rests on nothing more firm than 'seems' (*bis*, cf. 1273ᵇ41).

There are hypotheses without number to account for this curious state of affairs (see Schütrumpf's balanced account, ii. 362–9, Bertelli (1977) 79–81, Keaney (1981)). Though some or all of the material may well have been assembled by one or more of Aristotle's pupils under his supervision, the sharp discrepancies of content and manner with the rest of the book make it hard to believe that he is responsible for it as a whole, unless it is mere jottings of raw matter for subsequent elaboration (though **2–4** look like a finished product). One is perfectly free to suppose that the chapter is the hotch-potch of a pupil who hoped to parade his independent but uncoordinated research into lawgivers by tacking it on to the end of a completed section of the Master's work.

However, let us attempt to reconstruct the thoughts of the writer, as charitably as possible. He believes: (i) That something 'right and useful' can be learned from a study of admired historical, not merely contemporary, constitutions, even if they have deteriorated; at least one may see the reasons for that deterioration. This is much in the spirit of e.g. 1269ᵇ39–1270ᵇ6. Hence he discusses Solon, who did not appear in the rest of the book, apart from one brief comment (1266ᵇ16). (ii) That *non*-constitutional law is important too: in particular, isolated measures produced by individual lawgivers are just as crucial for the quality of life as formal constitutions are (see comment on **1**). (iii) That originality in this respect can occur when a lawgiver works under the stimulus of living in a foreign state; at any rate, the transfer of ideas, laws, and institutions from one state to another, and therefore naturally their modification for a new context, are part of the process of advance. Hence the migrant lawgivers of **5** and **6**, and the listing of features 'peculiar' to the various lawgivers in **6–8**.

1 (1273ᵇ27–34) For the distinction between public and private persons, cf. vii *init.*; 'nearly all', i.e. Plato, Hippodamus, and probably Phaleas. The distinction between (*a*) the laws *of* a constitution, which is a system of distributing offices, and (*b*) the laws administered *under* it, is set out at 1289ᵃ11–25 (cf. comments on 1265ᵃ1–10), where the point is made that the latter set must be consistent with and subserve the former. One wishes Aristotle had explored their relationship further (though obviously he thinks it should be tight: 1282ᵇ6–13, VIII i); our present author presumably takes it entirely for granted. In the first sentence, he means 'constitution' in a wide sense, to include laws both of type (*a*) and of type (*b*); in the last, he means it in a narrow sense, to embrace type (*a*) only. Outside 2–4 his chief concern is apparently not with theoreticians, but with the type (*b*) laws of practical men, though in fact at least some of the legislators in 5–8 were private persons (see 7).

2 (1273ᵇ35–1274ᵃ3), 3 (1274ᵃ3–11), and 4 (1274ᵃ11–21)   In general, Aristotle admired Solon (1296ᵃ18–20). The main sources for his constitution (594 BC) and its development are four: (*a*) his own poems, in which he justifies his measures, (*b*) the 'Aristotelian' *Constitution of the Athenians*, chs. 5–12, (*c*) these three paragraphs, (*d*) Plutarch's *Life of Solon*. The historical detail, and the relationships between the sources, are complex and often controversial: see Rhodes (1981) esp. 118–20; in particular, (*c*) is substantially similar to (*b*), but there is one perhaps significant discrepancy.

The text is crowded with allusion, and guidance is more than usually necessary. 2 *Slavery*: the extreme economic and political domination by landed aristocrats, which Solon ended by forbidding debts on the security of the person. *Ancestral*: a Protean slogan, see Finley (1971). On *mixture*, cf. e.g. IV ix, and comments on 1265ᵇ26–1266ᵃ22 and 1270ᵇ17–28. *Areopagus*: composed of former archons, appointed for life; much respected, but its wide general powers were cut down to homicide cases alone by Ephialtes and Pericles, 462–1. *Courts*: Solon permitted appeals from the decisions of aristocratic judges sitting alone to the popular assembly, *heliaea*, which in time formed numerous courts with jury panels; these became, in virtue of their popular composition and inappellable decisions, powerful legally and politically; brief account in Saunders (1991) 90–3. 3: for *popular leaders* (demagogues) as 'a structural element in the Athenian political system', see Finley (1962) 19. 4 *Scrutinies*: see comment on 1271ᵃ6–8. *Slave and foe*: cf. 1264ᵃ11–40, 1268ᵃ14–29, 1281ᵇ28–30, 1320ᵃ14–17. *Property-qualifications*: details in Rhodes (1981) 136 ff.; the point is the decisive shift to gradations of wealth alone as qualifications for office.

2 reports, with two corrections, the views of Solon's admirers (moderates, perhaps Plato especially, Morrow (1960*a*) 80–6), 3 those of his critics (who?). 4 defends him by arguing that he did not intend the undesirable results to which his constitution led, witness the limited power he accorded the people (cf. 1281ᵇ21 ff., 1318ᵇ27 ff.). In short, the question posed is, was Solon a conservative and moderate, or not?

The answer, while clearly 'yes', has two connected oddities. (*a*) It makes no difference to the moderate *character* of Solon's constitution whether the Areopagus and the practice of electing officials were inherited by him and allowed to survive (2), or whether he invented them; in either case they are an integral part of the 'package'. Yet our author goes out of his way to insist that only in the matter of the courts did Solon innovate. (*b*) In order to establish that Solon did not innovate in the matter of elected officials, he has to fudge the difference between the pre-Solonic and post-Solonic modes of election, which according to *AP* III i, VIII i–ii were sharply different. Before Solon, appointment to the archonship was made

(i) by and from among wealthy and aristocratic families; after, (ii) by the tribes, by a preliminary election of a 'slate' of candidates, who were then subject to (democratic) sortition. In both processes, there was of course choice; but (ii) is a fairly radical departure from (i), in its electors and in the use of the lot. On the accuracy of *AP* as against our passage, see *Rhodes* (1981) 146–8.

Why then does our author perform this manœuvre? Partly, no doubt, to show that Solon was a moderate, in preserving, in the shape of elections, the aristocratic principle of merit. But *if* we are to look for a conceptual, not just an external, connection (lawgiver) with **6–8**, he has in effect established an *idion*, 'peculiarity', for Solon: the innovation in regard to courts; for on his account Solon was in all other respects a moderate and a traditionalist. On the meaning and significance of *idion*, see comment on **6**.

5 (1274ᵃ22–31) Chronology: Zaleucus, probably mid-7th century; Charondas, probably 6th century; Onomacritus, probably he of Her. VII 6, late 6th cent., far too late to be the 'first' expert in lawgiving; Thales: *not* the philosopher of Miletus; Lycurgus, 7th cent.(?), perhaps only a legendary figure. The reported interest in the origins and development of legislation may be partly academic, but more probably arose mainly from a motive of patriotic (here Cretan) pride; cf. 1271ᵇ20–32.

6 (1274ᵃ31–ᵇ5) This erotic and picturesque story is in the style of a tourist guide-book (cf. Keaney (1981) 99); but at any rate we learn why Philolaus legislated in a foreign state. The victory of Diocles was in 728. For the belief that dead men can look out from inside the tomb, cf. *Laws* 872bc, Saunders (1991) 239.

The Greek of the last sentence of the paragraph is not quite clear, but probably Philolaus' 'peculiarity' is legislation not merely to keep the number of estates constant (cf. 1265ᵃ38 ff., 1266ᵇ14–24, *Laws* 740a ff., Asheri (1963) 1 ff.), but to do so by laws of adoption (i.e. by preventing their amalgamation into larger units when they lack an heir (Asheri 6 ff., cf. 1309ᵃ23–6, *Laws* 740c). However, Pheidon of Corinth, 'one of the earliest of lawgivers' (1265b12–16: late 8th cent.?), wished to keep the number of households and the number of citizens the same; the means he used are not stated. Now *if* he, or simply Corinthian practice, was the inspiration of Philolaus, a Corinthian, when he legislated in Thebes, then perhaps here is an example of a transfer of an idea from one state to another and of its being brought into connection with some other and local area of legislation (adoption). If that is so, our author sees fruitful interaction between the laws of two states.

But what exactly does it mean to ascribe a 'peculiarity', *idion*, to a lawgiver? Aristotle himself, though seeing that originality is not necessarily meritorious (cf. 1260ᵇ33–6, 1265ᵃ10–13, 1268ᵇ22 ff.), shares the widespread interest of the ancients in the 'first finders' in various fields of knowledge (e.g. *Soph. Ref.* 183ᵇ17 ff., 1253ᵃ30–1, 1267ᵇ29); but *idion* ought to indicate not mere priority but uniqueness. Yet it is clear from the account of Charondas' 'peculiarity' in **7** that others too availed themselves of it (the 'objection' was a procedure in use later in Athens); in fact, *idion* is *glossed* as 'first'. Perhaps the notion is that priority is (necessarily) 'peculiar', since there cannot be more than one 'first'; it is that which stands out as original in a lawgiver's total body of work (cf. *Met.* 987ᵃ29 ff., on the 'peculiarities' of Plato). Our author is however aware that peculiarity is not a necessary index of importance (**7** *fin.*); nevertheless, he seems to feel, peculiarities ought to be recorded: they may prove useful. When he uses the term of a law or an institution, he perhaps implies that he has studied enough of the rest of that legislator's work to know that none of it is peculiar to him or distinctive in any way; and that he knows enough of the work of *all* other legislators to be sure that that law is not contained in it (cf. Keaney (1981) 98). And are we to suppose that no legislator has more than one law or institution peculiar to him?

7 (1274ᵇ5–18) The wording of the opening is slightly curious, as obviously in theory a litigant can bring a suit for false witness without the preliminary 'denunciation', *episkēpsis*, of his testimony; the point may be that Charondas' invention of the denunciation led to the creation of formal suits in which its justification could be tested; cf. Harrison (1971) 192–7. Whether the 'finish' (cf. comment on 1271ᵇ20–32) of his laws was a once-for-all achievement at the time of the framing of a code, or arose empirically (as a result of e.g. problems of equity: see comments on 1269ᵃ8–12), is not clear.

The reversion to Phaleas and Plato (ii–vii) is slightly startling; but the author is concerned to isolate their 'peculiarities'. The point about intoxication sounds trivial or even silly, but is in fact important; for Plato wishes to use drinking-parties both to test and strengthen moral character: *Laws* 645c–650b, 666a, 671a–674c, see Belfiore (1986). As for ambidexterity, our author takes Plato's remarks literally, perhaps rightly (*Laws* 794d–795d); but they may also be a whimsically oblique way of urging that women too, not just men, ought to be utilized to the full in the life of the state (see Morrow (1960a) 329).

Draco gave Athens her first written laws in 621–620. The notoriety of the severity of his punishments (e.g. *Rhet.* 1400ᵇ22–3) tells us something of Greek disapproval, whether instinctive or calculated, of extreme retaliation (see Saunders (1991) 17–18, 94 nn. 22–3, 127–33).

8 (1274ᵇ18–28) Pittacus: of Mytilene, d. 570. A nice conflict between equity and the social need for repression and deterrence. Drunkenness could be urged in excuse as a kind of ignorance; but to have become drunk is one's own fault: see *Rhet.* 1402ᵇ8–12, *EN* 1113ᵇ30–3; Saunders (1991) 111 has further references and discussion. Does 'all the more' imply that among offenders who deserve pardon drunkards deserve it especially, or that even sober offenders are regularly entitled to it (cf. D.L. I 76), though less so than drunkards?

Of Androdamas we know nothing but what is said here.

APPENDIX

THE ALLEGED OLIGARCHIC BIAS IN PLATO'S LAWS
(*see pp. 134–5*)

1. Members of the Council. Aristotle's account (1266ᵃ14–22) of their appointment (756b–e) is somewhat lacunose but essentially accurate. The entire procedure lasts 5 days, a strong incentive to poorer persons not to attend and vote when they do not have to. The persons of 'better quality' are *voters*, not candidates. *If* the higher classes are smaller than the lower, then they have some edge in representation (Morrow (1960*b*) 151). Note that 'choose' throughout 1266ᵃ14–22 means in effect only 'nominate'.

2. Attendance at the Assembly, 764a: all males aged 20 and over are members, but the wealthier are fined for non-attendance; see 1297ᵃ14–35 for this as an 'oligarchical device', and cf. Saunders (1993) 57.

3. Temple treasurers, 759e–760a.

4. Market Wardens, 763e.

5. City Wardens, 763d.

6. Umpires of Athletic and Equestrian Contests, 765cd.

7. Guardians of the Laws, 753b ff.

Some points relevant to Aristotle's thesis emerge: (i) The powers of the Council and the Assembly are decidedly attenuated, as compared with Athenian practice (Morrow (1960*a*) 157–78). (ii) Office (6) perhaps calls for experience (see 765ab) of horses, which are expensive. (iii) Offices (3)–(5) presumably call for financial expertise, which wealthy persons may be expected to have (Morrow (1960*a*) 181); yet for (4) and (5), after an initial selection of a 'slate' of candidates, the final choice is left to the lot (in general accordance with the policy of 1294ᵇ6–14, cf. 1298ᵇ9, *Laws* 757e). (iv) Office (7) is very powerful. Plato probably intended, however, to include the light-armed (poorer) troops as electors, in addition to the (richer) heavy-armed (cf. comment on 1265ᵇ26–1266ᵃ5 (*a*), and Morrow (1960*b*) 151). But if that is not right, the choice of the Minister of Education, a vital official, from among the Guardians of the Laws would be indirectly oligarchical (766b). Moreover, a moderately costly ceremony at the end of the Guardians' election may be intended to exclude poorer voters from the final stage. (v) Office (5): the reason given is that the holders will have, in virtue of their wealth, leisure to go in for public affairs (a principle which is of course readily extendible to *any* oligarchic selection). Further discussion in Brunt (1993) 272–5.

LIST OF DEPARTURES FROM THE OXFORD CLASSICAL TEXT

	This translation	OCT
1255ᵇ7	delete square brackets	
1256ᵃ16	ἡ δὲ	ἤ γε
1256ᵃ17–18	οἰκονομικῆς	χρηματιστικῆς
1258ᵃ18	αὕτη	αὐτή
1260ᵃ4	ἀρχομένων	ἀρχόντων
1261ᵇ2	comma after ἄρχειν	full point
1262ᵃ31	γνωριζόντων	γνωριζομένων
1264ᵃ37	comma after διώρισται	full point
1266ᵃ16	ἴσως	ἴσους
1266ᵃ17	τοὺς	τοῖς
1268ᵃ25–6	delete quotation marks	
1269ᵇ2	delete ταῖς	
1273ᵇ5	ἄρχειν	ἀργεῖν

BIBLIOGRAPHY

This bibliography is limited to works cited in this book. A fuller bibliography of the *Politics*, divided by topic, is in Saunders (1981); the fullest available are in Schütrumpf (1991–) i. 135–70, and ii. 119–48.

TEXT

Ross, W. D. (1957), *Aristotelis Politica* (Oxford Classical Text).

TRANSLATION

Saunders, T. J. (1981), *Aristotle, The Politics*, translated by T. A. Sinclair, revised and re-presented by Trevor J. Saunders (Penguin Classics Series, Harmondsworth).

COMMENTARIES
(cited by name, volume, and page only)

Newman, W. L., *The Politics of Aristotle*, with an introduction, two preparatory essays and notes critical and explanatory (4 vols., Oxford 1887–1902).
Schütrumpf, E., *Aristoteles, Politik*, übersetzt und erläutert, vol. i, with extensive introduction, on book I, vol. ii on books II and III, both 1991; in progress (Berlin).

BOOKS AND ARTICLES

Ackrill, J. L. (1981), *Aristotle the Philosopher* (Oxford).
Allan, D. J. (1965), 'Individual and State in the *Ethics* and *Politics*', in *La 'Politique' d'Aristote* (*Entretiens sur l'Antiquité Classique*, XI Vandœuvres–Genève, 31 août–5 sept. 1964, 53–85 (discussion, 86–95).
Andrewes, A. (1966), 'The Government of Classical Sparta', in *Ancient Society and Institutions, Studies presented to V. Ehrenberg on his 75th birthday* (London), 1–20.
Annas, J. (1977), 'Plato and Aristotle on Friendship and Altruism', *Mind*, 86, 532–54.
—— (1981), *An Introduction to Plato's Republic* (Oxford).
—— (1988), 'Self-love in Aristotle', *Southern Journal of Philosophy*, 28, suppl. 1–18 (with comment by R. Kraut, 19–23).

ANNAS, J. (1990), 'Comments on J. Cooper' (see below), in Patzig, 242–8.

ARETHUSA (1975), *Population Policy in Plato and Aristotle* (= *Arethusa*, 8).

ASHERI, D. (1963), 'Laws of Inheritance, Distribution of Land and Political Constitutions in Ancient Greece', *Historia*, 12, 1–21.

BADIAN, E. (1958), 'Alexander the Great and the Unity of Mankind', *Historia*, 7, 425–44.

BALME, D. M. (1987), 'Teleology and Necessity', in A. Gotthelf and J. G. Lennox (eds.), *Philosophical Issues in Aristotle's Biology* (Cambridge), 275–85.

BARNES, J. (1990), 'Aristotle on Political Liberty', in Patzig, 249–64 (with comment by R. Sorabji, see below.)

—— SCHOFIELD, M., and SORABJI, R. (1977), *Articles on Aristotle, 2: Ethics and Politics* (London).

BELFIORE, E. (1986), 'Wine and Catharsis of the Emotions in Plato's *Laws*', *Classical Quarterly*, 36, 421–37.

BENSON, J. (1990), 'Making Friends: Aristotle's Doctrine of the Friend as Another Self', in A. Loizou and H. Lesser (eds.), *Polis and Politics: Essays in Greek Moral and Political Philosophy* (Avebury), 50–68.

BERTELLI, L. (1977), *Historia e Methodos: Analisi Critica e Topica Politica nel Secondo Libro della 'Politica' di Aristotele* (Turin).

BRUNSCHWIG, J. (1980), 'Du mouvement et de l'immobilité de la loi', *Revue Internationale de Philosophie*, 34, 512–40.

BRUNT, P. A. (1993), *Studies in Greek History and Thought* (Oxford).

BURNS, A. (1976), 'Hippodamus and the Planned City', *Historia*, 25, 414–28.

CAMBIANO, G. (1987), 'Aristotle and the Anonymous Opponents of Slavery', in M. I. Finley (ed.), *Classical Slavery* (London), 22–41.

CARTLEDGE, P. (1981*a*), 'Spartan Wives: Liberation or Licence?', *Classical Quarterly*, 31, 84–105.

—— (1981*b*), 'The Politics of Spartan Paederasty', *Proceedings of the Cambridge Philological Society*, 207, 17–36.

—— (1987), *Agesilaos and the Crisis of Sparta* (Baltimore).

CHAN, J. (1992), 'Does Aristotle's Political Theory rest on a "Blunder"?', *History of Political Thought*, 13, 189–202.

CLARK, S. R. L. (1982), 'Aristotle's Woman', *History of Political Thought*, 3, 177–91.

COOPER, J. M. (1990), 'Political Animals and Civic Friendship', in Patzig, 220–41 (with comment by J. Annas, see above).

DAWSON, D. (1992), *Cities of the Gods: Communist Utopias in Greek Thought* (New York).

DE STE. CROIX, G. E. M. (1975), 'Aristotle on History and Poetry (*Poetics* 9, 1451ª36–ᵇ11)', in B. Levick (ed.), *The Ancient Historian and his Materials, Essays in Honour of C. E. Stevens on his seventieth birthday* (Farnborough 1975), 45–58. Repr. in A. O. RORTY (ed.), *Essays on Aristotle's Poetics* (Princeton 1992), 23–32.

DEPEW, D. J. (1995), 'Humans and Other Political Animals in Aristotle's *History of Animals*', *Phronesis*, 40, 156–81.

DOVER, K. J. (1978), *Greek Homosexuality* (London).

EDELSTEIN, L. (1967), *The Idea of Progress in Classical Antiquity* (Baltimore).

ENGBERT-PEDERSON, T. (1983), *Aristotle's Theory of Moral Insight* (Oxford).

ENGLAND, E. B. (1921), *The Laws of Plato*, the text edited with introduction, notes, etc. (2 vols., Manchester).

EVERSON, S. (1988), 'Aristotle on the Foundations of the State', *Political Studies*, 36, 89–101.

FINLEY, M. I. (1962), 'Athenian Demagogues', *Past and Present*, 21, 1–23. Repr. in id., *Studies in Ancient Society* (London 1974), 1–25, and id., *Democracy Ancient and Modern* (New Brunswick and London 1985), 38–75.

—— (ed.) (1968), *Slavery in Classical Antiquity: Views and Controversies* (Cambridge and New York 1960; repr. with suppl. to bibl.).

—— (1970), 'Aristotle and Economic Analysis', *Past and Present*, 47, 3–25. Repr. in id., *Studies in Ancient Society* (London 1974), 26–52, and in Barnes *et al.*, 140–58.

—— (1971), 'The Ancestral Constitution', Inaugural Lecture, University of Cambridge. Repr. in id., *The Use and Abuse of History* (London 1975), 34–60.

—— (1980), *Ancient Slavery and Modern Ideology* (London).

—— (ed.) (1981), *Economy and Society in Ancient Greece* (London).

FORREST, W. G. (1980), *A History of Sparta 950–192 BC* (2nd edn., London).

FORTENBAUGH, W. W. (1977), 'Aristotle on Slaves and Women', in Barnes *et al.*, 134–9.

GOLDSCHMIDT, V. (1973), 'La Théorie aristotélicienne de l'esclavage et sa méthode', in *Zetesis, Album Amicorum, Festschrift É. de Stryker*, Antwerp), 147–63.

GRAHAM, A. J. (1964), *Colony and Mother City in Ancient Greece* (Manchester and New York).

GUTHRIE, W. K. C. (1962–81), *A History of Greek Philosophy* (5 vols., Cambridge).

HALLIWELL, S. (1993), *Plato, Republic 5*, with an introduction, translation, and commentary (Warminster).

HANSEN, M. H. (1991), *The Athenian Democracy in the Age of Demosthenes* (Oxford).

HARRISON, A. R. W. (1968–71), *The Law of Athens* (2 vols., Oxford).

HARVEY, F. D. (1965, 1966), 'Two Kinds of Equality', *Classica et Mediaevalia*, 26, 101–46; 27, 99–100.

HODKINSON, S. (1986), 'Land and Inheritance in Classical Sparta', *Classical Quarterly*, 36, 378–406.

HOROWITZ, M. C. (1976), 'Aristotle and Woman', *Journal of the History of Biology*, 9, 183–213.

HUMPHREYS, S. C. (1978), *Anthropology and the Greeks* (London).

HUSS, W. (1985), *Geschichte der Karthager* (Munich).

HUXLEY, G. (1971), 'Crete in Aristotle's *Politics*', *Greek, Roman and Byzantine Studies*, 12, 505–15.

IRWIN, T. H. (1985), 'Moral Science and Political Theory in Aristotle', in P. A. Cartledge and F. D. Harvey (ed.), *Crux: Essays Presented to G. E. M. de Ste. Croix on his 75th birthday* (Exeter) = *History of Political Thought*, 6 (1985), 150–68.

IRWIN, T. H. (1988), *Aristotle's First Principles* (Oxford).

—— (1991), 'Aristotle's Defense of Private Property', in Keyt and Miller, 200–25. (A revised version of 'Generosity and Property in Aristotle's *Politics*', in *Social Philosophy & Policy*, 4 (1987), 37–54 = E. F. Paul *et al.*, *Beneficence, Philanthropy and the Public Good* (Oxford and New York, 1987), 37–54.)

JOHNSON, C. (1988), 'Aristotle's Polity: Mixed or Middle Constitution?', *History of Political Thought*, 9, 189–204. (Rev. version in id., *Aristotle's Theory of the State* (London, 1990), 143–54.)

KAHN, C. H. (1981), 'Aristotle and Altruism', *Mind*, 90, 20–40.

KEANEY, J. J. (1981), 'Aristotle, *Politics* 2.12.1274^{a}22–^{b}28', *American Journal of Ancient History*, 6, 97–100.

KEYT, D. (1991), 'Three Basic Theorems in Aristotle's *Politics*', in Keyt and Miller, 118–41. (Revised version of 'Three Fundamental Theorems in Aristotle's *Politics*', *Phronesis*, 32 (1987), 54–79.)

—— (1993), 'Aristotle and Anarchism', *Reason Papers*, 18, 133–52.

—— and MILLER, F. D. (1991), *A Companion to Aristotle's* Politics (Oxford and Cambridge, Mass.).

KOCK, T. (1880–8), *Comicorum Atticorum Fragmenta* (3 vols., Leipzig).

KULLMANN, W. (1991), 'Man as a Political Animal in Aristotle', in Keyt and Miller, 94–117. (Slightly enlarged version of 'Der Mensch als politisches Lebewesen bei Aristoteles', *Hermes*, 108 (1980), 419–43.)

LANA, I. (1949), 'L'utopia di Ippodamo di Mileto', *Rivista di Filosofia*, 40, 125–51.

—— (1950), 'Le teorie egualitarie di Falea di Calcedone', *Rivista Critica di Storia della Filosofia*, 5, 265–76.

LEWIS, T. J. (1978), 'Acquisition and Anxiety: Aristotle's Case against the Market', *Canadian Journal of Economics*, 11, 69–90.

MACDOWELL, D. M. (1975), 'Law-making at Athens in the Fourth Century B.C.', *Journal of Hellenic Studies*, 95, 62–74.

—— (1978), *The Law in Classical Athens* (London).

—— (1986), *Spartan Law* (Edinburgh).

MAHONEY, T. A. (1992), 'Do Plato's Philosopher-rulers sacrifice Self-interest to Justice?', *Phronesis*, 37, 265–82.

MAYHEW, R. (1993a), 'Aristotle on Property', *Review of Metaphysics*, 46, 803–31.

—— (1993b), 'Aristotle on the Extent of the Communism in Plato's *Republic*', *Ancient Philosophy*, 13, 313–21.

MEIKLE, S. (1991a), 'Aristotle and Exchange Value', in Keyt and Miller, 156–81. (Revised version of 'Aristotle and the Political Economy of the Polis', *Journal of Hellenic Studies*, 99 (1979), 57–73; repr. in M. Blaug (ed.), *Aristotle (384–322 B.C.)* (London, 1991), 195–220.)

—— (1991b), 'Aristotle on Equality and Market Exchange', *Journal of Hellenic Studies*, 111, 193–6.

—— (1994), 'Aristotle on Money', *Phronesis*, 39, 26–44.

—— (1995), *Aristotle's Economic Thought* (Oxford).

MILLER, F. D. (1989), 'Aristotle's Political Naturalism', in T. Penner and R. Kraut (eds.), *Nature, Knowledge and Virtue: Essays in Memory of Joan Kung* (Edmonton) (= *Apeiron*, 22 (1989)), 195–218.

—— (1991), 'Aristotle on Property Rights', in J. P. Anton and A. Preus (eds.), *Essays in Ancient Greek Philosophy*, IV: *Aristotle's Ethics* (Albany), 227–47.

—— (1995), *Nature, Justice, and Rights in Aristotle's* Politics (Oxford).

MILLER, R. W. (1981), 'Marx and Aristotle: A Kind of Consequentialism', *Canadian Journal of Philosophy*, suppl. vol. VII, 323–52.

MORROW, G. R. (1960*a*), *Plato's Cretan City* (Princeton); repr. 1993 with new foreword by C. H. Kahn.

—— (1960*b*), 'Aristotle's Comments on Plato's *Laws*', in I. Düring and G. E. L. Owen (eds.), *Plato and Aristotle in the Mid-fourth Century* (Göteborg), 145–62. Repr. in P. Steinmetz (ed.), *Schriften zu den Politica des Aristoteles* (New York, 1973), 378–95.

MORSINK, J. (1979), 'Was Aristotle's Biology Sexist?', *Journal of the History of Biology*, 12, 83–112.

MULGAN, R. G. (1970), 'Aristotle's Sovereign', *Political Studies*, 18, 518–22.

—— (1974), 'Aristotle's Doctrine that Man is a Political Animal', *Hermes*, 102, 438–45.

—— (1977), *Aristotle's Political Theory* (Oxford); 2nd edn. 1987.

—— (1994), 'Aristotle and the Political Role of Women', *History of Political Thought*, 15, 179–202.

NATALI, C. (1990), 'Aristote et la chrématistique', in Patzig, 296–324.

NUSSBAUM, M. C. (1986), *The Fragility of Goodness: Luck and Ethics in Greek Tragedy and Philosophy* (Cambridge).

PARKER, R. (1983), *Miasma: Pollution and Purification in early Greek Religion* (Oxford).

PATZIG, G. (ed.) (1990), *Aristoteles' 'Politik': Akten des XI. Symposium Aristotelicum, Friedrichshafen/Bodensee, 25.8–3.9.1987* (Göttingen).

PEĆIRKA, J. (1967), 'A Note on Aristotle's Conception of Citizenship and the Role of Foreigners in Fourth Century Athens', *Eirene*, 6, 23–6.

PERLMAN, P. (1992), 'One Hundred-Citied Crete and the "Cretan πολιτεία" ', *Classical Philology*, 87, 193–205.

POLANYI, K. (1957), 'Aristotle discovers the Economy', in K. Polanyi, C. M. Arensberg, and H. W. Pearson (eds.), *Trade and Market in the Early Empires* (New York and London), 64–94. Abridged version in G. Dalton (ed.), *Primitive, Archaic and Modern Economies* (Boston, 1968), 78–115.

PRICE, A. W. (1989), *Love and Friendship in Plato and Aristotle* (Oxford).

RHODES, P. J. (1981), *A Commentary on the Aristotelian Athenaion Politeia* (Oxford). New edn. 1993, with addenda.

ROBINSON, R. (1962), *Aristotle's* Politics, *Books III and IV*, translated with introduction and comments (Clarendon Aristotle Series, Oxford); rev. edn. 1995 by D. Keyt.

Rose, V. (1886), *Aristotelis qui ferebantur Librorum Fragmenta* (Leipzig).

Rowe, C. J. (1977), 'Aims and Methods in Aristotle's *Politics*', *Classical Quarterly*, 27, 159–72. Rev. and repr. in Keyt and Miller, 57–74.

—— (1989), 'Reality and Utopia', *Elenchos*, 10, 317–36.

Saunders, T. J. (1970), *Plato, the Laws*, translated with an introduction (Penguin Classics Series, Harmondsworth).

—— (1984), 'The Controversy about Slavery reported by Aristotle, *Politics*, I vi, 1255ª4 ff.', in A. Moffat (ed.), *Maistor: Classical, Byzantine and Renaissance Studies for R. Browning* (Canberra), 25–36.

—— (1991), *Plato's Penal Code: Tradition, Controversy and Reform in Greek Penology* (Oxford).

—— (1992), 'Plato's Later Political Thought', in R. Kraut (ed.), *The Cambridge Companion to Plato* (New York and Cambridge), 464–92.

—— (1993), 'Aristotle and Bagehot on Constitutional Deception', in H. D. Jocelyn (ed.), *Tria Lustra, Essays and Notes Presented to John Pinsent* (Liverpool), 45–57.

—— (1995), 'Women in the *Laws* of Plato', in A. Powell (ed.), *The Greek World* (London), 591–609.

Schofield, M. (1990), 'Ideology and Philosophy in Aristotle's Theory of Slavery', in Patzig, 1–27.

Schumpeter, J. A. (1954), *History of Economic Analysis* (New York).

Schütrumpf, E. (1994), 'Aristotle on Sparta', in A. Powell and S. Hodkinson (eds.), *The Shadow of Sparta* (London and New York), 323–45.

Sedley, D. (1991), 'Is Aristotle's Teleology Anthropocentric?', *Phronesis*, 36, 179–96.

Smith, N. D. (1991), 'Aristotle's Theory of Natural Slavery', in Keyt and Miller, 142–55. Earlier version in *Phoenix*, 37 (1983), 109–22.

Snell, B. (1971), *Tragicorum Graecorum Fragmenta*, i (Göttingen).

Solmsen, F. (1964), 'Leisure and Play in Aristotle's Ideal State', *Rheinisches Museum*, 107, 193–220.

Sorabji, R. (1990), 'State Power: Aristotle and Fourth Century Philosophy', in Patzig, 265–76 (= comment on J. Barnes (1990), see above).

Soudek, J. (1952), 'Aristotle's Theory of Exchange', *Proceedings of the American Philosophical Society*, 86, 45–75.

Spyridakis, S. (1979), 'Aristotle on Cretan πολυτεχνία', *Historia*, 28, 380–4.

Stalley, R. F. (1983), *An Introduction to Plato's Laws* (Oxford).

—— (1991), 'Aristotle's Criticism of Plato's *Republic*', in Keyt and Miller, 182–99.

Swanson, J. A. (1992), *The Public and the Private in Aristotle's Political Philosophy* (Ithaca).

Taylor, C. C. W. (1995), 'Politics', in J. Barnes (ed.), *The Cambridge Companion to Aristotle* (Cambridge), 233–58.

Tigerstedt, E. N. (1965–78), *The Legend of Sparta in Classical Antiquity* (3 vols., Stockholm etc.).

Vander Waerdt, P. A. (1991), 'The Plan and Intention of Aristotle's Ethical and Political Writings', *Illinois Classical Studies*, 16, 231–53.

von Fritz, K. (1954), *The Theory of the Mixed Constitution in Antiquity*

(New York).

WARDY, R. (1993), 'Aristotelian Rainfall or the Lore of Averages', *Phronesis*, 38, 18–30.

WEIL, R. (1960), *Aristote et l'Histoire: Essai sur la 'Politique'* (Paris).

WIELAND, W. (1975), 'The Problem of Teleology', in J. Barnes, M. Schofield, and R. Sorabji (eds.), *Articles on Aristotle, Science* (London), 141–60. (Trans. of *Die Aristotelische Physik* (Göttingen 1962, 2nd edn. 1970), ch. 16.).

WILLETTS, R. F. (1955), *Aristocratic Society in Ancient Crete* (London).

WILLIAMS, B. (1993), *Shame and Necessity* (Berkeley, Los Angeles, Oxford).

WOODS, M. (1982), *Aristotle's* Eudemian Ethics, *Books I, II and VII*, translated with a commentary (Clarendon Aristotle Series, Oxford); 2nd edn., 1992.

YACK, B. (1993), *The Problems of a Political Animal: Community, Justice and Conflict in Aristotelian Thought* (Berkeley, Los Angeles, London).

SELECTIVE GLOSSARIES

NOTES

1. These glossaries cover the translation only, and are confined to the more important institutions, offices, practices, and concepts, irrespective of frequency of occurrence.

2. Apart from certain pairs or clusters, mere cognates are omitted (e.g. *eleutheriotēs*, 'liberality' is listed, but not *eleutherios*, 'liberal'). Also omitted are 'ordinary' uses of words used technically (e.g. *ergon*, 'function', means ordinarily 'job', 'task' etc.).

3. Greek adjectives ending in *-ikos* are a trouble. P. Chantraine remarks of them (*Études sur le vocabulaire grec* (Paris, 1956) 152): 'Le même adjectif peut connoter à la fois l'appartenance à une catégorie, la caractérisation et l'aptitude.' Their clearest employment in the *Politics* is in the feminine singular, *-ikē*, with *technē* (art or skill) or *epistēmē* (knowledge) 'understood'; they then become virtually nouns in their own right, e.g. *oikonomikē*, the skill 'of household-management', *oikonomia*, or 'of the household-manager', *oikonomos*. But sometimes it is hard to be sure what nuance Aristotle intends; yet to take refuge in the non-committal rendering 'to do with' seems inadequate. In such cases I have ventured to adopt the locution that seemed right in the context (e.g. 'with the role of', 1252^{a}7–16, see commentary). The range of *politikos* is particularly wide; however, its most common use is as a noun, 'statesman'; cf. comment on 1252^{a}1–7 *fin.*, on *koinōnia politikē*, 'the association which takes the form of a state'.

ENGLISH–GREEK

absence of Cosmoi	akosmia	ἀκοσμία
acquisition	ktēsis	κτῆσις
knowledge or art or skill of acquiring property	ktētikē	κτητική
knowledge etc. of acquiring goods or wealth	chrēmatistikē	χρηματιστική
cf. property		
action	praxis	πρᾶξις
affection	philia	φιλία
agreement	homologia	ὁμολογία
ancestral	patrios	πάτριος
cf. traditional		
appetition	orexis	ὄρεξις
arbitrator	diaitētēs	ὁμολογία
aristocracy	aristokratia	ἀριστοκρατία

182

Assembly	*ekklēsia*	ἐκκλησία
association	*koinōnia*	κοινωνία
cf. common		
participate in or share in	*koinōnein*	κοινωνεῖν
assumption	*hupothesis*	ὑπόθεσις
benevolent	*philanthrōpos*	φιλάνθρωπος
Boards of Five	*pentarchiai*	πενταρχίαι
capacity	*dunamis*	δύναμις
cf. faculty, power		
category	*eidos*	εἶδος
cf. kind		
change (*active verb*)	*kinein*	κινεῖν
changing-round, technique of	*metablētikē*	μεταβλητική
to do with changing-round	*metablētikos*	μεταβλητικός
choice (= choosing), chosen aim	*prohairesis*	προαίρεσις
citizen, *see* state		
coin(age)	*nomisma*	νόμισμα
common, communal	*koinos*	κοινός
cf. association		
common meals, messes	*sussitia*	συσσίτια
concord, conducive to	*homonoētikos*	ὁμονοητικός
constitution	*politeia*	πολιτεία
cf. polity, state		
contentious	*eristikos*	ἐριστικός
convention	*nomos*	νόμος
Cosmoi	*kosmoi*	κόσμοι
Council	*boulē*	βουλή
courage	*andreia*	ἀνδρεία
court	*dikastērion*	δικαστήριον
democracy	*dēmokratia*	δημοκρατία
desire	*epithumia*	ἐπιθυμία
deviation	*parekbasis*	παρέκβασις
disposition	*hexis*	ἕξις
doing well	*eupraxia*	εὐπραξία
dominion	*archē*	ἀρχή
education	*paideia*	παιδεία
Elders	*gerontes*	γέροντες
elect, choose	*haireisthai*	αἱρεῖσθαι
chosen by election	*hairetos*	αἱρετός
end	*telos*	τέλος
Ephors	*ephoroi*	ἔφοροι
equal	*isos*	ἴσος
essential	*anankaios*	ἀναγκαῖος
estate	*klēros*	κλῆρος
cf. lot		
exchange	*allagē*	ἀλλαγή
faction	*stasis*	στάσις

faculty	*dunamis*	δύναμις
cf. capacity, power		
fallacy	*paralogismos*	παραλογισμός
feelings	*pathēmata*	παθήματα
force	*bia*	βία
free	*eleutheros*	ἐλεύθερος
friendship	*philia*	φιλία
function	*ergon*	ἔργον
general (*noun*)	*stratēgos*	στρατηγός
good	*agathos*	ἀγαθός
good life	*eu zēn*	εὖ ζῆν
goods	*chrēmata*	χρήματα
cf. money		
government by good laws	*eunomia*	εὐνομία
Guardians	*phulakes*	φύλακες
habit	*ethos*	ἔθος
happiness	*eudaimonia*	εὐδαιμονία
heavy-armed troops	*hoplitai*	ὁπλῖται
heiress	*epiklēros*	ἐπίκληρος
helots	*heilōtes*	εἵλωτες
honour	*timē*	τιμή
household	*oikia, oikos*	οἰκία, οἰκός
household-management	*oikonomia*	οἰκονομία
household-manager	*oikonomos*	οἰκονόμος
art or skill of household- management	*oikonomikē*	οἰκονομική
to do with household- management	*oikonomikos*	οἰκονομικός
ideal	*kat' euchēn* ('according to prayer')	κατ' εὐχήν
impulse	*hormē*	ὁρμή
interest	*tokos*	τόκος
juryman	*dikastēs*	δικαστής
justice	*dikaiosunē*	δικαιοσύνη
kind	*eidos*	εἶδος
cf. category		
King, king	*basileus*	βασιλεύς
knowledge	*epistēmē*	ἐπιστήμη
law	*nomos*	νόμος
lawgiver	*nomothetēs*	νομοθέτης
leisure	*scholē*	σχολή
liberality	*eleutheriotēs*	ἐλευθεριότης
licence	*anesis*	ἄνεσις
limit	*peras*	πέρας
lot, chosen by	*klērōtos*	κληρωτός
cf. estate		

love	*erōs*	ἔρως
master (of slaves)	*despotēs*	δεσπότης
means (towards an end)	*ta pros to telos*	τὰ πρὸς τὸ τέλος
mechanic	*banausos*	βάναυσος
mind	*nous*	νοῦς
moderation	*sōphrosunē*	σωφροσύνη
monarchy	*monarchia*	μοναρχία
money	*chrēmata*	χρήματα
cf. goods		
nation	*ethnos*	ἔθνος
nature	*phusis*	φύσις
Naval Commanders	*nauarchoi*	ναύαρχοι
need (*noun*)	*chreia*	χρεία
noble birth	*eugeneia*	εὐγένεια
non-Greeks	*barbaroi*	βάρβαροι
office	*archē*; also *timē*	
	(*cf.* honour)	ἀρχή, τιμή
official (*noun*)	*archē*	ἀρχή
oligarchy	*oligarchia*	ὀλιγαρχία
one	*mia*	μία
overlap	*epallattein*	ἐπαλλάττειν
part	*meros, morion*	μέρος, μόριον
peculiar (to)	*idios*	ἴδιος
cf. private		
people (common)	*dēmos*	δῆμος
cf. democracy		
peripheral people	*perioikoi*	περίοικοι
perjure	*epiorkein*	ἐπιορκεῖν
philosophy	*philosophia*	φιλοσοφία
polity	*politeia*	πολιτεία
cf. constitution, state		
popular leader	*dēmagōgos*	δημαγωγός
cf. people		
possession	*ktēma*	κτῆμα
power	*dunamis*	δύναμις
cf. capacity, faculty		
power-group	*dunasteia*	δυναστεία
practical wisdom	*phronèsis*	φρόνησις
private, peculiar (to)	*idios*	ἴδιος
production	*poiēsis*	ποίησις
property	*ktēsis*	κτῆσις
cf. acquisition		
property-class	*timēma*	τίμημα
public	*dēmosios*	δημόσιος
public service	*leitourgia*	λειτουργία
reason	*logos*	λόγος
cf. speech		

reciprocal	*antipeponthos*	*ἀντιπεπονθός*
resources	*ousia*	*οὐσία*
respectable	*epieikēs*	*ἐπιεικής*
restraint	*sōphrosunè*	*σωφροσύνη*
cf. moderation		
rule (*verb*)	*archein*	*ἄρχειν*
(*noun*)	*archē*	*ἀρχή*
cf. dominion, office		
scrutiny	*euthuna*	*εὔθυνα*
self-engendered	*autophuton*	*αὐτόφυτον*
self-sufficiency	*autarkeia*	*αὐτάρκεια*
sensation, sense	*aisthēsis*	*αἴσθησις*
skill	*technē*	*τέχνη*
skilled worker	*technitēs*	*τεχνιτής*
slave	*doulos*	*δοῦλος*
sophisticated	*charieis*	*χαρίεις*
soul	*psuchē*	*ψυχή*
sound (*adjective*)	*spoudaios*	*σπουδαῖος*
sovereign (*adjective*)	*kurios*	*κύριος*
speech	*logos*	*λόγος*
cf. reason		
state	*polis*	*πόλις*
citizen	*politēs*	*πολίτης*
constitution	*politeia*	*πολιτεία*
statesman	*politikos*	*πολιτικός*
to do with state or citizens		
or statesmen	*politikos*	*πολιτικός*
engage in state affairs		
(or similar)	*politeuesthai*	*πολιτεύεσθαι*
syllogism	*sullogismos*	*συλλογισμός*
tool	*organon*	*ὄργανον*
trade	*kapēleia*	*καπηλεία*
traditional	*patrios*	*πάτριος*
cf. ancestral		
tyrant	*turannos*	*τύραννος*
vexatious prosecution	*sukophantia*	*σμκοφαντία*
village	*kōmē*	*κώμη*
virtue	*aretē*	*ἀρετή*
voice	*phōnē*	*φωνή*
whole	*holos*	*ὅλος*
wholly	*holōs*	*ὅλως*
written rules	*grammata*	*γράμματα*

GREEK–ENGLISH

ἀγαθός	*agathos*	good
αἱρεῖσθαι	*haireisthai*	elect, choose

αἱρετός	*hairetos*	chosen by election
ἀκοσμία	*akosmia*	absence of Cosmoi
αἴσθεσις	*aisthesis*	sensation, sense
ἀλλαγή	*allagē*	exchange
ἀναγκαῖος	*anankaios*	essential
ἀνδρεία	*andreia*	courage
ἄνεσις	*anesis*	licence
ἀντιπεπονθός	*antipeponthos*	reciprocal
ἀρετή	*aretē*	virtue
ἀριστοκρατία	*aristokratia*	aristocracy
ἄρχειν	*archein*	rule (*verb*)
ἀρχή	*archē*	rule (*noun*), dominion, office, official
αὐτάρκεια	*autarkeia*	self-sufficiency
αὐτόφυτον	*autophuton*	self-engendered
βάναυσος	*banausos*	mechanic
βάρβαροι	*barbaroi*	non-Greeks
βασιλεύς	*basileus*	King, king
βία	*bia*	force
βουλή	*boulē*	Council
γέροντες	*gerontes*	Elders
γράμματα	*grammata*	written rules
δεσπότης	*despotes*	master (of slaves)
δῆμος	*dēmos*	(common) people
δημαγωγός	*dēmagōgos*	popular leader
δημοκρατία	*dēmokratia*	democracy
δημόσιος	*dēmosios*	public
διαιτητής	*diaitētēs*	arbitrator
δικαιοσύνη	*dikaiosunē*	justice
δικαστήρον	*dikastērion*	court
δικαστής	*dikastēs*	juryman
δοῦλος	*doulos*	slave
δύναμις	*dunamis*	capacity, faculty, power
δυναστεία	*dunasteia*	power-group
ἔθνος	*ethnos*	nation
ἔθος	*ethos*	habit
εἶδος	*eidos*	kind, category
εἵλωτες	*heilōtes*	helots
ἐκκλησία	*ekklēsia*	Assembly
ἐλεύθερος	*eleutheros*	free
ἐλευθεριότης	*eleutheriotēs*	liberality
ἕξις	*hexis*	disposition
ἐπαλλάττειν	*epallattein*	overlap
ἐπιεικής	*epieikēs*	respectable
ἐπιθυμία	*epithumia*	desire
ἐπίκληπος	*epiklēros*	heiress
ἐπιορκεῖν	*epiorkein*	perjure
ἐπιστήμη	*epistēmē*	knowledge

ἔργον	ergon	function
ἐριστικός	eristikos	contentious
ἔρως	erōs	love
εὐγένεια	eugeneia	noble birth
εὐδαιμονία	eudaimonia	happiness
εὖ ζῆν	eu zēn	good life
εὔθυνα	euthuna	scrutiny
εὐνομία	eunomia	government by good laws
εὐπραξία	eupraxia	doing well
ἔφοροι	ephoroi	Ephors
ἴδιος	idios	private, peculiar (to)
ἴσος	isos	equal
καπηλεία	kapēleia	trade
κατ' εὐχήν	kat'euchēn	ideal
κινεῖν	kinein	change
κλῆρος	klēros	estate
κληρωτός	klērōtos	chosen by lot
κοινός	koinos	common, communal
κοινωνία	koinōnia	association
κοινωνεῖν	koinōnein	participate in or share in
κόσμοι	kosmoi	Cosmoi
κτῆσις	ktēsis	acquisition (of property), property
κτητική	ktētikē	knowledge or art or skill of acquiring property
κτῆμα	ktēma	possession
κυριος	kurios	sovereign
κώμη	kōmē	village
λειτουργία	leitourgia	public service
λόγος	logos	reason, speech
μέρος, μόριον	meros, morion	part
μεταβλητική	metablētikē	technique of changing-round
μεταβλητικός	metabletikos	to do with changing-round
μία	mia	one
μοναρχία	monarchia	monarchy
ναύαρχοι	nauarchoi	Naval Commanders
νόμισμα	nomisma	coin(age)
νόμος	nomos	law, convention
νομοθέτης	nomothetēs	lawgiver
νοῦς	nous	mind
οἰκία	oikia	household

οἰκονομία	oikonomia	household-management
οἰκονόμος	oikonomos	household-manager
οἰκονομική	oikonomikē	art of skill of household-management
οἰκονομικός	oikonomikos	to do with household-management
ὀλιγαρχία	oligarchia	oligarchy
ὁμολογία	homologia	agreement
ὁμονοητικός	homonoētikos	conducive to accord
ὅλος	holos	whole
ὅλως	holōs	wholly
ὁπλῖται	hoplitai	heavy-armed troops
ὄργανον	organon	tool
ὄρεξις	orexis	appetition
ὁρμή	hormē	impulse
οὐσία	ousia	resources
παθήματα	pathēmata	feelings
παιδεία	paideia	education
παραλογισμός	paralogismos	fallacy
παρέκβασις	parekbasis	deviation
πάτριος	patrios	ancestral, traditional
πενταρχίαι	pentarchiai	Boards of Five
πέρας	peras	limit
περίοικοι	perioikoi	peripheral
ποίησις	poiēsis	production
πόλις	polis	state
πολίτης	politēs	citizen
πολιτικός	politikos	statesman; to do with state or citizens or statesmen
πολιτεία	politeia	constitution, polity
πολιτεύεσθαι	politeuesthai	to engage in state affairs (or similar)
πρᾶξις	praxis	action
προαίρεσις	prohairesis	choice (=choosing), chosen aim
σπουδαῖος	spoudaios	sound (adjective)
στάσις	stasis	faction
στρατηγός	stratēgos	general (noun)
συκοφαντία	sukophantia	vexatious prosecution
συλλογισμός	sullogismos	syllogism
συσσίτια	sussitia	common meals, messes
σχολή	scholē	leisure
σωφροσύνη	sōphrosunē	moderation, restraint
τέλος	telos	end
τὰ πρὸς τὸ τέλος	ta pros to telos	means
τέχνη	technē	skill

τεχνιτής	technitēs	skilled worker
τιμή	timē	honour
τίμημα	timēma	property-class
τόκος	tokos	interest
τύραννος	turannos	tyrant
ὑπόθεσις	hupothesis	assumption
φιλάνθρωπος	philanthrōpos	benevolent
φιλία	philia	affection, friendship
φιλοσοφία	philosophia	philosophy
φρόνησις	phronēsis	practical wisdom
φύλακες	phulakes	Guardians
φύσις	phusis	nature
φωνή	phōnē	voice
χαρίεις	charieis	sophisticated
χρεία	chreia	need
χρήματα	chrēmata	goods, money
χρηματιστική	chrēmatistikē	knowledge or skill of acquiring goods or wealth
ψυχή	psuchē	soul

SELECTIVE INDEX

Most references are to the Greek text, sometimes to whole chapters, but usually to particular lines or short passages. The Bekker system of lineation, and its application to the translation, are described on p. xiv; in this index the first two digits of the Bekker numbers, being invariable, are omitted. Since the sections of the commentary match those of the translation and display the same Bekker numbers, the index may be used to locate topics in the commentary also. There are some supplementary page-references to the commentary alone: they lead to comment not readily traceable by the above means.

The references to proper names are confined to *ancient* persons and places.

Broad indications of the subject-matter of each chapter are given in the 'Guide to Translation and Commentary', pp. viii–ix.

acquisition:
  by exchange   I ix–x
  in household-management   I viii, x
  modes of   I viii–xi *passim*
action 54^a1–8
affection, *see* friendship
Alexander   161
Androdamas 74^b23
animals 56^b7–26, 64^b4–6
anthropology, historical and
   comparative   I ii, 62^a18–24, 64^a1–
   11, 68^b31–69^a8
Areopagus, Council on 73^b39, 74^a7
Ares 69^b28
aristocracy 70^b16, 73^a4–6, 21, 32
  Plato's   132–3
Aristophanes 62^b11
Assembly 72^a10–12; 155, App.
association, taking form of state
   52^a1–7
assumption 61^a16, 63^b30, 69^a32, 71^a41,
   73^a4; 104–6, 149, 162
Athens 67^b18, 68^a10
Auxiliaries   107

barter   88–9
benevolence 63^b15
biology   69–70
Boards of Five 73^a13

Callicles   56, 63, 81
Callipolis   106
Carthaginian(s)   II xi
changing-round 57^a9, 15, 58^b1, 4, 21,
  29
Charondas 52^b14, 74^a23, 30, $^b5$

children:
  moral virtue of   I xiii
  in *Republic*   II i–iv, 62^b41, 64^a17,
   66^a34
  see also rule
coin(age) 57^a31–$^b40$, 58^a38–$^b8$
commensurability, in exchange   88
common meals, messes 63^b41, 64^a8,
   65^b6–10, 66^a35, 71^a26–37, 71^b41–
   72^a4, 12–27, $^b34$
communal wives, children, and
   property in *Republic*   II i–v,
   66^a34–6
communism   136
communitarianism   56
concord 61^b32
consent, of governed   134
constitution(s):
  of Callipolis   II i–v
  of Carthage   II xi
  of Crete   II x
  education for 60^b8–20
  elaboration of 71^b23–4
  of Hippodamus   II viii
  and laws 70^b32–4
  of Magnesia   II vi
  middle 65^b28
  mixed 65^b33–66^a5, 73^b39; 154–5
  of Phaleas   II vii
  of Sparta   II ix
  writers on 73^b27–34
  see also aristocracy, democracy,
   kingship, monarchy, oligarchy,
   polity, power-group, rule, tyranny
contemplation   129
contractualism   56

Cosmoi 72^a4–12, 27–^{b}11
Council 66^a14, 72^a8, App.
courts 67^b39–68^a5, ^{b}8, 73^b41, 74^a3–11
Crete 63^b41, 64^a20, 69^a39, 71^a29, II x, 72^b28

demand 88–9
democracy 65^b26–66^a30, 70^b16, 73^b38; 136, 166
desire 67^a2–12
deviations 73^a3, 31; 162
Draco 74^b15

economics I viii–xi
   see also acquisition, barter, coin(age), exchange, household-manager, money-lending, monopoly, trade
education 60^b8–20, 63^b36–64^a1, 29–40, ^{b}37–65^a1, 7, 66^b24–67^a2
Elders 70^b24, 35–71^a18, 72^a7, 12, ^{b}34, 73^a8
ends 52^b31–53^a1, 57^b25–30; 92
Ephialtes 74^a8
Ephors 70^b6–35, 72^a5, 29, 41, ^{b}35
Ephorus 158
equality:
   in economic theory 88–90
   of education 66^b32–8
   in office-holding 61^a30–^{b}6
   of property II vii
equity 144–5, 170
exchange I ix
expiations 62^a32

faction 62^b8, 64^b8, 73^b18
finance, public 71^b11
food-supply 56^a19–^{b}20
force I vi
Forms 57–8, 106
friendship/affection 55^b13, 59^b11, 62^a40–^{b}24, 63^a40–^{b}7
function 52^a34–^{b}5, 53^a23, 73^b9–10; 165

generals 68^a22, 71^a40, 73^a30, 37
geography 159
good life 52^b30, 56^b32, 58^a1–2
Gorgias 60^a28
government by good laws 60^b30
Guardians II i–v passim, 64^b37–65^a1
Guardians of the Laws 135, App.

happiness 64^b15–24, 69^b14; 55–6, 62, 67
helots 64^a35, 69^a38, ^{b}12, 71^b41, 72^b19
Hippodamus II vii
history, see anthropology
Homer 52^b22, 53^a5, 59^b13
homosexuality 69^b27, 72^a24–5
household:
   double 65^b24–6
   historical 52^b9–15, 57^a20
   structure and rule I iii, xii–xiii; 78
household-manager I iii, viii–x, xii–xiii passim
Hundred 73^a14

induction 75–6, 84–7

justice 53^a31–9
   of slavery I vi

king(ship) 52^a7–16, ^{b}19–27, 59^b10–17, 65^b37, 70^b15, 23, 71^a19, 39–41, 72^a8, ^{b}33, 37–^{a}13, 29–37
knowledge:
   political 55–9
   possessed by slave-master I vii

labour value 90, 95
Lacedaemon(ians) 63^a35, ^{b}41, 64^a10, 65^a35, 69^a29, 71^b17, 72^a36, 73^a2, 20, ^{b}24, 35
Laconians 65^b32, 69^a38, ^{b}31–70^a1, 71^a29, ^{b}22–72^a2, 13, 27, ^{b}26
land 63^a3–8, 65^b21–6, 66^b17, 67^b10, 33–7, 68^a19, 34, 70^a19, ^{b}5; 130–2, 159
law(s) 55^a5–7, 22, 64^a38, 65^a1, 67^b37
   changes to 68^b22–69^a28
   and constitutions 73^b32–4
lawgivers II xii
leisure 69^a35, 73^a33
liberality 63^b7–14, 65^a28–38
life, styles of 65^a20–38
   see also good life
limit 56^b31–57^a1, 57^b23–58^a18
lot, chosen by 66^a9, 73^a18, 74^a5
love 62^a32–40
Lycophron 56, 141
Lycurgus 70^a7, 71^b25, 73^a33, 74^a29; 121, 169

means 57^b27
Meno 100
military matters 55^a25, 56^b26, 65^a20–8,

67^{a}17–37, 68^{a}17–^{b}4, 69^{b}36, 70^{a}29–34, 71^{a}41–^{b}6, 72^{a}8–10
minimalism 56
monarchy 65^{b}36–7, 66^{a}5, 23
money-lending 58^{b}2–8, 25
monopoly 59^{a}6–36

nations 52^{b}20, 57^{a}25, 61^{a}28, 63^{a}5
nature, natural:
  in economics I viii–ix
  ladder of 86
  applied to slaves I vi
  applied to state I ii
Naval Commanders 71^{a}37–41
need 56^{b}6; 88–9
non-Greeks 52^{b}5–9, 55^{a}28–36, 57^{a}25; 161

oligarchy 73^{a}13–30, ^{b}36; 134–5, App.
oneness II ii–iii

part and whole 53^{a}18–29, I iv, 55^{b}9–12, 64^{b}15–25
pay for office 73^{a}17
peculiarities II xii
people 70^{b}9, 73^{a}6–13, 74^{a}12–15
Pericles 74^{a}8–9
peripheral populations 69^{b}2, 71^{b}30, 72^{a}1, 18, ^{b}18
Phaleas II vii, 74^{b}9
Pheidon 65^{b}12
Philolaus 74^{a}31–2, 41, ^{b}2
philosophy 67^{a}12
Pittacus 74^{b}18
Plato 61^{a}6, 66^{b}5, 71^{b}1, 74^{b}9; 56–9
pluralism, see specialization
polity 65^{b}28, 73^{a}5
popular leaders 74^{a}9–15
population policy 65^{a}13–^{b}17, 66^{b}8–14, 70^{a}29–^{b}6, 72^{a}24, 73^{b}18–26, 74^{b}2–5
power-group 72^{b}1–15
practical wisdom 157
production 54^{a}1–8
profit 57^{b}5; 88–89, 92
property:
  in Callipolis II i–v
  on Crete 72^{a}12–27
  in Hippodamus' state 67^{b}33–7, 68^{a}19, 34
  in Magnesia 65^{a}28–^{b}17, 21–6, 66^{b}5–8
  in Phaleas' state II vii
  at Sparta 70^{a}11–34

prosecutions, vexatious ('sycophancies') 68^{b}25
psychology 54^{a}34–55^{a}3, 54^{b}5–9, 22–4, I xiii
Pythagoras 140–1

reason 54^{b}22–4, 59^{b}28, 60^{a}19
reciprocity, see equality
restraint 63^{b}9–10, 67^{a}10
rule:
  varieties of 52^{a}7–16, 31–4, I v, vii, xii–xiii
  by turns 61^{a}32–^{b}6, 64^{b}6–15
  see also constitutions

scrutiny 71^{a}6–8, 74^{a}17
self-love 63^{a}41–^{b}5
  see also friendship
self-sufficiency 52^{b}27–53^{a}1, 26–9, 56^{b}4, 32, 57^{a}14–19, 30, 61^{b}10–15
skill 68^{b}31–69^{a}8
skilled workers 60^{a}36–^{b}7, 62^{b}26, 64^{a}27, ^{b}15, 23, 34, 67^{b}15, 32, 68^{a}17
slave-master, see rule, varieties of
slaves 52^{a}34, I iii–vii, 56^{b}23–6, I xiii
socialism 136
Socrates, views held by:
  in Laws II vi
  in Republic II i–v
Solon 56^{b}32, 66^{b}17, 73^{b}34–74^{a}15
soul, see psychology
sovereignty 52^{a}1–7
Sparta II ix
Spartiatae 70^{a}37, ^{b}2, 71^{b}11, 13
specialization 52^{a}34–^{b}9, 73^{b}8–17; 91, 122
state:
  as association 52^{a}1–7
  historical growth and essential characteristics I ii, II ii
  parts of 52^{a}17–23
statesman, see rule, varieties of

teleology 57^{b}1–3; 85–6
Thales, (i) of Miletus 59^{a}6, 18, 32, (ii) 74^{a}28–9
Third Class 62^{b}24–36, 64^{a}11–^{b}6; 107
Thrasymachus 56, 81
tools I iv, 56^{b}35–7
totalitarianism 71
trade 57^{a}41–58^{a}18, 38–^{b}2
tyranny 65^{b}40, 66^{a}2, 70^{b}14, 74^{a}6

SELECTIVE INDEX

utopias   104–5

verdicts   68ᵇ4–22
villages   52ᵇ15–30, 57ᵃ19–28, 61ᵃ28
virtue   I xiii, 71ᵃ41–ᵇ10

war, *see* military matters

women   52ᵃ24–ᵇ9, 54ᵇ13–14, 59ᵃ40–ᵇ3,
    I xiii, II i–v, 64ᵇ37–9, 66ᵃ34–5,
    69ᵇ12–70ᵃ34, 72ᵃ23–4
workfare   117

Zaleucus   74ᵃ22, 29